Working Miracles

She could work miracles, she would make a garment
   from a square of cloth
in a span that defied time. Or feed twenty people on a
   stew made from
fallen-from-the-head cabbage leaves and a carrot and a
   cho-cho and a palmful
of meat.

Lorna Goodison, 'My Mother'

Edna Manley, *Market Women*, 1936 (Mahogany, height 16″)
Collection of: Spelman College, Atlanta
Photographer: Maria La Yacona

Working Miracles

Women's Lives in the English-speaking Caribbean
OLIVE SENIOR

Institute of Social & Economic Research
University of the West Indies, Cave Hill, Barbados

Published in association with

James Currey
LONDON

Indiana University Press
BLOOMINGTON & INDIANAPOLIS

Institute of Social & Economic Research
University of the West Indies, Cave Hill, Barbados

Published in association with

James Currey Ltd
54b Thornhill Square
Islington, London N1 1BE

Indiana University Press
601 North Morton Street
Bloomington, IN 47404-3797

British Library Cataloguing in Publication Data
Senior, Olive
  Working miracles : women's lives in the English-speaking
Caribbean.
  1. Caribbean region. Society. Role of women
  I. Title
  305.42091821

  ISBN 0-85255-209-2 (James Currey Cloth)
  ISBN 0-85255-208-4 (James Currey Paper)

Library of Congress Cataloging-in-Publication Data
Senior, Olive.
    Working miracles : women of the English-speaking Caribbean / Olive
Senior.
      p. cm.
    Includes bibliographical references and index.
    ISBN 0-253-35136-7. — ISBN 0-253-28885-1 (pbk.)
    1. Women—Caribbean, English-speaking. 2. Women—Caribbean,
English-speaking—Economic conditions. 3. Women—Caribbean,
English-speaking—Social life and customs. 4. Women—Caribbean,
English-speaking—Socialization. 5. Women in the Caribbean Project.
    I. Title.
    HQ1501.S46 1991
    305.4'09729—dc20   91-4013

1 2 3 4 5   95 94 93 92 91

Map by Almac
Typeset in 10/11 pt Baskerville by Colset Pte Ltd, Singapore
Printed by Villiers Publications, London N6

Contents

List of Illustrations, Map & Tables

Illustrations

Details of these sculptures have been used on the front cover
and jacket

Map

Tables

Acknowledgements

I would like to thank:

• the women who shared their life stories and provided an understanding of the miracles performed by Caribbean women

• the entire team of the Women in the Caribbean Project and the staff of ISER (EC)

• the staff of the ISER documentation centre, UWI, Mona, the documentation centre, School of Education, UWI, Mona and the National Library of Jamaica

• Dorian Powell, Erna Brodber, Rhoda Reddock and Maxine Henry, who all at various times gave me access to their unpublished material

• Elsa Ettrick, for typing the first drafts of the manuscript, and the staff of Institute of Jamaica Publications Ltd, for being helpful and supportive at critical times

• Hyacinth Evans, who read and commented on early drafts of the first three chapters, and members of the Women and Development Studies Group, UWI, Barbados, who also commented on three of the chapters during an interdisciplinary seminar in 1987

• Herman McKenzie, who read and commented on the entire manuscript and made a great deal of material available to me

• Joycelin Massiah, for her unflagging support, advice and confidence in me over the many years it took to complete this book

• the Carnegie Foundation, which funded this project, and Jill Sheffield, former programme officer of the foundation, who believed in it.

Foreword

Joycelin Massiah
Director, Institute of Social & Economic Research
(Eastern Caribbean)

Popular perceptions of Caribbean women as being strong, assertive, independent, self-reliant matriarchs are being constantly challenged by growing evidence of the structural and ideological factors which hinder Caribbean women's achievement of social and political advancement. Gender-based division of labour within and outside the household, the dual burden of reproduction and production borne by women and gender ideology which favours men are some of the factors often cited as inhibiting Caribbean women's potential for advancement. Caribbean women do exercise considerable power and authority through their domestic and maternal roles, in the process acquiring a measure of autonomy which sets them apart from their sisters in the developing world. To a large extent legal impediments to their participation in society have been dismantled, although several areas still merit reform. But, from an overall perspective, it cannot be denied that, in the Caribbean, as in so many other parts of the world, it is a man's world.

Present economic crises in the region, occasioned by recessions in the international economic system and structural adjustment efforts of individual Caribbean territories, have done much to illustrate and intensify the weak position of Caribbean women, particularly the poorest among them. *Working Miracles* therefore appears at a particularly opportune moment. It is the first attempt to provide a comprehensive overview of available literature from the social sciences, the humanities, the creative arts and women themselves in order to facilitate an understanding of the realities of the lives of Caribbean women.

The Women in the Caribbean Project (WICP), which provided the impetus for the present work, had set as one of its objectives the task of generating data relevant to policy-making for women. In a process involving the collection, collation and analysis of documentary material, review of past research and multi-level interviewing, the project generated a wealth of data which the project team felt needed to be made available to the general public in non-technical form. The project itself had developed and implemented a multi-media dissemination programme aimed at the women interviewed in the project territories, planners, decision-makers, Women-in-Development practitioners and researchers in the region.[1] Yet

---

1 The programme included national seminars in project territories, information brochures for distribution by non-governmental organizations (NGOs), a regional conference, a video tape, a slide tape presentation, monographs and a special issue of *Social and Economic Studies*, the academic journal of the sponsoring Institute.

there still remained a sense in which it was felt that the project findings were not reaching a wide enough cross-section of the societies. And so *Working Miracles* was born — an attempt to translate the WICP findings and their meaning into clear, easily assimilated prose for the benefit of the general-interest reader.

In her interpretation of what *Working Miracles* should be, Olive Senior has gone much further. Although guided by the constraints of the academic whose conclusions must be based on observations and disciplined deductions, she has not allowed her creative imagination to be fettered. Rather, she has used her skills and experience as a writer of short stories, a poet, a journalist and an editor to try to get into the hearts and minds of the women who were the subjects of the study. Her explanations of some of the commonalities and contradictions of the data reflect a refreshing personal identification with the subjects. As she says: 'In reading and re-reading these life histories . . . I experienced no sense of strangeness about these women: it was as though I already knew them' (Conclusion).

It is perhaps this oneness with the subjects which provides the major element of attractiveness about *Working Miracles*. Olive Senior's ability to humanize the study of women without fictionalizing their experiences and without straying too far from the body of evidence available is particularly attractive. Her method has been to adopt, wherever possible, a life-course perspective linking specific issues (e.g. socialization, gender relations, sources of livelihood) to the relevant infrastructure (e.g. the law), to women's perceptions of themselves, their experiences and their society and to society's expectations about women. Thus the book begins with an examination of the legal and domestic setting into which Caribbean girl babies are born and ends with an exploration of possible impacts of recent global changes (e.g. information technology, economic adversity) on the contemporary Caribbean women (e.g. interpersonal relationships, women's autonomy).

Because it is grounded in a specific and comprehensive data set and is supported by a wide range of other sources, this approach serves to shed a more cohesive light on the issues affecting Caribbean women than has been available in any single text to date. During the period when *Working Miracles* was being written a number of general-purpose texts, apart from the WICP publications, have appeared which have begun to fill the gap in published information about women in the region. Patricia Ellis' (ed.) *Women of the Caribbean*, Patricia Mohammed & Cathy Shepherd's (eds.) *Gender in Caribbean Development* and Keith Hart's (ed.) *The Sexual Division of Labour in the Caribbean* were collections of essays, the latter two being revised versions of papers presented at seminars bearing the same titles. Two other important publications have been Sistren's *Lionheart Gal: Life Stories of Jamaican Women* and Neesha Haniff's *Blaze a Fire: Significant Contributions of Caribbean Women*. These were collections of life stories, the former of members of a women's collective, the latter of 'visible' and 'invisible' women in the region. *Working Miracles* joins this growing literature not as a definitive statement, but as a start 'in outlining the complex mosaic which needs to be created if we are to understand the reality of women's lives'.

Olive Senior has herself identified a number of pieces of that mosaic which require further investigation. These include the influence of culture and religion on women's lives, childhood socialization, agents and impact of gender-role stereotyping, linkages between race, class and gender, impact of recent socio-economic and political changes, women's health and sexuality. This list is instructive not only for its recognition of gaps in our knowledge about women, but also for its recognition that knowledge about women permits a conceptual understanding of a wider social reality. In this connection, *Working Miracles* speaks directly to the significance of the

Caribbean as an area for the study of the role of women.

The particular historical heritage of the Caribbean has been instrumental in forging the framework within which Caribbean women have functioned. The history of women in this region is a history of women developing strategies and techniques to defy a system which took their submission for granted. The variety of family forms, for example, in which women developed relationships with their men, their children and other relatives, represents a consistent refusal to be encompassed in the simple nuclear family form which was supposed to be universal. The tradition of economic autonomy amongst women has never been abandoned. Rather, the contemporary Caribbean woman seeks to strengthen this autonomy, though — and this is a point often overlooked — in the context of a relationship of interdependence with her man. The Caribbean woman has used techniques similar to those used by men to confront adverse situations. But she has also used techniques peculiar to her state of being a woman. She has refused to cede her responsibility for maintaining herself and her household, even in the presence of a male partner; she has transformed educational opportunities into opportunities for skills enhancement and self-advancement; she has reserved the right to speak out.

It is no accident that women like Mary Seacole, Lucille Mair, Dame Nita Barrow or Dorienne Wilson-Smillie have emerged from the Caribbean on to the international arena. They are the product of a region which Keith Hart has described as 'an avant-garde crucible of modern social movements and cultural forms' (Hart, 1989, p. 5). Within that crucible, despite structural and cultural constraints, women's strengths are recognized and approved. Women have access to the key social institutions and to a variety of resources; women can and do make use of available opportunities. Some have been eminently successful, but it remains true that the vast majority struggle daily against an ideological gender system which has not yet freed itself from according low status to women's activities. Thus, the autonomy which is so widely believed to be typical of Caribbean women is, in fact, reality for a few, a dream for the many.

Working Miracles challenges the view that reliance on economic solutions are sufficient to promote gender equality. Cultural factors, prevailing gender ideologies, women's perceptions and global economic changes are all factors to be taken into account. Olive Senior has speculated on all of these. She has provided no definitive answers. But she has demonstrated how the interplay between these factors has produced contradictions both in the lives of Caribbean women and in their position in their societies. She has also demonstrated how important it is to pay attention to the views of Caribbean women who are only just beginning 'to speak for themselves, to name their experiences and to make their own connections'. We should sit up and listen.

Patricia Ellis (ed.) (1986) *Women of the Caribbean*, London & New Jersey: Zed Books.

Patricia Mohammed & Cathy Shepherd (eds.) (1988) *Gender in Caribbean Development*, Mona, Jamaica: University of the West Indies, Women and Development Studies Programme.

Keith Hart (ed.) (1989) *The Sexual Division of Labour in the Caribbean*, Mona, Jamaica: University of the West Indies, Consortium Graduate School of the Social Sciences.

Sistren (1986) *Lionheart Gal: Life Stories of Jamaican Women*, London: Women's Press.

Neesha Haniff (1988) *Blaze a Fire: Significant Contributions of Caribbean Women*, Toronto: Sister Vision.

Map The English-speaking Caribbean

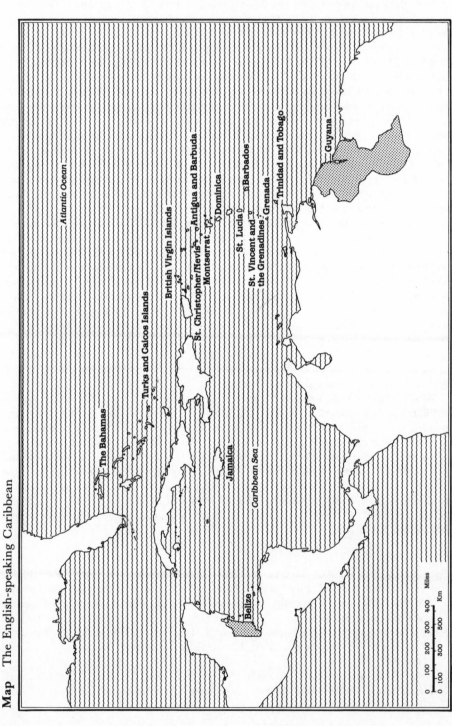

Introduction

This book examines some of the issues affecting the Caribbean woman: issues centred around her socialization and education, domestic and family life, sources of livelihood and interactions with men and the wider society.

It utilizes formal research findings, examples from literature, popular and folk culture, and the voices of women themselves. In the organization of the book an attempt has been made to link specific issues to the life cycle, where this was possible.

The Women in the Caribbean Project (WICP)

Working Miracles arose out of the first multidisciplinary, multinational examination of women's lives and work in the countries of the English-speaking Caribbean[1] — the Women in the Caribbean Project (WICP). The Project was undertaken between 1979 and 1982 under the auspices of the Institute of Social and Economic Research, University of the West Indies (UWI), with funding from regional and international agencies. It involved a team of scholars of both sexes, drawn from the UWI and the University of Guyana, who covered the fields of anthropology, Caribbean literature, demography, history, sociology and political science.

Although a significant amount of sociological and anthropological research on Caribbean lower-income families and households exists from which information on Caribbean women is available, the WICP was the first to attempt woman-centred research, i.e. to involve women in defining their own reality.

The methodology involved four levels of data collection:

1 Collection and review of documentary material on a regional basis.
2 Semi-structured interviews of national samples of 1,600 women in three project territories: Antigua, Barbados and St Vincent.
3 Detailed life-histories obtained from 38 of the women.
4 In-depth interviews to examine in detail issues related to kinship and friendship networks among women (Jamaica); survival strategies of poor women (Barbados); life-histories of older women (Jamaica); male perceptions of women (Barbados); rural women (Guyana); and successful women in public life (eastern Caribbean).

---

1 The territories are: Antigua, Barbados, Belize, British Virgin Islands, Cayman Islands, Dominica, Grenada, Guyana, Jamaica, Montserrat, St Christopher-Nevis (St Kitts), St Lucia, St Vincent and the Grenadines, Trinidad and Tobago, Turks and Caicos Islands. The older term West Indies is used interchangeably with Caribbean.

Table i   Selected Social and Economic Indicators for Four Caribbean Territories, *c* 1989

	Barbados	Guyana	Jamaica	Trinidad & Tobago
Life expectancy (years)	74.9	66.1	73.9	69.8
Infant mortality rate	12.4	43.9	18.0	20.0
Percentage of women in labour force[a]	47.4	25.1	45.7	29.9
Total fertility rate[b]	1.9	3.3	3.4	2.9
Average annual growth rate in per capita GDP[c]	0.8	−3.2	0.4	−4.9
Unemployment rate	18.0	n/a	18.7[d]	23.0
Average annual growth rate in consumer prices	6.2	80.0	14.2	11.4

Source: ISER (EC).
Note: Except where otherwise stated, all data refer to preliminary estimates for 1989.
a 1990; b 1985; c 1981–89; d 1988.

Much of the research material generated by the WICP is in the form of unpublished papers and publications as listed separately in the bibliography. The final papers were published in a two-volume issue of the journal *Social and Economic Studies*, University of the West Indies (35:2, June 1986; 35:3, September 1986). The reader is referred to these volumes for a detailed overview of the project, discussions of methodology, statistical details, proposals emanating from the project, as well as conclusions and recommendations of the WICP, which have been omitted from the present volume.

Aims of the book

A decision was taken early in the Women in the Caribbean Project to communicate the findings to a wider readership than the exclusively academic, and to pull together the extensive material generated by the project in one convenient volume. In doing this, I have gone beyond the scope of the WICP research and used material from a wider range of sources as I felt this was necessary to present a more rounded picture and to explore certain issues, especially those related to socialization, which were not direct research interests of the project. The aim of this book, then, is to examine, within the limitations of the available data, the Caribbean woman as she performs various roles in her life and to try to seek explanations for her behaviour, which sometimes appears contradictory and seemingly at odds with her ideology.

Working Miracles does not in any sense pretend to be definitive; I rather hope that, by pulling together material from very disparate sources, by taking risks in imbuing some of this varied material with explanatory power, by combining and contrasting the formal academic research with women's own narratives and with the views sometimes expressed by the wider society, I have made a start in outlining the complex mosaic which needs to be created if we are to understand the reality of women's lives. I hope that, if it does nothing else, this work will reveal the many missing elements that now need to be documented and researched in order to arrive at a truer and more complete picture.

In putting together this book, I am conscious of perhaps too heavy a reliance on the literature of the black lower-class family, with too little about others, especially since I identify throughout the text the importance of racial, ethnic and social stratification in all countries and at all levels, through time. This reliance, however, reflects the bias of previous research efforts. The problem of not providing enough data about other ethnic and social groups becomes most serious in relation to Guyana and Trinidad, which both have significant East Indian populations (the largest ethnic group in the one, and approaching numerical equality in the other), and in relation to Belize, which has a more mixed population. We should bear these factors in mind but they should not obscure the fact that, in the other territories, the high visibility of white and light-skinned racial and ethnic minorities in positions of leadership and power and in urban areas often masks the reality: that the majority of the population consists of black people and that the people of lower socio-economic status in these countries are mainly black. For instance, the racial proportions in the samples in the three WICP survey territories of Antigua, Barbados and St Vincent (which closely matched that of the regional census) were as in Table ii.

One of the enigmas posed by a study of Caribbean women is that, while most official barriers to female achievement in these societies have now been dismantled, and although many young, upwardly mobile women are taking advantage of this, the large masses of women still appear to be handicapped not only by the invisible barriers which still exist in a male-dominated society but by the barriers in their heads. Probing these barriers will be part of our task throughout.

We take as our starting-point the fact that the Caribbean woman is born to equal rights, since each country's Constitution, the supreme law of the land, guarantees fundamental rights and freedoms to all individuals — regardless of gender. Indeed, the Guyanese Constitution adds a ringing declaration of equality: 'Women and men have equal rights and the same legal status in all spheres of political, economic and social life. All forms of discrimination against women on the basis of their sex are illegal.' Article 29 goes on to spell out how women's rights are to be ensured:

> by according women equal access with men to academic, vocational and professional train-
> ing, equal opportunities in employment, remuneration and promotion and in social,
> political and cultural activity, by special labour and health protection measures for women,
> by providing conditions enabling mothers to work and by legal protection and material
> and moral support for mothers and children, including paid leave and other benefits for
> mothers and expectant mothers.

How far this equality of status 'guaranteed' at birth continues to find expression in the objective reality of her life, will form the basis for our examination of that life as she moves from childhood and adolescence to the assumption of adult responsibilities. We might find, for instance, that the various Constitutions have not in fact cancelled out existing laws which might run counter to her rights and interests and that actual practice in institutions, at the workplace or in the home might give the lie to rhetoric. We will nevertheless bear in mind the guarantees listed above as constituting a package of women's rights which can be used as the yardstick for measuring women's status in Caribbean societies.

The most striking feature of the Caribbean woman observed by researchers,

Table ii Race of the Survey Population (percentages)

	Antigua	*Barbados*	*St Vincent*
Negro/black	95.4	87.9	75.9
White	0.8	3.7	1.7
Indian	—	0.8	2.1
Mixed	3.2	7.3	19.4
Other	0.6	0.3	9.0

and, indeed, visible to outsiders, is how fraught with contradictions is her existence. The crux of these contradictions has been identified as the lag between behaviour and the self-images, perceptions and consciousness which women seem to have (LeFranc WICP 1983): between female performance and female ideology.

Because of the persistence of the contradictions (to be examined throughout this work) *Working Miracles* begins by looking at how the Caribbean woman is socialized, to see what light this might throw on her behaviour.

This is not an easy task, for, although linkages between early childhood experiences and socialization and later adult behaviour have been identified, there has been little exploration of these links in Caribbean female consciousness. This is partly a commentary on the lack of investigation in such areas as socialization or psychology, but it is also due to the fact that Caribbean women are only just beginning to find their own voices, to speak for themselves, to name their experiences and to make their own connections. This 'naming' of experience only began around the 1940s, first in speeches or tracts advocating the rights of women, in plays, poetry and stories, later in novels and in the historical and sociological literature.

Until the early twentieth century, the views — and voices — of women were filtered through a metropolitan perspective: resident or visiting planters, travellers, missionaries or officials sent from the metropolis to investigate conditions in the colonies. This perspective was for the most part male, with exceptions such as Mrs Carmichael and Lady Nugent. Generally, the women of the Caribbean — black women, mulatto women, white women, East Indian, Amerindian or Chinese women — were not directly heard from in the pages of history, with the brilliant exception of the brown Mary Seacole and her best-selling *Wonderful Adventures of Mrs Seacole in Many Lands*, published in England in 1857 (reissued 1984). While Mrs Seacole's book is more concerned with describing her adventures than with direct self-revelation, she early on identifies one tendency: 'All my life long I have followed the impulse which led me to be up and doing; and so far from resting idle anywhere, I have never wanted inclination to rove, nor will powerful enough to find a way to carry out my wishes' (Seacole 1984, p. 56). She is thus identified with an archetypal image of the creole woman as 'powerful', 'dominant', 'managing'. In this work, we will examine whether or not this is an accurate picture or a stereotype, what other stereotypes might exist, and what might be woman's 'true' situation. Is she the 'managing bitch', the emasculating mother, the honoured matriarch, the woman in search of fulfilment exclusively through marriage and family, the woman who daily 'works miracles' in her reproductive role? Or the one who finds that:

> Sometime when yuh no have notten and yuh have di pickney dem and dem a look to yuh fi food and fi shelter, yuh haffi do sometings weh yuh no really waan fi do, just fi survive. Sometimes a better yuh cyaan do, mek yuh tek certain man. Sometime yuh really in need. A man might use dat fi ketch yuh. Yuh might know a so it go, but yuh in need. Yuh want it, so yuh haffi tek it.
>
> (Sistren 1986, p. 201)

Organization of the book

Working Miracles is divided into four parts.

Part I consists of three chapters which are concerned with childhood and socialization.

Chapter 1 deals with the domestic setting into which the Caribbean woman is born and in which she bears and rears her children, and highlights the fluidity of such arrangements. It looks at the ambiguous and multiple roles played by the mother and the strategies she uses to care for and support her children — often both her responsibilities. These include utilizing the traditional grandmother and kin networks and the process of child-shifting. The role of the father is also examined, especially the high incidence of paternal absence and the phenomenon of 'inside/ outside' children, and the possible effects of such factors on the child.

Chapter 2 looks more closely at the socialization process and specifically at the acquisition of gender identity. In the first section, we examine factors affecting socialization, including culture and socio-economic status, social expectations and values and child-rearing practices, also the value conflicts which can arise from these and from generational differences. The second section is devoted to gender-role learning, that is, how perceived gender differences influence the rearing of children. In the Caribbean the female role is well defined compared with the male role and the implications of this are examined, as are the sometimes contradictory roles played by both males and females as socializing agents. Finally, gender-role stereotyping and identity formation are examined, especially the part played by agents such as the media.

Chapter 3 looks at women's access to education and progress through the system and at the role played by gender-role stereotyping and other internal and external factors in shaping educational and occupational choices. The historical process which shaped the ideology of female education and the cultural, economic and social factors which impede or facilitate women's progress in the system today are examined, as well as attainment, performance and occupational choices. Women's own educational experiences and expectations are also explored.

Part II (chapters 4 and 5) is concerned with women in their familial and domestic roles — as mothers, partners and household heads.

Chapter 4 begins by examining the contradictory pressures on young women to avoid early pregnancy and at the same time prove their womanhood by getting pregnant. Attitudes to childbearing are first examined, and then the preparation for motherhood, specifically how information on sexual relationships and the facts of life are transmitted; the contradictory and often ambivalent nature of this transmission is discussed. The second section turns to the social context of childbearing and examines the mothers' own reactions and that of others to their first pregnancy and their feelings about children, as well as the way they utilize kin and other networks as a means of coping. Finally, some socio-economic trends that affect childbearing and the mothers' ability to cope are briefly noted.

Chapter 5 looks at women in their domestic and conjugal roles. It highlights the distinction between family and household and the role of the woman in each. In the first section, types of union common to the Caribbean and women's attitudes to and expectations from each type — visiting, common-law, married and single — are described. Attitudes to marriage are then discussed in some detail because marriage represents the norm by which other relationships are measured and the status that women hope to acquire — eventually. The legal aspects of relationships are also discussed. The second section deals with the important distinction between family and household and uses WICP research to re-examine concepts relating to decision-making in the household and the special status of female household heads.

Part III (chapters 6 and 7) focuses on women's economic role performance and, specifically, their varied sources of livelihood.

Chapter 6 looks at women in the world of work and the ideology of work, specifically what is women's work, why women work, and how work is perceived and experienced. First, we look at the historical dimension of female labour and how women's role and status in the labour force have been structurally determined. In the next section we look at how women's work is defined through census and surveys, and then at another way of defining it suggested by the WICP. We also examine women's own perception of what constitutes work and the meaning of work, especially in relation to their notions of independence and the female self-image and the challenges women face in balancing the demands of job and home. The final section looks at women in the labour force and the types of jobs available, with special emphasis on two of them — one traditional (domestic labour) and the other an outgrowth of the modernization process (export-processing industries). The occupational structure of the region's labour force is highlighted to show both the post-war changes that have given women much broader opportunities and the sexual stratification which still exists. Characteristics of working women and women's perceptions of their jobs close this chapter.

Chapter 7 focuses on informal sources of livelihood — the means women employ to survive outside of the formal labour force and to supplement family income. Women's survival strategies that are examined here include 'making do', sources of support identified as male support, kin and friendship networks, pooling resources in the family home, support from adult working children, and institutional benefits. The final section, on women's ownership and management of resources, reveals how few resources most women have and their preference for using informal credit and savings associations such as 'sou sou' rather than formal institutions such as commercial banks.

Section IV (chapters 8 and 9) looks at women in two critical areas: their interactions with the wider society and their relationships with men.

Chapter 8 looks at women in the public and political arenas. It begins by examining the historical role played by 'rebel' women as active participants in public struggles from slavery up to the disorders and civil disturbances of the modern period. 'Decent' women of whatever race and class were expected to participate only in the public roles defined for them — in social work and charitable organizations. Women's entry into politics and the wider social arena is therefore fairly recent. While such participation is now widespread, women have virtually no impact at the higher decision-making levels of society. Some reasons are advanced as to why this might be so, including the ways in which Caribbean women conceptualize gender identity and 'women's issues'.

Chapter 9 examines the complex and not always happy interactions between men and women, and the fact that this is regarded as the domain in which women are most vulnerable. We look, first, at general views of male/female behaviour, particularly as expressed in literature and popular culture such as in calypso. Then, male perceptions of women are examined. Attitudes and expectations of males and females towards each other are contrasted with their actual behaviour and experience, particularly in the realms of fidelity, the assumption of family responsibilities and the phenomenon of male sharing by women. The changing role of women and the implications for male/female relationships are examined and explanations for these relationships are suggested. Finally, there is a brief examination of the development of a women's movement in the 1970s and 1980s.

In the **Conclusion (chapter 10)**, an attempt is made to pull together the various elements that characterize the lives and work of Caribbean women and to suggest areas for future research.

Childhood & Socialization

Edna Manley, *The Message*, 1977 (Ciment fondu, height 45″)
Collection of: Commonwealth Secretariat, London, used with permission of
  the Commonwealth Secretariat
Photographer: Maria La Yacona

1 *The Household Setting*

The social and economic circumstances of her mother will largely determine the kind of household unit into which the Caribbean child is born and the manner in which she is raised, and what ultimately her 'rights' and her 'freedoms' will be.

The mother is paramount because only about one-quarter of the region's children are born into what conforms to the nuclear family, i.e. with father, mother and their children together under one roof. More often than not, the Caribbean child is born and raised in a household rather than a family unit. Although many definitions have been offered as to what constitutes a household, for our purposes a household consists of a group of people residing under one roof and sharing at least one meal a day, who may or may not be family (see White WICP 1986). Nearly one-half of Caribbean households are headed by women, a status deriving largely from the absence of an adult male (see chapter 5). This leaves the woman as principal, often only, breadwinner. In some territories or enclaves, female household heads are in the majority.

For the child, the source of power and authority in the home will depend on the household setting. In many homes, the mother not only fulfils the traditional maternal and domestic roles but is also the provider — sometimes the only one — as well as the authority figure or 'pseudo-father' (Blake 1961). 'My mother who fathered me', the phrase used by Edith Clarke as the title for her now classic study of Jamaican rural communities in the 1950s, was coined by Barbadian novelist George Lamming to describe his own situation: 'My father who had only fathered the idea of me left me the sole liability of my mother who really fathered me' (Lamming 1970, p. 11). The paradigm of absent father, omniscient mother, is central to the ordering and psyche of the Caribbean family.

Trinidadian novelist Merle Hodge, in noting the dominant presence of strong and capable mother figures in the emerging Caribbean literature from the 1950s, observes that she discovered in retrospect that her own novel (*Crick, Crack! Monkey*) is full of these strong women, that the men 'are either absent or unnoticeable' and that 'I had once intended to give the children a grandfather — Ma's husband — but I had conceived of him as an invalid in a rocking chair, ably looked after by Ma!' (Hodge 1974, p. 116).

In real life as in literature, it is the child who often bears the brunt of the mother's frustrations arising from her inability to fulfil her multiple roles manless, jobless and sometimes hopeless. In many homes, the idealized image of motherhood can become distorted by the mother's assumptions of the functions which in most societies are normally provided by the father — including disciplinary ones (see chapter 2). Children growing up in these homes sometimes hold mothers and mother substitutes in awe and fear. Instead of natural closeness, social distance can result (see, for example, Blake 1961; Brodber 1968; Sistren 1986). One WICP informant, a Vincentian washerwoman, said of her mother:

> She ain't easy you know, she ain't easy at all at all, she ain't easy with we at all. She beat we, don't give us no food, lock we out many nights to sleep, don't talk no talk. If we don't go to grandmother she don't give us any food. Every one she used to do the same. She ain't easy. Up to now she still hasty and everything.[1]

Child-caring

Because of all the demands on her time and attention, the working mother might not in fact be able to devote much time to the raising of her children. Although there is legislative provision in some Caribbean countries for paid maternity leave, the law is not easily enforced (Forde WICP 1981) and in some cases does not cover domestic service, in which a significant number of working women are engaged.

Thus the time the female breadwinner can spend at home even with her newly born is sometimes severely limited. As Rodman (1971) expresses it, when the father opts out of providing for the child, the mother has to both care for and mind it. She usually cannot perform both roles simultaneously so she takes on the job of provider and shifts caring to someone else. In the widespread absence of formal child-care facilities,[2] female relatives are the primary carers followed by older siblings, neighbours and friends. In better-off homes, children are looked after by domestic servants, who, in order to work out, must themselves delegate their own child-care responsibilities.

Of course, care of children by their mothers is projected as the ideal situation. Where this is economically possible, many mothers do give up their jobs or interrupt careers or abandon studies in order to take care of their children (WICP survey).

Some women find it possible to combine child-care and work responsibilities, depending on the type of work they do and the way in which they can allocate their time. A Guyanese farm woman in the WICP study was found to care for her baby while she worked by taking him along with her to the field, for, as she explained, 'no trouble at all, with minding baby and care fuh plants at the same time'. What she did was 'build one lil shelter, juk two posts and tie baby hammock near to where me look after dem beds. When me gan too far, me move he and tek he near up again. When he get bigger, me put he in one box to sit down under the shade' (Odie-Ali WICP 1986, p. 274).

Home-based activities — making handicrafts or preserves for sale, cooking, laundering for others, sewing — also afford the mother a means of combining child-care with income-earning activities:

---

1 Unattributed quotations throughout this work are from in-depth interviews with 38 women in the WICP project territories — Antigua, Barbados and St Vincent. The quotations have been substantively edited for length, and punctuation has been imposed, but nothing has been added to the women's speech nor has anything been changed; the author's interpolations are included within square brackets. Names and locations within countries have been altered to protect identities.

2 In 1980, less than 10 per cent of the children of the required age in the territories other than Barbados and Jamaica were enrolled in day care and/or early childhood educational institutions (Grant 1980, vol. I). The WICP survey found day nursery facilities in the three survey territories 'totally inadequate'.

I knew her as the figure
who sat at the first thing I learned to read: 'SINGER'
and she breast-fed
my brother while she sewed; and she taught us to read
while she sewed and
she sat in judgement over all our disputes as she sewed.
                                                    (Goodison 1979)

Because many women tend to enter into stable relationships, including marriage, when they are older and have had several children (see chapter 5), the burden of the first children is often borne single-handed or shared with female kin. More than half of the children in the 1,600 homes in three eastern Caribbean countries surveyed by the WICP were found to be cared for by female relatives, especially grandmothers. About 50 per cent of Caribbean women begin childbearing while they are still teenagers (Powell WICP 1982; see also chapter 4, this work) and the chances are that the first child will be born under the roof of the maternal grandparents. This child is most likely to be looked after by its maternal grandmother, much less often by the father's kin. Child-caring becomes more of a responsibility shared with a partner as the number of children increases. Thus the chances are high that, while the first children will be cared for by others or by the mother alone, later children will increasingly have a father present.

As older children grow, they themselves become the primary minders of younger siblings. This sometimes occurs at very early ages. A Jamaican survey found that in most low-income families children in the age range 9–14 had care of their younger siblings while their mothers were at work.[3] The leaving of infants with very young children, or sometimes on their own, frequently leads to tragic consequences reported in newspaper headlines. Other forms of child-caring might be just as makeshift — older neighbours, older, sometimes enfeebled or handicapped, persons in the home, or the child might become casually 'everyone's child' in a tenement or 'yard' situation.

Older children, especially girls, in a large household can find their own childhoods cut short and their options curtailed by the demands made by their families on their time and energy. Many women interviewed by the WICP attributed their lack of education and life options to the assumption of household responsibilities — and income-earning activities — at an early age. One bitterly complained, 'Every year my mother have a baby, she had 14 in all. I have to stop from school to let her go to work . . . if I didn't have to look after baby, baby, baby, I wouldn't get pregnant so early' (Powell *et al.* WICP 1982; see also chapter 3, this work).

Child-rearing

Grandmother and kin networks

While child-caring is usually a shared responsibility between mother and others, in many cases another does become the substitute mother, moving from caring for to rearing the child. One contributory factor is the process of migration, which is a characteristic feature of Caribbean family life. Women — like men —

---

3 VOUCH, Report on Survey of Age-range of Older Siblings as Child-minders. Quoted in Grant (1974).

frequently migrate from their home villages to the towns, to other islands and to the metropolis in search of work, leaving children with relatives for longer or shorter periods. Edith Clarke in her study of Jamaican village life over thirty years ago noted the significant role played by the grandmother and the diminished role of the mother in the child's life, as a result of migration and other processes:

> Suckling the infant may be the only act which establishes the exclusive maternal relationship: providing for its other needs, fondling and playing with it, may be shared with, or largely taken over by, the grandmother or another relative. When the baby is weaned and the mother goes away (or is sent away) as is usual in these cases, the grandmother assumes all the functions of the real mother who is seen only on rare visits.
>
> (Clarke 1957, p. 142)

One 64-year-old worker on an arrowroot estate in St Vincent, who had her first child as a teenager a generation before Clarke's study, described this process in her own life:

I. Who helped you care for the child because you were quite young, you were about eighteen . . . ?

R. My grandmother.

I. When did your grandmother come into the picture? Did your mother live with her mother?

R. Yes.

I. So you brought the child home to your mother?

R. Yes.

I. And your grandmother cared for it?

R. Grandmother cared the child. I left him about nine months old and went back to work.

I. Did your grandmother teach you anything about childcaring?

R. No, she didn't teach me. All she did to the child was to take care of it because I didn't know one thing about it so she took it over and care it.

I. So you didn't bathe the child?

R. I didn't even know how to bathe it but in her bathing she will show me, you understand, how it is to be done. In those days, the navel couldn't [get] wet but now they does wet them. Then she would be particular to let it dry. So she had the whole care of him and then he was a little boy and everyone in the home . . . Well, I didn't hardly have him you know because everyone want him. I only had to work and maintain him, and they stay at home and care the child.

While it is the 'absent father' who is most frequently remarked upon, the 'absent mother'[4] has become sufficiently institutionalized to be also a theme in West Indian literature:

> Every year we expected my mother home on vacation, and every year she wrote that she was sorry that she couldn't make it. But she always sent, as if to represent her, a large round box that people insisted on calling a barrel. It was full of used clothes of all sorts, obviously chosen with little regard for my size or my grandmother's size . . . Every year we expected my mother home on vacation. But she never came. The year I was in Third Form they flew her body home.
>
> (Pollard 1974)

---

4 Nevertheless, it should be emphasized that the absence of the mother cannot be equated with that of the father. Foster-mothers, unlike foster-fathers are plentiful in Caribbean cultures.

A Vincentian, who was 26 at the time of the WICP interview and whose mother had migrated overseas in search of work and left her and her brother to be raised by their grandmother, gives an insider's perspective on this phenomenon:

I. So when you were growing up your mother was away?

R. Yes.

I. And who raised you?

R. My grandmother. She was more or less my mother because she was the only person that I really knew.

I. You don't remember when your mother left for the first time?

R. No, nothing at all. I couldn't even remember her.

I. How did you feel when you saw her for the first time again?

R. Well, my grandmother told me and my mother told me the same thing, [that] when she came back I told her plainly that she was not my mother. I said plainly, 'This is not my mother'.

I. Who did you think was your mother, your grandmother?

R. My grandmother. Because when I was growing up when I came home from school she would be there, wherever I go she was there, and if anything happen she was there. So I thought, really, that was my mother. She never let us call her Mummy, she let us call her Gran or Granny, whichever she felt like, and she made a statement that she wasn't our mother, right, that she was only our grandmother. But, still, for having to accept a stranger to be your mum!

I. How did you get along with your mother when you first saw her?

R. At a distance. I would just sit down and I would watch her. But to go near her like she was my mother, no I wouldn't. We were just at a distance. But then, growing, we realise she is our mother, then we change.

The WICP survey showed that less than 50 per cent of first children grow up with their mothers. However, the presence and power of the grandmother usually lessens with each succeeding child. In examining the pattern of child-rearing among women in the WICP sample, Powell (WICP 1982) observed that, as the number of children increased, a common pattern emerged: 'a decline in the proportion of mothers-only parenting and an increase in the proportion of both parents with each additional child. Grandmothers feature more strongly in earlier than later childbearing.' Increasing mobility and dispersal of families has also contributed to the weakening of the 'grandmother household'.

Child-shifting

In many cases, parenting is carried out by perfect strangers: informal 'adoptions' of children into households of strangers as well as kin is another well-established feature of Caribbean family life. These 'adoptions' are not necessarily stable and many children might end up passing their childhood years in a succession of households. The impulses to parenting are seemingly endless:

I. When do they usually take them and why they take them?

R. See them and like them.

I. Oh. You see a child and you like —

R. Like the little child, and the parents is embarrassed by . . . if they could go to work, you know, and me mother and even the other strange person see that it is a little inconvenient for the mother, she say, 'give me the baby, nuh'.

I. And just take it like that?

R. Yes . . . 'I'll keep it for you.' Sometimes she keep it just for the day or two, and after that, what happen? They don't give it up at all.

I. They just keep it until it is a grown person?

R. Until it get big. I know my mother had children until they get big now and the parents . . . she say, 'well the child can help you now. She can sweep the house, she can carry water, so you can come back and take you child.'

I. Oh, the woman who took it gives it back to the mother willingly?

R. Yes. They give it back to her for she can help.

(Brodber WICP 1986, p. 27)

A childless woman might wish to mother a child and 'borrows' one from someone else. Children are sent off to be 'company' to ageing grandparents. A lonely older woman requires a companion and takes a child from a large family. Children in need — motherless or homeless — will be taken by relatives or others. Children unwanted in a home because of a new 'stepfather' might be sent away to live with a grandmother, an aunt or the father's relatives. Mothers who are finding it hard to make ends meet in the city to which they have migrated might send their children to stay in the country with relatives and might disperse them in the process. Illness or death of the mother might also lead to family dispersal. Mothers might simply abandon their children — to the elements or to temporary minders. A Jamaican survey in the 1970s showed the economic situation of the mother to be a significant deciding factor in child dispersal (Roberts and Sinclair 1978, p. 166).

In the shuffle, some children will be subjected to the extremes of total abandonment or be turned over to the authorities for care by the state or become 'street-corner boys' or other manifestations of children left to fend for themselves in cases of acute family distress. A researcher on abandonment of children in Jamaica noted that:

'Passing on' as a means of dealing with problems of children seems to be an accepted solution. Leaving a child in a borrowed toilet, at a busy street corner, in someone's car, does not suggest an attempt to solve problems of child-caring by infanticide but are only more extreme forms of passing on to a father, a cousin, or a woman who needs a child to help her in the market.

(Brodber 1974, p. 49)

Fortunately for some children in need of a home, there are many women in need of parenting yet another child. A number of women were asked by WICP researchers to describe the complex processes whereby they came to be raising the children of others, or others came to be raising theirs. An Antiguan woman described her shift from caring to parenting a 3-year-old whom she started looking after when she was 18 years old:

R. His mother was working and he had all sort of rash on his skin. It seems as if she was trying to get away from him. So when she brings it on mornings, I will see to it. She finish work at four and she never used to come for it until seven at night. After a time it was left with me altogether.

I. Did she make some arrangements for leaving the child?

R. No. No arrangements at all, because the night when I was looking for her to come for it she didn't come.

After two years the mother took the child and sent him to his grandmother. This informant went on to raise eight children of her own, but also took in another child — simply because she liked him:

R. Let me tell you how that started out. He's from a family of maybe eight. His mother is something like mine; she had a lot of different children. She's married herself but her husband and her fell out years ago [and] so as to get support for these children, she go to another man and she gets pregnant and its just a cycle . . . she ends up with a lot of kids of her own and the little boy used to be what we call a handiboy around the neighbourhood. And I used to have sheep and I used to pay him a little dollar per week to look after, run them out of the pasture, and another little dollar a week to sweep up the yard you know. So it just happened like this. He comes and he gets his little dollar and his little food and I can't even tell you where it began, where we got so attached, but coming and coming and coming, he gets his food. Now and then I'll buy him a little shirt. And its just a cycle. He moved in and moved in and he's living here altogether.

I. What's the relationship you have with the mother?

R. We don't even say hello.

Another woman explained that she had taken a boy because:

My boys met him, they seem to know him and he came with them one day and I fell in love with him, start wondering who his parents were. His aunt went and told the mother how I love this child so much. She have a lot of them, eleven, so she say well if she love him let her keep him. Just like that.

The boy has been living with her for the past ten years. This woman also raised her sister's oldest child until he was 18 years old. When asked how this came about, she said that her sister had come to her house for the birth of her two children: 'When she was getting the first one she came. That was when she was about three months making her. So both of them born in my yard so they come like my own, I love them so much.' Her sister in turn raised our informant's son:

I. How did he come to be living in Trinidad with your sister?

R. She was always fond of him. She always used to go and come and when he was about 8 years old she told me to send him to spend some time with her. I asked her to send him back. She say when she was ready she would bring him. She kept him for six years. When he got big he must be started giving her trouble, you know, so I told her to send him home to me.

A woman in her sixties described her own adoption and that of her sisters:

I. Why is it that you were taken from St Vincent at the age of 3 and sent to Trinidad and lived with a guardian?

R. Well you see my parents were poor people and she had one child that a god-mother took from her and took to Trinidad. And a friend in Trinidad asked her to get another child for her so she came and took me.

I. So your parents didn't know . . . [her guardian].

R. No, no, no, no. They knew nothing about her.

I. So their friend got you for her?

R. For her.

I. How long did you live with your guardian?

R. I lived with her until I came back here around 12 to 14 because she died. And she left it on record that I must be returned to my mother.

I. How many children did your mother have?

R. Five.

I. Did your mother keep all your other brothers and sisters?

R. No. Three was in Trinidad. Another friend saw me and asked the same person to get another for them and so that person came back and took another so I have a sister in Trinidad now.

The recipients and minders of others' children might themselves have many children of their own and/or be having a hard time making ends meet or be even destitute. While economic factors might force mothers to hand over their children to someone else, of some importance too is the fact that the children are often wanted by the recipients and fill a place in the household. One WICP informant, a motherless child, described how she casually took the place of another girl in a relative's household:

R. Going to watch the TV the people don't mind me watching the TV but TV used to stop at nine o'clock and it was pretty dark at nine and I used to stay and sleep until morning and sleep until morning until I eventually live, live in with the people.

I. So it started from going by after school, eating, staying and watching TV. TV is late, you stay and you sleep?

R. Yes. Why I wanted to stay was because there's a cousin who lived there and her mother lived in Canada and she was going to Canada for good so I just fit in to take her place in the home.

As Erna Brodber notes of an earlier period when child labour was more common, 'dispersion of a child was not intended to mean permanent subtraction from its natural parents but rather the loan of its energies to a needy household in return for good treatment' (Brodber 1984, p. 57).

The experiences of the St Vincent informant who was taken to live in the household of a childless woman in Trinidad seems to embody both views: 'My *work* [our emphasis] was to keep her company as she didn't have any children.' This woman herself later raised four grandchildren after her only son died and, though poor, regarded them as a welcome addition to her then single household.

Of course, facilities for formal (legal) adoption do exist. The route of formal adoption is usually followed by married couples of means and, increasingly, childless single women. Official foster care is also covered by legislation. But 'child-shifting' as a widespread process exists outside legal sanction.

The nature of child-shifting   The fact that so many children spend their formative years with people other than their parents and are often shifted back and forth between households has many implications for their socialization. Although no study of this phenomenon could be found, the extent and nature of child-shifting is thrown into high relief by a number of researchers. From a survey conducted in Jamaica in the 1970s, Roberts and Sinclair (1978) estimated that about 15 per cent of the population under the age of 15 are shifted. Between one-third and one-quarter of the 1,600 women in the WICP survey had raised children other than their own; in most cases the women had raised several such children.

Erna Brodber in her study of Jamaican families examined the detailed life-histories of 37 women, and established that, of the 37, 10 had never lived at any time in units that contained both parents. Seven of the 10 had lived with their mothers and three with their fathers:

Twenty-six persons had lived for some time with both or one parent. Only seven of these continued to live with both parents consistently past teenage. Seven lived at some stage with both parents and at other times with neither parent. Only 14 of the 37 women —

seven with mother and seven with both parents — had experienced no change in primary group personnel through subtraction or addition of parents or self. Twenty-two or a little more than 61 per cent therefore were subject to change . . . For the women who grew up for some time with a parent or both parents:

in 9 cases there were also grandparents in the unit

in 4 cases there were also aunts

in 2 cases there were also cousins

in 1 case there was also a stepfather

in 1 case there was also a father's wife's sister.

The seven whose parents both shifted from them lived with grandmother in three cases

cousins in two cases

grandparents in one case; and

a stranger/grandmother in one case.

(Brodber WICP 1982b, pp. 6–7)

All the women in Brodber's sample had raised children other than their own, the number of children passing through a woman's care being as high as 30. A study by Dorian Powell of the present generation in Jamaica reveals a similar pattern of parenting. A collective profile of 100 teenage mothers showed:

• 40 grew with parents
• 27 raised by mother alone
• 16 raised by grandmother
• 17 raised by other relatives   (Powell 1982).

Some surveys suggest that most cases of child-shifting occur among women in 'visiting' unions, i.e. unions with no resident partners. Roberts and Sinclair in their study of Jamaican women found that an overwhelming majority of children being cared for away from their mothers' homes came from this type of union (1978, p. 246) and that 'visiting' women depend most on sources outside the family for aid for their children (p. 173).

Child-shifting in various forms is characteristic of lower-income Afro-American families, is widespread throughout the Caribbean and, indeed, the African diaspora (see Herskovits 1958, ch. 7; Rodman 1971; Roberts and Sinclair 1978; Brodber WICP 1986; WICP survey 1982) and is strongly embedded in our history. Historical antecedents for the practice might be sought both in some West African countries where a child belongs to a tribe and a nation and the concept of 'orphan' is unknown, and in the earliest experiences of the African family in the diaspora. Under the system of chattel slavery which existed throughout the Caribbean, the concept of family hardly existed; dispersal of family members was the norm. Up to a certain age, children would be kept with their mothers, but, during the daytime hours when the female slave was expected to labour, parenting was assigned by the slave-owner to others. Mrs Carmichael, a Scotswoman who resided five years in the West Indies in the closing years of slavery and wrote a book on the 'domestic manners and conditions' of the population, noted that:

Children who are too young to be employed, are all brought up by women, whose sole office is to take care of them. They return to their parents at night, but not until then. Their food is given by the manager to the nurse and the woman who has the care of them, keeps them together all day in a building appropriated for them. Every mother has time allowed her in the morning to wash, dress and suckle her infant — that is when she again returns from her confinement to work. The nurse keeps the baby and attends upon the mother from three to four weeks, as may be requisite. One or more nurses are required for the estate, according to the number and ages in the nursery.

(Carmichael 1833, vol. I)

In seeking to arrive at explanations for child-shifting and other aspects of contem-porary lower-class family life, one researcher, Hyman Rodman, suggested that child-shifting is permissible in this subculture because of the lack of a strong feeling that it is the biological mother alone who must bring up the children:

> The mother's mother, mother's sister, and many others may, and frequently do, bring up the child. If there were a strong feeling that the mother should bring up her own child, it would be more difficult and guilt-provoking to turn one's child over to another's care. The lack of such a feeling makes it possible to maintain the child-shifting pattern, and therefore makes it possible for the woman whose husband has left her to arrange for the care of her child.
>
> (Rodman 1971, p. 184)

In other words, child-shifting can be seen as a guilt-free problem-solving mechanism indulged in by a mother who is left by the father to provide and care for the child and who cannot do both. In a further extension of this adaptation, the society provides women — older women especially — who specialize in the child-rearing role (Rodman 1971, p. 184).

The effects of child-shifting   Although we now have a fair idea of the diversity of family forms that exist and some of the patterns of parenting, we have very little knowledge of the treatment accorded the child by proxy parents and the effects on its emotional life and socialization. The experiences seem to vary widely. One of Brodber's informants noted that 'adopted' children were treated the same way as children of the family: 'Same school. Same bed. They don't sleep otherwise. Everybody in the children's room. And sleep same way and they eat everything same way. And if you get a farthing, everybody get a farthing . . . Even strangers, beside my mother, treat children same so' (Brodber WICP 1986, p. 26).

Other WICP informants cited different types of experiences. A 23-year-old who was raised by an aunt recalled the treatment by her cousins:

I. Some of the girls used to beat you up?
R. Yes.
I. Why?
R. Well, I don't know if it's because they want me to come do it all. Because, well, she feel like she could hit me and nothing to it. Sometimes they don't even talk to me if they feel like just hitting me for certain things. Sometimes they have some people take advantage of other people's children because they know it's not their children.
I. You said that sometimes they wouldn't let you use certain things because you were from a poor family. What kinds of things they wouldn't let you use?
R. Like their bathrooms and their toilets.
I. So what bathroom did you use?
R. Sometimes I had to bathe outside. Well, you know I was young so nobody would take any notice. I used to have to go by my mother to use the toilet or probably I might do it in school.

What these examples perhaps do not fully convey are the shifting residences, relationships and emotional centres to which many children are exposed during childhood and the lack of bonding to mother or another adult figure that might result. A telling indication might be that children frequently address their mothers as 'aunt', 'sister' or by other kin names but not as 'mother' (see, for example, Braithwaite 1953; Rodman 1971; Roberts and Sinclair 1978). Additionally, the 'adoption' might not be a stable one and the child might be shifted back and forth between homes as circumstances dictate. Even when a child grows up in one household, the composition of that household might change with alarming rapidity.

One older woman who had raised many children described a specific case of child-shifting:

> Well, sometimes some of them don't want to go. I have a little one . . . and she never want to go back to her Mammy. No. I tell her, 'Yes. She is your mother.' And I say, 'Your mother still counts.' And a next one again she leave her child. She was working and she ask me say, 'Mek she stay with you for me until I can get somewhere.' Because they never want any child staying at the yard where she was living. And I say to her, 'Alright.' And when the mother came here one day I say, 'She getting big now, why don't you give it . . . to the auntie? The auntie is better off than I and now I am not working and I have to be living with my son. If I was working I wouldn't send her back.'

The mother eventually took the child, to the minder's satisfaction, for:

> She is better off, for the school that she is going, I wouldn't be able to school her . . . And she go far up, for she went for Senior Cambridge and expect to marry now. And she look nice. She came here Saturday.

(Brodber WICP 1986, p. 28)

But when is the child really 'better off'? What little has been published on the effects of child-shifting identifies it as deleterious to the personality development of the child (see studies cited in Grant 1980; also Wray and McLaren 1976; Feldman and Marriott 1979). Other research suggests that the long-term effect of maternal separation might be modified by a great many factors such as duration of and reasons for separation, age of child and quality of foster care (Landman *et al.* 1983); what we do know is that a great deal more research is needed to evaluate such effects.[5]

Paternal absence

The unsettled nature of the child's existence might be further exacerbated by its relationship to a father who is usually absent from the household, whose contact with the child might be limited or perfunctory or who might even be unknown. In place of the father there might be a constant shift of male partners ('stepfathers'), a situation which sometimes leads to emotional and physical abuse of another man's child and, especially in the case of girls, sexual abuse.

If, as is often the case, men have children with several women, then, even if the desire to play the father role is present, the time he can spend in any one household is limited. The absent father has become such a common feature of Caribbean life that society itself sometimes takes for granted his physical absence. One woman who was 'adopted' recalled:

> The woman, my guardian, always tell me I have a mother, but she never tell me I have a father so I didn't know much about a father. But when I came back I went there to look for him to tell him I arrive. He took me quite nice and glad to know me and from that we go alright until he dead, we never had any falling out, never had.

Another was asked to describe her relationship with her father:

---

5 The reader is referred to Sistren's *Lionheart Gal* (1986), which is a virtual source-book on the socialization of poor rural girl children especially, in Jamaica.

R. Well I never live with him you know he live by himself so he never say nothing cause he glad for grandchildren because is only me alone he have.

I. So what was his reaction when the baby was born?

R. Well he glad and he lift them up and kiss them.

I. Did he used to help you with them?

R. No, no.

I. He didn't help in any way?

R. No. The onliest helping he do he just give a . . . if they want exercise books and they go to him he will give them. But like, to say, chip in with money or food, not he. Me mother alone.

Nevertheless, we ought to treat the question of paternal absence with some caution for, as the body of literature on the West Indian family grows, there is increasing evidence that the 'absent father' might play a larger role in the welfare and socialization of the child than has been suggested.

The typology which has been developed for the Caribbean census classifies unions as 'married', 'common-law' and 'visiting' (described more fully in chapter 5). It is assumed that a man is present in both married and common-law unions while the 'visiting' type has no resident male. This represents about one-quarter of Caribbean unions. The visiting union is commonly described as unstable with little or no contact between father and child. However, a recent investigation of patterns of reproduction and family among Jamaican women suggests another look at visiting relationships. In-depth interviews with 500 women in a study by Roberts and Sinclair (1978) showed that the contact maintained between father and child in visiting unions is 'considerable'. That partners spend about three hours per day in each other's company suggests that many important decisions are arrived at jointly. The fathers were found to spend an average of four hours per week with their children. The authors argue that their findings make a 'strong case' for a sub-category of visiting union which they describe as a 'casual relationship'. This is usually a first relationship for a woman and is called a union only because it involves sexual contact from which a child results; usually afterwards the man is not seen again. It is children from these unions, Roberts and Sinclair argue, who are most subjected to the 'absent father' syndrome. They concluded that:

> Many discussions of the family are concerned with whether it performs satisfactorily such functions as the socialization of the child and the part a non-residential father plays in these processes. While full elucidation of these issues cannot be obtained from this study, the extensive contacts between the father and his children and between him and his partner indicates that current opinion often appreciably understates his role in these important aspects of the family.
>
> (Roberts and Sinclair 1978, p. 243)

More recent research in a suburban area of Kingston, Jamaica, also suggests greater paternal participation in child-raising than has been reported (Landman et al. 1983). R.T. Smith using a different methodology — genealogies of 51 individuals from Jamaica and Guyana — also suggests a new approach to the concept of 'male marginality' in these societies. He says, 'What these data show is that the existence of non-legal and unstable unions, low occupational status and high birth rates does not entail an erosion of kinship ties and does not lead to the disappearance of males from kinship networks and genealogies' (Smith 1975).

It might be argued that a father who visits is a father who is 'present'. Nevertheless, father absence does play a role in family problems. For instance, a study of 444 female clients of the Family Court in Jamaica showed that only 40 of the women were married; over half (59.7 per cent) were single, one-third (30.4 per cent) were separated and the rest divorced. Their problems included child support, behavioural problems and child care. In most cases problems of maintenance arose when the relationship broke down and the father was not seen again. The researcher Jean Jackson noted that it was these single parents who experienced the most stress (Jackson WICP 1982).

'Inside/outside' children

For the child, another confusing element in family life might be the problematic nature of kin relationships, especially in small societies. This stems from the practice of both men and women having children with different partners.[6] The complexities which can result from such relationships is well illustrated by one Antiguan young woman's story. She is the eighth of 13 children her mother had with five different men and she was raised by an aunt. Her father had five children with five different women.

> **R.** One day I'm in church. I was small at the time and a lady kept staring at me and I didn't know why. So after church she came and ask me if I was a Sharpe. I told her yes. She ask me if I am a Sharpe from Main Road. I said yes. She said, 'That Sharpe he is my brother.'
>
> **I.** So it was your aunt?
>
> **R.** Yes. Look, I met my parents very funny. He had some other children, you know, and he had grandchildren. And this girl she's older than I am, we were playing at school; we were good friends [but] didn't know that we were related. So this day she came up to me and ask me what's my title. I said Sharpe, because we used to play and didn't even know each other's names. And she ask me who's my father. I told her. She said, 'You know, he's my grandfather.' And she invited me [home] and I met my big sisters and a big brother.
>
> **I.** What kind of relationship did you have with your father's son?
>
> **R.** He met me in town. I didn't know him, right. He met me in town and ask me, 'Are you a Sharpe?' I say, 'yes'. He say, 'I'm your brother, you know.' I looked at him and could see he was a Sharpe.

There is usually no problem in identifying a woman's children, though in 'respectable' families an unplanned child born out of wedlock to a young woman might be passed off and reared as someone else's child, even in the same household. But this is nowadays increasingly rare. A man's activities, however, might well be covert and half-siblings might only gain contact with and knowledge of each other by accident or in adulthood, especially since under most circumstances the illegitimate child will bear the surname of the mother. Most legislation in the Caribbean (inherited from English law) distinguishes between 'legitimate' children born in wedlock and those who are 'illegitimate'. Where children are born out of wedlock, the name of the father will not appear on the birth certificate unless the father goes to register the

---

6 Thus at least one analyst has argued that 'the attribution of the concepts "legitimacy" and "illegitimacy" to a society where extramarital relations and parenthood are more common than those within family is analytically inappropriate and misleading' (Joseph Manyoni, 'Legitimacy and illegitimacy: misplaced polarization in Caribbean family studies', *Canadian Review of Sociology and Anthropology*, 14:4, 1977).

child and consents to have his name registered or otherwise formally acknowledges paternity by signing a paternity certificate. The child might also be registered in the mother's name but be known by the father's name, or might have a 'pet name' by which she is always called but which does not appear on the birth certificate. Half-siblings on both sides of the family can therefore end up with a bewildering array of names and might not even know each other, as the song 'Shame and scandal in the family' narrates. There might be effort on the man's part to hide his activities which result in what are called throughout the Caribbean 'outside children', i.e. children born outside his stable residential union. One middle-class older informant recalled that as a child she knew that her father had 'outside children' but not how many:

> R. My mother didn't talk very much about it, you know. Children were not sup-
> posed to be brought into these things. But we knew that there were outside
> children. It's only recently since I'm an adult that I've come to learn of one
> or two of the others. There were one or two who were accepted by my mother
> because she knew before [she got married]; she knew that these children
> existed and so they visited. There's one particularly that we're close to, an
> older one. I think there is another one. But just recently when I was in Canada
> somebody called me and said, 'Your sister is here,' and I said, 'sister?' And
> she called me up and she said, 'Hi, old So-and-so was a son of a something,
> he was something else.'
> I. Referring to your father?
> R. Yes.
> I. And you had never laid eyes on her?
> R. Up to now I haven't seen her because I was not able to meet with her that
> day. She was visiting from New York. But she said, 'come and see me any
> time and this is my address and this is my telephone number' sort of thing.
> So I know that there is another one and there must be many others because
> you know West Indian men. Then those that I knew about growing up as a
> child were the ones he had after, he had five children after.
> I. So there were two sets of 'outside'; the ones before he married your mother
> and the ones after?
> R. Yes.

The way an outside child will be treated will depend to a great extent, it seems, on the status of the people involved, as the varied experiences related below by women in different countries and of different ages and life styles show. Generally, the notion of legitimacy/illegitimacy does not seem to be an issue among lower-income families; they recognize the legal but not the social aspects of this status (Rodman 1971). Among the middle and upper strata where marriage is the norm, and values are derived from metropolitan countries, considerable social stigma once attached to illegitimacy, though, generally speaking, this is not the case today. It should also be borne in mind that the concept of 'inside/outside' children refers not so much to their legal status as to whether they are born inside a union (whether married or common-law) or outside it.

One woman spoke of her husband's children which he had with another woman before they were married:

> They come now and again to spend time. He has a son and a daughter, the
> daughter and I are closer than the son. The son's mother is in England. She left
> him when he was a year and she never sent for him. She went to do nursing and
> she is qualified now; she could have made an effort to send for her child. She

never did. She came home last year and she wanted me to take him. I said, 'No way. I have three. I got mine very young and I sacrifice a lot. I think now is the time for you to have him. He's growing up, he's fourteen now.' She said she is going to some other course for another two years and if I could keep him for the two years. I said, 'I need a break too so why not let me go for the two years and come back and then we'll change.' She didn't say anything but I didn't take him so he [her husband] took the child and left him with his mother.

A teacher describes the situation of a child fathered by her husband before their marriage:

I. How did she come to be living with you?

R. The mother of the child used to meet him [her husband] and run him down all the time. He wouldn't give the child anything and I felt sorry for the child because it's his, no two ways about it, and I took it. First he said I mustn't bring the child there; he doesn't want this child to mix with his children and [he] go out and tell them she's nothing to them and things like that. And I say, 'No, no, no. You not bringing that against her because of my children. She's your child. You had it before you were married and it's their half sister, see.'

The same woman (who came from a close nuclear family) talks of her own father's 'outside child':

R. He tried to hide it from us. Of course it eventually came out. He never brought the child home, he never mentioned the child at home and if my mother should say anything about it he tried to change the conversation as quickly as possible. But we understood that he used to support the girl. The first time that he really spoke to me about her, she passed common entrance to go to secondary school and he came and asked me if I had any books to give her. I said, 'You don't give the child books that I don't want. What do you mean by that? When we went to school you never bought a secondhand book for us. Go and buy a new book for the girl.' And his words were, 'She's a secondhand child.' These were his exact words. There was never any big thing about it but he said, 'She's a secondhand child.'

I. But he never brought her in and never . . . ?

R. No.

Another middle-class father took a different approach. As his daughter recalled:

R. She was of lower status of course and he insisted that the children got the same sort of education that we got. He insisted that we should go to secondary school and he also insisted that they should go to secondary school too.

I. Did you go to the same secondary school?

R. Yes. We were older. But we did meet. We lived very near to one another and it was not an easy relationship because this woman and the second family lived very near to my [maternal] grandmother. And I always remember my mother saying, 'When you go out that street, walk on the other side.' My mother was a lady, incidentally. So we knew that these people were there but, you know, it was sort of dinned into us that there wasn't to be any relationship between us and them. They were there but we were to keep as far as possible from them. That has coloured our relationships more or less and so our lives.

Then there are the effects on the children themselves. A teacher informant recalled:

R. Women are famous for giving the illegitimate children the name of the man, whether he is married or separated. And we had it where one child would say, 'She is carrying my father's name but she better don't carry my name.' Sometimes we would call a name and they would say, 'She is not my sister, Miss.' They would come right out and tell me this. And I know they are innocent but I have to try and make these two children learn to accept each other and learn to share what they had; even though there were different mothers they were the same father.

I. Did you know anything about the history of these children?

R. One girl was a year older than the other and the father always brought this child from outside home to spend weekends and vacations. And the mother never wanted it and it cause disturbance in the home. But the mother had to do what he wanted. So this child resented this other one because at times it lead to blows because of this child.

Although the social implications of this aspect of family life have not been studied, obviously there are such implications for both the 'inside' family and the 'outside' children. There must be serious social/psychological consequences for the individuals concerned, for the quality of family life and for society in general. Children might well be guaranteed equality under the Constitution of their land, but their social and in many cases their legal status are in fact determined by their birth status. For example, an older light-skinned, middle-class informant recalled that during her childhood:

If you were an illegitimate child you couldn't go to certain schools, [get] certain jobs, you couldn't go to the grammar schools and the girls' high school. This girl had a child for a very . . . not a white man but he was very high brown, and this girl was very fair, and the school mistress would not admit this girl if she were living with the mother, so the mother asked my mother to board her. The school only took in children who were boarding in certain circumstances which they felt were decent enough and the school would not accept her if she continued living with her mother.

The phenomenon of child-shifting, i.e. rearing outside the family home, and the complications of 'inside/outside' children are some of the factors which lead to the pain of separation and lack of family unity which persist into adult life. One middle-class woman, whose two older children were raised by her parents, touches on the seemingly schizoid nature of Caribbean domestic life as she looks forward to the day when her entire family might be reunited:

At times you don't have this sense of oneness, so they would be with me, go out to spend a weekend or vacation or whatever. We will live together. We will sleep under one roof. Because my entire family, my five children, my husband and myself, we have never yet one day slept under one roof as a whole family by ourselves in our twenty-five years of marriage.

And yet, as we will discover when we come to look more closely below at the lives of Caribbean women, these seemingly fragmented manifestations of family life mask much stronger bonds than at first appear. Although children might be shifted around frequently, might grow up in households rather than nuclear families and in situations where the concept of family appears tenuous, kin relationships are nevertheless a potent force in the lives of most individuals. Caribbean family ties are extensive (though they might be shallow) and because of widespread migration are geographically far-reaching. Through family networks, women especially can develop a resource base which enables them to cope with their child-rearing and economic responsibilities.

Erna Brodber has argued that the processes described, especially child-shifting and consequent 'lack of fixed emotional centres', do encourage independence since they require adjustments of the emotional self and help to develop flexibility in dealing with the world (Brodber WICP 1986). These factors also encourage what Brodber calls 'emotional expansiveness', which enables women to always find room for children — theirs and those of others. But, it can be argued, they also create feelings of anomie, of displacement, of anger, of worthlessness, of guilt, which can consume a great deal of creative energy as children struggle to rebuild wounded psyches (see, for example, Senior 1986; Sistren 1986).

While the information collected on the Caribbean family structure and family formation over the last few decades is now quite extensive, the same cannot be said regarding the internal dynamics of the family and the effects of the processes described on the development of self-identity and on socialization. In the next chapter we will nevertheless attempt to describe how the child is socialized within these varied domestic settings and specifically how male/female roles are transmitted.

2 Socialization & Gender-Role Learning

The socialization process

The way a girl child is raised from birth, the differences emphasized between her and a boy child, will determine to a great extent the manner in which she will later manage her life, resources and social and sexual encounters.

An examination of gender-role socialization — the process by which we learn gender identity — might provide an answer to some critical questions frequently asked about Caribbean women and examined in this work. Questions such as: Why do Caribbean women place such a high premium on child-bearing? (chapter 4). What accounts for the so-called irresponsibility of the Caribbean male? Why do Caribbean men treat their women the way they do and why do women 'accept' such treatment? (chapter 9). How do we account for the fact that Caribbean women now have equal access to education at nearly all levels — and perform academically as well as men (chapter 3), yet continue to make 'safe' and 'female' low-paid low-status occupational choices? (chapter 6). That women are recognized as 'power-ful' in the domestic sphere (chapter 5), function powerfully (though unrecognizably so) in the economic sphere (chapter 6 and 7) but continue to take a back seat in the public domain? (chapter 8).

It is now well established that our values, attitudes, behaviour, choices and performance as men and women owe a great deal to the manner in which we learn or absorb the specific role which society associates with the male or female sex. Gender-role learning is an important part of our socialization, which is the process by which 'Every society tries to raise its young so that they will accept the values and ideas of that society . . . Socialization experiences in childhood prepare people for the social roles they will be expected to assume as adults' (Romer 1981, pp. xv–xvi).[1] The gender role is one of the most important of these roles, for it determines our behaviour as men and women.

The way children develop gender identity will be based mainly on the influence of significant others at various stages of their development. Children learn not only from those who consciously teach them but also teach themselves through observing the social world around them. Because of a desire to 'fit in' with society, argues Romer, the individual becomes a partner in the process of gender-role socialization. In the narrow world of infancy, parents, family and family friends and child-care personnel will be the child's principal influences. But, as the child

---

1 The theoretical orientation in this section draws heavily on Romer (1981).

grows older and moves into adolescence, other agents assume greater importance. Principal among these agents will be the school and teachers, but peers, books, television and other media also assume larger roles, coming to exert a more significant influence than the family circle.

The way parents, teachers and others contribute to the socialization process will to a great extent reflect the social and cultural norms and expectations of the wider society in which they live as well as how they themselves were socialized. Thus the social categories of race, ethnicity, socio-economic status or class will affect how the gender role is defined. Nancy Romer speaking of American society gives an example which is also applicable to Caribbean society of how social categories could affect a woman's socialization:

> a wealthy woman would be socialized to fulfill a different social role as an adult than a poor woman would be. The two would probably have different expectations of the kinds of lives they will lead as adults, and they will have different socialization experiences: one may attend a small, private school, while the other goes to an overcrowded public school; one may take music lessons, and the other may work part-time after school. The wealthy woman may expect to go to college and marry a factory owner, while the poor woman may drop out of school and go to work in that very factory. While one of the women may fully expect to be provided for by the advantaged man in her life, the other may realize that she must provide for herself because the poor economic circumstances of the men and women around her do not offer a cushion for support. These different experiences will help to socialize these two women into very different types of adults.
>
> (Romer 1981, p. xx)

Before we look specifically at how the Caribbean female learns gender identity, we will first look at the socialization of the Caribbean child within the family or household. We will then look at gender-role learning in the home — how the girl child learns to prepare for adulthood and the specific roles she will play as a woman; we will also examine the sometimes contradictory roles played by adults in the home circle.

Very few studies of socialization in the Caribbean have been published to date. Information on the subject presented below is heavily drawn from the many studies on the Caribbean family which have been published over the last few decades. At best, this permits only the grossest generalizations. More than anything else, it makes us realize how inadequate is our knowledge of this very important subject.

Factors affecting socialization

Culture Cultural factors will play a particularly significant role in the socialization process since it is through these that the ideas and values of a society are most frequently expressed. By 'culture' here we simply mean the rituals, behaviour and organizations which distinguish particular peoples and are transmitted from generation to generation. Some cultures are homogeneous, i.e. all accept the same norms and values. Others, such as those of the English-speaking Caribbean, are more complex. Though these societies are held together by institutions which are shared by all, different sectors might adhere to different value systems. The socialization process in the multicultural Caribbean might be complicated by the fact that individuals often teeter between two or more racial and cultural ideals: on the one hand the received white European culture of these territories, on the other the culture based on blood and ethnic origins — especially African or Indian — which has been partly or largely suppressed or 'submerged'. The result for many is severe cultural imbalance (see, for example, Nettleford 1970; Brathwaite 1974). For this reason the socialization of the Caribbean child has been described variously as contradictory (Henriques 1953), frustrating (Kerr 1952) and full of tension (Hodge WICP 1982; see also Sistren 1986).

The first of the cultural factors to be emphasized is the significance of race and ethnicity and the correlation between race and class. The social structure — and racial perceptions — have been changing in recent times for a number of reasons:

1 the broadening of opportunities through education;
2 growing upward social mobility in some societies through the acquisition of quick wealth;
3 the black power movement of the 1970s, which brought questions of race and class into the open and helped to challenge concepts of physical beauty (Hodge 1974);
4 increasing political nationalism, of which the emphasis on indigenous culture and new recognition of the African and Indian elements in the heritage are manifestations.

Despite changes and more open attitudes, both skin colour and ethnicity and people's perceptions of the roles these play in power and status in Caribbean societies are still of tremendous importance. Recent studies of self-concept and self-identity among young people in Jamaica, for instance, show that the Caucasian ideal or a close approximation is still operative (in a country which is over 90 per cent black) (see Miller 1969, 1973).

The pervasive influence of the mass media, with content heavily influenced by metropolitan programming and advertising concepts, and the role these play in shaping or reinforcing certain racial, cultural and sexist biases are also of tremendous significance (see Cuthbert 1981).

Notions of colour and status are underscored by the perception that the educational system itself still reinforces the European or white bias as the ideal and, up to recently, implicitly or explicitly denigrated the black or African, though the introduction of a regionally structured curriculum is now helping to change this. Since education is perceived as an important contributor to upward social mobility, parents of lower socio-economic groups have high aspirations for their children to raise themselves out of their poverty-stricken conditions by success in this sphere (see chapter 3). But the school system — textbooks, curricula, teaching methodology — is based largely on European values, which are often at odds with the reality of the world and the environment of the working-class child. Thus there might be conflict between the two principal agents of socialization: home and school (e.g. Henriques 1953; Rubin and Zavalloni 1969).

The family has been regarded as the main agent for transmitting the values of a society regarding skin colour and racial values (Braithwaite 1953), especially the mother, since it is the Caribbean female who has in the past carried the burden of moving the family to higher status. Many have done it by 'lightening' the colour of their offspring through liaisons with lighter-skinned males, or by raising their status through marriage to men of high professional status. Not only do children learn racial values through unconscious assumptions of maternal values, but there is also sometimes explicit indoctrination by the mother, who defines who are desirable playmates and why. Such definitions will often be based on descriptions such as 'good skin', 'nice complexion', 'good' or 'bad' hair, etc. (Braithwaite 1953, p. 100). Discrimination not only is directed towards outsiders but sometimes exists within the family itself. Quite often families will openly acknowledge a favourite child — in many cases this is the fairest child. Thus from an early age children are able to see and probably internalize the disadvantages in the society of being black as opposed to being white or fair-skinned (Braithwaite 1953, p. 64).

Aside from race and European biases, other cultural factors such as religion are often of importance in the socialization process. We can only mention this in passing since we are not aware of any studies done so far on these aspects of socialization. Nevertheless, we might assume that the socialization of, for example, Rastafarian children and of those coming from families which adhere to orthodox beliefs will differ in degrees and particulars from those of other children. Religion is still a vital force in Caribbean life, with pentecostal and other fundamentalist sects which demand adherence to strict codes of personal and community behaviour, the fastest-growing elements.

Socio-economic status   Poverty and wealth are significant determinants in the process of socialization. As we have seen, socio-economic status will shape the way people perceive their options. It will also help to determine the extent to which children in early childhood are afforded the opportunity for optimum mental, physical and creative development and to learn how to interact with the world around them.

The child born into the middle or upper socio-economic group will most probably grow up in a nuclear family rather than the household settings previously described and will have its basic needs of shelter, food, clothing and toys well taken care of, in some cases in luxurious fashion, and will be pampered and sometimes indulged. The child will normally be exposed to stimulating learning experiences from an early age: books, toys, games, travel, even home videos and computers. The child is more likely than not to attend a private kindergarten and then preparatory school equipped with the best learning facilities.

But this describes the reality of the minority of children. The vast majority of children in the region are in fact born into conditions of abject poverty and deprivation[2] — between 30 and 50 per cent in households headed by the mother. One-third of employed mothers are in domestic service, earning minimum wages in their respective countries. The fact that family responsibilities are forcing more and more mothers (including married ones) into the labour force and that the extended family, which afforded a network of kin support in child-rearing, is being eroded contribute to childhood deprivation. More and more children are being born to teenage mothers — with deleterious effects on their physical condition at birth and their subsequent physical and mental development (Grant 1980).

Generally, children are born into large families and in quick succession. In 1980, a Caribbean-wide survey by the Project for Early Childhood Education (PECE) noted that 'among the survey children of the poor there is every possibility that a sizeable fraction of them continue to live and grow with some form of illness sufficiently harmful to cause deficit in their physical, behavioural and cognitive development' (Grant 1980, vol. I, pp.27–8).

Housing for these children is usually substandard and overcrowded. The poorest children might grow up in one or two rooms with many adults and children and

---

2 We will use the definition of deprivation/disadvantage used by the Project for Early Childhood Education (PECE) study in 1974, which limits the term to 'the environmental deficits in terms of the material and attitudinal conditions at home' (Grant 1974; see also Grant 1980). Much of the material in the following section is drawn from these PECE studies, which sought to identify the home-life conditions of Basic school children in the Caribbean.

might spend much of their time confined indoors. Children might share a bed with several siblings or with adults. Household composition or location is frequently unstable. For children brought up in such conditions, there might be little bonding or social patterning and adult behaviour and social dynamics might be unpredictable. For example, in conditions of poverty, there might be no set meal-times and the concept of a meal as a family activity might be unknown. The young in household structures might be cared for by many people; householders' interaction with the child might be at random, and discipline might depend on shifting moods of parents as well as shifting minders.

The use of reward and punishment is an important mechanism for socialization, i.e. the passing on of values, attitudes and ideas. As a process it can have positive and negative consequences, though our knowledge of its effects is still limited. Reward as a method of child-rearing is infrequently used by the poor — at least with the pre-school children studied (Grant 1974; Landman *et al.* 1983), partly because poor parents have little to reward children with. There is also little active praise of the child, though parents will boast of their children's academic and other achievements. A PECE study noted that where reward was given there was no discrimination between boys and girls, though the light-skinned child of either sex ('brown-skin pickney') might be favoured over the darker child (Grant 1974).

A significant feature of child-rearing practice is the use of corporal punishment to reinforce parental discipline, especially in lower-class families, a factor which will be discussed more fully in the context of gender-role learning. Equally important is the fact that threats are frequently used and there is little of 'quiet, gentle-spoken admonition' (Clarke 1957; see also Kerr 1952; Grant 1974; Landman *et al.* 1983).

This does not necessarily signify a lack of love and affection. The PECE study found that adverse living conditions did not make a great deal of difference in the quality of love which mothers show to their children (Grant 1974).

One concomitant of socialization in a poverty-stricken household is the lack of stimulation which the child receives. Because very few parents are able to purchase toys, there is an almost complete absence of these in the household; illiteracy combined with poverty leads to the almost total absence of books and other reading material and there might be a lack of constructive play (see Grant 1974; Landman *et al.* 1983). Both playtime and social interaction derived from play might also be curtailed for poor children because of their heavy involvement with household chores — or, in the very poorest families, income-earning activities. Lower-class children are also discouraged, for reasons to be discussed below, from too much 'mixing' with other children.

Early childhood educators have noted the effects of stimulus deprivation on children from poorer homes. Such deprivation includes a lack of 'desirable exposures' to a variety of experiences — contact with places outside the home, exposure to books, motivation of desire to read and to enjoy radio and television programmes, the development of social skills through the use of toys and games in the company of other children (Grant 1974).

Poor children often attend poor schools, which are inadequate to compensate for the home environment and which lack facilities for constructive play. Grant notes of these 'deprived child care institutions' that they too fail to provide sensory and linguistic stimulation. Children in these situations grow up to be deficient in discrimination of speech sounds, inattentive to sensory stimuli and deprived of adequate language expression (Grant 1974).[3] All of these factors will impinge on boys and girls equally and the degree to which they exist will serve either to limit or to enhance the child's potential.

Social expectations and values   Although the material condition of children will differ substantially between classes, certain aspects of the socialization process will differ only in degree. A number of factors contribute to this:

1 In the Caribbean, occupational status is nowadays used as a prime determinant of class status.[4] We have noted that there is common aspiration towards a middle-class life style whether or not there is the means to achieve this.

2 Though patriarchic family structures might be changing, authoritarian and repressive discipline is still a feature of Caribbean family life, though this might be manifested differently among classes.

3 The Caribbean middle class has expanded considerably since World War II, with new avenues for the acquisition of wealth and professional qualifications over the last few generations. But persons moving from lower to higher status carry within them the seeds of their own socialization — a step or two removed perhaps from peasant and working-class origins — and might, even subconsciously, pass these values on to their children.

4 This process might be helped along by the fact that the grandmother and other older females still play a significant role in the upbringing of children and will contribute to the continuation of conservative child-rearing practices.

5 Overriding everything else is the fact that females are the chief agents of socialization in all classes.

Even in a society as stratified as Trinidad in the immediate post-colonial era, when race was still a strong determinant of status, Lloyd Braithwaite observed similarities in child-rearing between middle- and lower-class families, especially the strong role played by the mother and the weak role played by the father:

> Although the status of the kinship group derives largely from the social and occupational status of the father, within the home itself the mother's authority is supreme. In all matters concerned with the rearing of children her word is law. In this respect even the word of the grandmother is of more importance than that of the father; for in childbirth and in the rearing of offspring there is a strong tendency to fall back on the mother's mother. In most middle-class families the 'father' is relatively subordinate, so that psychologically speaking there is sometimes no man in the home. The emotional attachment to the father is as marked in the middle-class home as in many working-class families where there is no man in the home. The mother is the main source both of affection and discipline.
> (Braithwaite 1953, p. 98)

Finally, the fact that many upper- and middle-class children are raised and socialized by women of the lower classes should not be overlooked. Fernando Henriques in his study of the Jamaican family at about the same time as Braithwaite's study of Trinidad notes this as a significant element contributing to the similarity in some aspects of child-rearing in the upper-class and lower-class child (and, we might add, as more and more middle-class mothers go out to work today and leave children in the care of domestic helpers, in the middle-class child). Henriques noted:

> The nanny usurps the function of the mother. The mother is preoccupied with duties of a social nature and has little time to devote to the child except for a few months after its

---

3 The importance of early childhood stimulation with regard to mental development is underscored by the results of a home-visiting project which aimed at helping poor mothers to interact with and stimulate their children. After a maximum of 29 visits, the children had made significant gains (average of 13 IQ points) compared with children in a control group (see Grantham-McGregor and Desai 1975).

4 For an attempt to provide another measure, see Leo-Rhynie and Hamilton (1982).

birth . . . during a very important formative period of the child's life it is very much influenced by the ideas of the lower class. In some cases, the rapport established between the nanny and the child may be more intense than that between the mother and the child.

(Henriques 1953, p. 155)

This significant role played by the nanny in the early childhood experiences of middle- and upper-class children has been explored in a number of Caribbean novels such as *Wide Sargasso Sea* by Jean Rhys, *The Orchid House* by Phyllis Shand Allfrey and *Christopher* by Christopher Drayton.

Child-rearing practice

Restrictive child-rearing practice has been identified by many observers as the lower-class ideal (Kerr 1952) and obedience and docility as the values most strongly encouraged in children. Since girls come most under the mother's watchful eye, they are far more the beneficiaries of such training than boys. Although both boys and girls are expected to conform to these expectations, a great deal more of repressive parental discipline is directed towards girls.

A study done in the early 1960s identified some of the behavioural ideals which women hold. Respondents were asked to list the ways in which they thought their children's upbringing should be similar to their own. The responses were grouped as in Table 2.1. Thus commands, such as 'stay at home all the time', 'come straight home from school', 'don't leave the yard' are stressed. Many WICP informants in the 1980s proudly boasted of their not loitering on the streets and of not 'keeping friends' or 'keeping company' as aspects of their own strict upbringing of which they approved and which, presumably, they will pass on to their own children.

Researchers in the 1960s found that working-class and peasant families especially seemed to perceive outside influences on their children as a threat, were suspicious of outside contacts, and thus forbade their children to mix and play with others outside the family unit and to visit or receive visits (see, for example, Blake 1961; Brodber 1968, p. 84). Cohen in the 1950s reported what admittedly might be an extreme case of a Jamaican village where for the first seven years of the child's life, until he goes to school, he does not play with anyone except his own siblings (Cohen 1955). Kerr (1952) and others writing in the fifties also noted the isolation in which young children were often reared in rural Jamaica. It can be assumed that many of these practices still persist, though they would have been considerably modified

---

Table 2.1 Behavioural Ideals Held by Women

	%
Have good manners, good behaviour, be decent	55
Go to church, Sunday School	51
Go to school	47
Be obedient	34
Stay at home all the time, come straight home from school, not leave yard, not keep friends	26
Have strict discipline	17
Know how to do housework, take care of the home (girls)	13
Have some home training	13
Not to steal	4

Source: Blake 1961, Table IV–1, p. 59.

by improved communications in all the territories. A recent study indicated that, in the urban setting, the child's social contacts might be more extensive (Landman et al. 1983).

Girls seem to suffer most from over-strictness of parents, especially with regard to their social lives and friendships. This was cited as one of the principal areas of conflict between adolescent girls and their parents in a number of studies on parent–child relationships in Jamaica (Phillips 1973). Even in the 1960s, when these studies were done, parents still voiced strong disapproval or approval of their children's friends. 'The adolescents reported that parents regarded their desire to have friends as a bad trait that ought to be discouraged' (Phillips 1973, p. 61).

The freedom allowed children will depend on their class and location and their sex, middle- and upper-class children and urban children of both sexes being allowed on the whole more freedom for social mixing. Girls of all classes have less freedom than boys of the same class. Virtually all children are expected to associate with children of families of which their families approve (though children are observed to play together freely where there is no family interference) (see, for example, Clarke 1957, p. 148; Brodber 1968). Approval of others will be based on favourable knowledge of the child's family, on race, colour and class, on whether the deport-ment of the other conforms to the strict standards of the home. For having good manners, or 'broughtuptcy' as it is called, is constantly stressed by 'respectable' lower-class and middle-class families. Obedience and helpfulness to parents are particularly emphasized. Since the respect of other adults is highly valued, children are pressured to conform in those areas which will impress the outside world (Grant 1980, vol. I). Children who display these virtues and their external manifestations in dress, deportment and speech are thought to reflect highly on the minder's ability as a raiser of children — being a 'good mumma' as Victoria Durant-Gonzalez's informant called it; successful child-rearing is one of the few avenues to high status within their own communities which lower-class women can acquire (Durant-Gonzalez WICP 1982).

While social values are emphasized, there might be, as Blake (1961) and others have observed, a corresponding lack of emphasis on those personal qualities such as intelligence and ambition which are conducive to occupational and social mobility. Independent and challenging behaviour is discouraged in girls especially.

Value conflict

Although parental and family influences are significant in the early childhood years, outside influences assume greater importance in the socialization process as the child grows older. These help to underscore the conflict which the child is bound to perceive and experience between the values which are being inculcated and the socially accepted patterns of behaviour which he observes. Especially stressful might be the conflict between the culture of the home and of the school, only one aspect of which — language — has so far been studied in depth (see work emanating from the University of the West Indies).

The fact that as urbanization increases a great deal of the socialization of even young children now takes place in the streets also creates serious conflicts between what the child might be taught in the home and at school and what he observes out-side. The situation becomes extreme in, for example, certain areas of Kingston, Jamaica, where violence has become institutionalized and gang warfare, gunplay, drug-dealing and open criminality are the order of the day. Within subcultures, certain individuals, e.g. gang leaders, might enjoy high status, but this high status is contrary to the general scale of values (see, for example, Braithwaite 1953; Grant 1984).

The fact too that much of the culture to which children are exposed at all ages — primarily via television and films — consists of mass-produced programmes made for consumption in the USA or UK and reflects the images, norms and values of these societies must also pose another serious area of conflict. The rapid proliferation throughout the Caribbean of television 'satellite' images, which multiply the availability of external programmes, has significant implications for the future. Reading material is also to a great extent 'imported'. Children growing up with such alien exposure might very well become so divorced from their own culture that they might become 'orphans of the imagination'.

A final area of conflict that we can only touch on but which is nevertheless of great importance is the generational one. Grandmothers and other older women who are primary child-minders are passing on to their charges the socialization of two generations ago. Value conflicts are bound to arise when what children are learning elsewhere is often so different from 'grannie's' expectations and standards.

Gender-role learning

In the previous section we described generally some important aspects of the upbringing of Caribbean children but touched only peripherally on areas in which there is gender differentiation. We will now look specifically at the important area of gender-role learning.

Although women in the WICP survey indicated no preference as to the sex of their children, there is evidence from other sources (for example, Justus 1981, p. 434; Rodman 1971) that mothers are more closely attached to their daughters because it is felt that they will have more concern for their parents' welfare, and that this attachment might affect their differential treatment.

Many observers have found that, like most mothers everywhere, Caribbean mothers distinguish between their boy and girl children from an early age. Davenport notes that male and female children receive differential treatment from birth but that this first becomes obvious when toilet training and lessons in personal modesty are taught to the toddler (Davenport quoted in Henry and Wilson 1975). What are considered appropriate forms of 'masculine' and 'feminine' behaviour will also be encouraged. Little girls will be dressed and encouraged to act like 'little dolls', boys are dressed and encouraged to act like 'little men'. Where children are provided with toys, these are usually sex-typed. Popular games with little girls are those in which they imitate female roles; boys will often imitate adult male activities, such as driving heavy-duty vehicles.

Small children are to a great extent confined to home or 'yard', whether this describes the communal 'yard' of the urban ghetto or the space around the single family dwelling. Basic or nursery schools are few in number and might not be affordable. Public parks and playgrounds and recreational areas in the Caribbean hardly exist and small children, especially, are housebound. In the process they are constantly interacting with their mothers or minders in fulfilling tasks of fetching and carrying even at an early age (Clarke 1957). Pre-school children are allowed to play together and 'help' around the house with no obvious sexual differentiation until the age of 5, which is the age at which researchers have noted that similarity in upbringing ends and role training for girls begins. Five is the age at which children from poor families begin to be assigned household chores and it is these chores which will largely facilitate gender-role learning (see, for example, Cohen 1955; Justus 1981).

Joyce Justus, for example, in a study in Dominica, noted that at that age, 'while boys are permitted, and expected, to continue to be "babies" and are allowed to play, girls are confined to the home and learn women's work, first by imitation, later by deliberate instruction' (Justus 1981, p. 437). Clarke (1957, p. 158) expressed this process in a different way: 'The girl child identifies itself with the mother while the boy has already begun to build up a type of behaviour which might be described as husband substitute.'

The levels of responsibility and the nature of the tasks assigned to children will vary greatly according to the socio-economic status of the parents, the level of infrastructural development in the particular territory or area, and whether the setting is urban or rural.

Upper- and middle-class children will assume fewer household duties or none at all compared with working-class and peasant children. There is usually domestic help to take care of chores and, since many mothers of this stratum are full-time housewives, they too will indulge their children by taking over many of the duties themselves. Upper-class homes are also likely to be fitted with modern labour-saving devices which reduce the need for child labour. Depending on the rules of the household, children may be required to make their beds and keep their rooms tidy but only when they reach adolescence will more be expected of them in the home. However, where upper- and middle-class children are assigned duties, these too will usually be assigned according to gender. Girls will help mothers with kitchen and domestic chores, boys will help their fathers in tinkering with cars and domestic appliances and 'outside' duties which are regarded as 'male' ones, such as cleaning the yard, lawn-mowing, hedge-trimming, etc.

Though child labour is no longer an institutionalized part of Caribbean life, children do engage in daily labour for their families. Rodman (1971) refers to the fact that his lower-class informants in Trinidad recognized the 'economic utility' of children. Thus the child in the lower-class family is assigned a role — that of being a household assistant — and this role is usually sex-differentiated from an early age.

As boys and girls get older, these tasks can absorb much of their time outside school hours and, in cases of extreme poverty, even during time that should be spent in school. In the village situation especially, 'children are seen as appendages of elders and have little existence of their own; rarely can they find occasions to slip away to play with neighbouring children . . . As their parents hire no help, and as there are no labour saving devices, their human energy is very highly valued and is not frittered away in play' (Brodber 1968, p. 60). Where there is no piped water, children are assigned the task of carrying water from a river or spring some distance from the house.[5] Where there is no cooking gas or electricity or other easily available fuel, seeking firewood — sometimes at a great distance — is a major daily task. Where there is no refrigeration and the family income arrives in a fragmentary way, running to the shop for basic items as needed is a constant activity. Caring for

---

5 This practice is still common though the situation will vary from country to country and between rural and urban areas. A study of three parishes in Jamaica showed that in rural areas children transported domestic water from one-half to three miles and, depending on family size, needed to make at least three trips a day to satisfy household needs (Grant 1974). The WICP survey showed that the survey areas were fairly well served with piped water.

domestic animals and garden plots, helping with laundry, cooking, cleaning and other housekeeping tasks and caring for younger siblings are all regarded as the duties of children.

The situation will be aggravated by the poverty of the household and the number of children in it, whether or not the mother is the household head and whether or not she works full-time. In large families, especially with children arriving in quick succession year after year, parents alone cannot cope with all that needs to be done to keep the family going.

These activities serve as a means of teaching older children, girls especially, child-caring and domestic skills and a sense of responsibility — and many assume such responsibilities before the age of 12. One WICP informant, now in her fifties, left school at 11 to help her mother, who had just had a baby. Her chores included taking care of the baby and washing diapers and baby clothes. She proudly recalled:

> I had to be there. She had people helping her and I had to be there so that I could watch and she didn't have to call or halloo or things like that. Then I started to help hold the child, feed it. I was very handy at the age of 11. I was able to cook and do quite a lot of things, make doughnuts and fudge at that age.

Childhood tasks are usually gender-differentiated. Fetching water and firewood, fetching and caring for animals and other outdoor tasks are usually assigned to boys. Girls' duties are usually home-based, though some, like going to the shop, might be assigned to any child. However, children of either sex might be assigned any task if no other child is available.

One study of gender-role learning in Jamaica noted differences between rural and urban boys in the allocation of tasks. In the urban areas, boys as well as girls would be mothers' helpers. In rural areas, girls helped their mothers while boys helped their fathers. But this, the researcher noted, could be partially explained by the presence of running water and the absence of yard space for the rearing of animals in urban areas, which severely cut down on boys' assignments (Brodber 1968, p. 101).

Yolanda Moses noted the same phenomenon in her study of a community in Montserrat. The unskilled woman often had no male to help her do a variety of tasks such as home repairs, yard work and vegetable gardening, which is often a part of her subsistence. Even in such situations, 'Male children are not enlisted to ease the burden'. The women themselves were found to discourage male participation at an early age, 'cultivating a kind of relationship in which the boys are made to feel like pampered strangers in the household, catered to by mothers and sisters' (Moses 1981, p. 507). There seems to be widespread acceptance of this practice among all classes, of females catering to males and of failing to make them assume responsibilities for domestic activities (see Cummins WICP 1982). Thus, within their own families, girls are cast in a subordinate position in the domestic sphere. As Merle Hodge (1977, p. 43) acidly notes: 'Boys are fledgling kings of the farmyard, bound by few rules, few commitments to the home, while their sisters may wait on them hand and foot and patiently tolerate their wildest vagaries. Girls are reared to be put upon.'

One researcher made the observation that most mothers in his study said that they wished their boys would learn household chores but that the boys refused to do so. He observed that:

> What the parents fail to report, and only observation discloses, is that the girls are just as reluctant as the boys to do this sort of work, but work they must. When a boy refuses to wash floors, his refusal is accepted and he is not troubled further. A girl may also begin

by refusing to do such things, but she is flogged for her refusal. This accounts for the fact that girls are reported to be more obedient and a greater help in the home than are the boys.

(Cohen 1955, p. 279)

Such gender-role expectations are further reinforced by other agents of socialization, especially the educational system, which sometimes allocates tasks and assigns curricula on a gender basis, especially at the vocational level. A final point in connection with the gender-typed allocation of household duties should be noted here. This is the fact that tasks which keep girls housebound also provide a way of keeping them under strict parental control and observation, a key element in the upbringing of the Caribbean female (which we will explore more fully in chapter 4).

Despite the unanimity of the observations cited above from research of the last thirty-odd years, one living within the culture cannot help but note changes which suggest that the rigid allocation of household duties on a gender basis is breaking down. More and more boys are learning to cook and otherwise fend for themselves. Research into this subject might reveal a link with the recent upsurge in women's consciousness, which has made them more vocal about their own rights and needs — and about the need to make their children aware of these issues.

Absent male/avenging female?

The evidence is strong that the main burden of child-rearing and of the socialization of both boys and girls is largely in the hands of women. This, many believe, has resulted in serious socio-psychological aberrations among males (see chapter 9) and possibly contributes to the contradictions perceived in women's self-definitions.

The role that the male plays as socializing agent is one that we know little about; the received theories that stress male marginality are currently being challenged, though little evidence has been presented so far; research into the real role played by the male in Caribbean family life is urgently needed. One of the findings of the WICP was that 'men are not the reluctant fathers that we have been led to expect'. There is no question that a substantial number of males in whatever form of union, of whatever age, class, race, ethnic origin or nationality, do take their family responsibilities very seriously and play a major role as nurturers and role models. There is also no doubt that a substantial number are reluctant or 'invisible' fathers. As we discussed in chapter 1, physical absence — or presence — does not define the real role that a man plays in family life. But the fact that most fathers are non-residential and that residential males are often not biological fathers of children in the household does complicate the issue. The situation is further compounded when we consider that we are not really certain of how the male role is defined by women or by men themselves. What do women expect of their men? And how do men conceptualize their roles as fathers?

Some scholars have forcefully argued that, in Caribbean societies, the role which society, his women and his children define for the man is an economic one: his manhood is defined in terms of his earning capacity. To play a family role, a man first has to fulfil his occupational role. Rodman in his study of a lower-class Trinidadian village found that the father is expected only to acknowledge paternity and to support his child; the mother 'feeds, clothes, and generally takes care of the child, almost to the exclusion of the father' (Rodman 1971).

Erna Brodber's study of gender-role learning in urban and rural settings in Jamaica also found the adult male role defined as an economic one. According to the youthful respondents, the father is expected to support the household whether or not he resides there and to take responsibility for community relationships, i.e. to regulate the relationship of the unit with the outside world, and, as a corollary, to express some interest in academic affairs. Urban and rural informants were found to perceive the male role differently. Urban children conceptualized the father role on a cash basis — he was expected to provide money for support and maintenance. In the rural area, the role of the father embraced a wider dimension as he was expected to provide shelter, food and money, probably reflecting the fact that the father is more integrated into rural families (Brodber 1968).

The narrow conceptualization of the male role is not confined to lower-class families. Although the middle- and upper-class father is more likely than not to be head of the household, he is also far more involved in work and other activities than in child care. Thus he functions either as the authority of last resort when the mother is unable to cope or as the person with whom the child has 'ritualised interactions' (Justus 1981). Little more than his financial support of the family is expected. His status within the family — like that of the lower-class male — hinges on his ability as provider.

But the provider role can only be fulfilled with certainty by men of higher socio-economic status. In the conditions of poverty and high unemployment which characterize the region, the lower-class male might be unable to fulfil this role because he is financially insecure — a condition which increasingly now describes the middle class. Inability to discharge this function means that the man 'is therefore unable to command the respect of his wife and children', though he is still 'expected to be the major figure of authority in the household, and he may use physical force in an attempt to obtain reluctant obedience. As a result the man's role within the family is not a satisfying one. He is often a marginal or absent member of the nuclear family group' (Rodman 1971, p. 80).

An argument among a group of boys in George Lamming's classic novel, *In the Castle of My Skin* (1970, pp. 44–45), bears this out:

> *Fourth Boy*: My father don't live in the same house . . . My father couldn't hit me 'cause he don't support me. An' that's why I alright. My mother won't let him hit me 'cause he don't support me. An' the courthouse won't let him either. The law says a father can't flog if he don't feed. Thank God for the law.
>
> *First Boy*: Mine don't support me, but if he beat me my mother would say it shows he wus still taking an interest.
>
> *Second Boy*: Mine won't.
>
> *Fourth Boy*: Nor mine . . . I rather not have a father around, believe me, I'd give anything to have a father out of the house at all times of the day. A father in the house is like a bear or a tiger or a lion. You can't talk an' laugh as you like, an' sometimes if you stay in the W.C. too long he come for you. Some fathers don't even want you to do what's nat'ral. They don't.
>
> *Third Boy*: Rat's father who's the tailor is like that. He support all of them good good good, an' they don't want for anything in this God's world. But they ain't got no freedom. When he ain't there the house is like a concert, 'cause the mother is a sweet woman who gives plenty jokes, but as soon as he put in his appearance, everybody stop talking. 'Tis funny the way it happens. You hear the talking talking talking, an' suddenly somebody say easy easy, daddy comin', an' suddenly everything is like a black-out for the ears. You don't hear anything at all. Not a sound but their father foot coming through the yard. An' it stay silent so till he go out again.
>
> *Fourth Boy*: We can do without fathers if that's what they like. I do without mine alright . . .
>
> *First Boy*: I don't see much of my father, but my second brother father is good. He don't

make no difference between us, me and my brother, 'cause he says we is both our mother children. How many fathers you got in yuh family?

In gender-role learning we have seen that the female role is well defined compared with the male role. The female role is conceived as the traditional one, as domestic and maternal: the woman is assigned child-bearing, child-caring and housekeeping functions. We do need to look more fully at the whole question of how adult males and females influence gender-role learning. For it is the girl socialized in this manner who will become the woman described in these pages, and the boy whose presence or absence as an adult male will determine the girl's future. Can a girl achieve complete self-definition in the absence of a father or other strong male role model in her life? How does she learn to relate to men? Boys are also growing up in situations where female gender identity is strong, and, where a father or other older male is absent, he might not be able to absorb notions of male status and identity through role modelling in the home. On whom does such a boy model himself?

If the father, for whatever reason, fails to play his role in family life, then the mother is forced to assume it. Household 'headship' and economic responsibilities for the family fall on her, as does the role of authority figure. In the process, she might be sending out to her children ambivalent or contradictory signals. As Blake points out, the dominance of the mother does not rest on any legitimizing power accorded to the woman by society as a whole. Though the mother might be head of household, in most cases the father is the real authority figure and the mother rules by default (Blake 1961). Even when the male is absent for a lengthy period of time, he can still regulate to a certain extent the woman's actions and behaviour (see, for example, Henry and Wilson 1975, quoting Della Walker; Moses 1981; WICP survey 1982). Thus the mother 'assumes' the father role but not necessarily the power and dominance that goes with it. To extent the analogy, even as she performs centre-stage in the family sphere, she is often acknowledged — and acknowledges herself — only as supporting actor (see chapter 5).

This perhaps comes out most clearly in the matter of parental discipline. Although Edith Clarke (1957, p. 158) observed that 'In all aspects of home training the mother is the principal actor' and children themselves recognize the mother as 'parent' regardless of family group (Brodber 1968), it is the father who is assigned the role of disciplinarian.

We mentioned earlier that a significant feature of child-rearing practice in the Caribbean has been identified as the authoritarian nature of parent–child relationships and the use of corporal punishment to reinforce parental discipline. Such discipline is often violent. Flogging or verbal abuse of children by adults is common. Clarke noted that 'Children are shouted at in a way which appears brutalising to anyone outside the particular culture. The child responds to this by equally noisy and violent outcries' (Clarke 1957, p. 156). There is in addition constant threatening of children and many childhood memories are of brutalizing floggings at home or at school. Recent studies confirm that these old patterns continue, though flogging is now used less and less in schools — in many, not at all. Flogging at home still seems to be widespread, though usually of children over the age of 3, which is regarded as the age at which real disciplining should begin. Of 803 mothers of preschool children interviewed by the PECE in Jamaica, 671 reported 'beating' their children (Grant 1974). Usually mothers are expected to punish the girls and fathers the boys, but, where there is no male present, the mother will punish both.

But, even though the mother punishes her boys, she acknowledges the father or some other male as the real authority figure, often by the nature of the threats she issues. In some families the traditional 'wait till your father comes home' might be extended to the more colourful 'wait till your father come home he will show you where water walk go a pumpkin belly', but the meaning is the same. Or she will threaten him with another authority figure: 'Wait till you go to school. Teacher will know what to do with you.' The 'hard-headedness' of boys especially will be ascribed to the absent parent.

When the male parent is around, even if he is only visiting, he is expected to deliver physical punishment. This contributes to the ambivalence with which the father figure is viewed, for, even though the mother's discipline is harsh, she might temper it with warm physical affection, even indulgence (Clarke 1957). It is only one side of her behaviour revealed. But the father's discipline might be harsh and impersonal and capable of leaving permanent mental and physical scars.

Power relationships in the home and the terms by which the father is expected to assume responsibilities are not lost on the children. A further discussion among the boys in *In the Castle of My Skin* (Lamming 1970, pp. 46–47) illuminates this:

> *Third Boy*: If there's one thing you ain't to do is tell yuh father a teacher lash you. It ain't wise to do it. By my dead grangran it ain't.
> *Fourth Boy*: Why ain't it wise or right or whatever you say it ain't'?
> *Third Boy*: 'Cause yuh father'll say that the teacher had a cause. That's what yuh father'll say. An' when you tell him you don't know the reason why the teacher do what he do, then yuh father'll tell you why. An' he won't only tell you why, but he'll tell you the teacher didn't lash you properly an' he'll do it all over again. He'll show you how the teacher ought to lash you, next time. It ain't wise to tell yuh father that sort of thing. I know what I saying. I know it ain't wise.

Some implications of gender-role learning

When there is no man around to carry out disciplinary functions, it is possible that the woman will give up on the job or shift the responsibility, just as she shifts child-rearing when she is unable to cope. For example, a sample of cases before the Jamaican Family Court showed that a large percentage were brought by mothers who were unable to deal single-handed with the behavioural problems of their children. Boys are perceived by some single mothers as more difficult to raise than girls, perhaps one reason why more of them grow up abandoned and in need of protection and before the court as adult offenders (Jackson WICP 1982). Boys also have a much higher rate of arrests and convictions for juvenile delinquency (Phillips 1973, p. 13; Barbados 1978, vol. I, p. 129). These differences a Caribbean educator attributes partly to the fact that more girls than boys remain in school during adolescence, and partly to the greater attention and concern shown to girls in the society. 'The girls respond by being diligent, ambitious and committed to improving themselves' (Phillips 1973, p. 131). This perception of malleable, disciplined girls probably accounts for the fact that they are found to be more easily fostered (Brodber 1968, p. 69) and adopted and more of them might end up growing up in the households of others.

The behavioural problems of the child might be compounded by the lack of moral and financial support from the father and by a succession of 'step-fathers' arising from the mother's attempts to secure reliable male support. The varied 'fathers' might play varied roles and might humiliate and ill-treat the mother. Hermione McKenzie (WICP 1982) has posed the important question of how these ambivalent views of adult behaviour, of male/female roles and of the mother's evident status weaknesses will affect the child's later behaviour. We might reiterate some of these ambivalences:

1 Society at all levels emphasizes the superiority of males. But for the child it is the mother who stands for security, often the only security (Clarke 1957).

2 Yet the mother herself is frequently exposed in the child's eyes as weak and vulnerable, especially in her dealings with men (see chapter 9), and is frequently powerless in her relationships with the wider world, e.g. her employers.

3 She stands for harsh discipline alternated with love and affection.

4 Although the mother is basically the most important person in the child's life, the father or another male has to be respected as if he were (Henry and Wilson 1975); i.e. the child is taught to respect and defer to males. Yet the man's behaviour often reflects harsh authoritarianism and distance, frequently untempered by love and affection. Additionally, if the father does not support his family or ill-treats his woman, the child will probably grow up absorbing his or her mother's suppressed or overt hostility to men:

> Me cyaan figat dem lickle tings weh me madda used to tell me. 'Member seh man a green lizard,' she used to say. 'Man is a ting weh change. De instant when dem see one next woman, dem no waan bodder deal wid yuh, especially when dem see yuh tight pon yuh money.' You see, she was disappointed by a man and dat cause her fi go tru a whole heap.
> (Sistren 1986, p. 45)

Brodber (1968) found that young males in her study of sex-role learning distinguished between (i) possible wives and (ii) older women and were ambivalent towards the former. They knew how to act towards older women and what were their obligations, but had acquired few skills in dealing with peers of the opposite sex.

What of the effect of the overwhelming presence of females on the socialization of girls? How does this affect female self-definition? Girls too are given little preparation for male/female interactions and little guidance in developing psychological maturity. The girl's upbringing is based more on the repressive measures of her parents than on the development of her own inner controls, a situation which frequently results in early and unplanned childbearing (chapter 4).

Despite the tentative nature of the investigation, we can now draw certain other conclusions which might throw some light on the lack of congruence observed between the role performance of Caribbean women and their ideology. Yolanda Moses (1981) has suggested that, through gender-role learning, both males and females learn contradictory ideal gender roles which they cannot fulfil. Girls are taught female tasks in the process of which they learn to be unassertive, dependent, controlled and subservient to the male. The ideal is that men should manage.

This is borne out by results from the WICP pilot survey, in which women were asked to list the characteristics of the ideal male/ideal female partner. The responses reflected the stereotypes of the woman as loving, gentle, warm, sensitive — and playing a secondary role to her man. She is generally supportive of her partner at various levels, a 'good' mother, a 'good' partner and a 'good' homemaker. The ideal male is given characteristics of competence. He is logical, active, competitive, strong, aggressive but self-controlled. Most important, the ideal male assumes the dominant role in the family as principal breadwinner (see Cummins WICP 1982). It is ideally believed and valued that men are and should be superior at providing and at decision-making.

But, due to lack of economic alternatives that men have to face in life, they might be unable to fulfil the ideal role and yet they are not being socialized by their mothers to adjust their behaviour to other modes and to other roles, e.g. parenting. Girls, it is argued, because they have more achievable goals, are actually better equipped to survive.

Gender-role stereotyping and identity formation

Since the ideal male and ideal female images being projected differ so substantially from the reality, we need to ask, how did the situation come about? Brodber explains this in terms of gender-role stereotyping. A stereotype results when an image held does not conform to real behaviour but people come to act as if it did. When individuals abandon real behaviour and act according to the stereotypes, they have internalized stereotyped behaviour (Brodber WICP 1982a, pp. 1–2).

Historically, the model for 'right behaviour' for women in the Caribbean was an imported one — the model which emerged elsewhere in Western society: that of woman as a being whose purpose is derived from the existence of another, whether husband, father, or extended family, and whose locus is the home or household. This is the model which emerged from Brodber's historical survey of the images projected in the press and church in the period 1838 to the present in three territories — Barbados, Jamaica and Trinidad. In Jamaica we also get the physical property of the image: a woman 'pale and delicate'.

While this image certainly described some women, it has never described the reality of most women's lives, as we shall see when we look at women workers (chapter 6). Even among the white women who came closest to the image, there were those among them who 'left their homes, managed businesses, sought jobs outside the home and sometimes supported themselves without recourse to males' (Brodber WICP, 1982a). Yet we catch very few glimpses of this 'other' woman, what we might call the 'real' woman, projected either in history books or the contemporary media or indeed in school texts.

Brodber argues that, while the models of 'right behaviour' were not culturally possible and were not performed by the majority of women, the models were nevertheless internalized as the 'right ones'. They are still part of women's psyches and influence their behaviour. The dualisms of the society have become manifest in women's interior landscape.

While the distance between stereotype and actual behaviour is not unique to this culture or its women, there are peculiarities which make behaviour more susceptible to the influence of stereotyping (Hodge WICP 1982, p. ix). Hodge argues that in other parts of the ex-colonial world — Africa, Asia, Indo-China:

> there existed before colonization and there continued to exist under colonization an independent traditional culture which had its own validated prescriptions for, among other things, female behaviour. The great majority of women were never touched by the official prescription. The culture which has developed in the Caribbean, however, is a culture which as yet does not recognize itself, which sees itself as (and is, in many of its features) largely derivative of the Western metropolitan culture which remains the official culture and the effective prescription-making culture of the region.

The understanding that 'a prerequisite for social mobility was the ability to adopt the life styles of the whites' (Brodber WICP 1982a, p. 21) has reinforced the internalization of the white ideal projected by press, church and other agents of socialization. Whether women — and men — act on this model depends on whether or not they have the economic means to operationalize it and the desire for social mobility: 'With the increase in the number of academically trained black men and their acceptance into the white collar jobs has come the cash base with which to acquire the "necessary appendage". Upwardly mobile women have become willing to design their lives to fit the stereotypes' (Brodber WICP 1982a, p. 2).

While for the majority of women the stereotype is not accessible and therefore does not determine their behaviour, it can nevertheless 'affect self-image, the person's assessment of his/her own worth', become 'part of the the psychic land-scape' (Hodge WICP 1982, p. ix).

Studies of contemporary agents of socialization show that the traditional stereotype is the one that is still being projected, especially in the regional media. As in the rest of Western society, another dimension of the image is being explicitly projected, woman as sexual object. And the idealized physical object is still 'pale and delicate'.

While Brodber's study was a historical one, the evidence from the contemporary media shows that the stereotyped image of woman has changed little. Peggy Antrobus has concluded that 'Anyone whose only access to Caribbean life is through the region's media, even the part of it that is Caribbean, will be hard put to recognise the reality of Caribbean women from its images' (Antrobus 1981, p. 38). A study of the portrayal and participation of women in the Caribbean media by Lorna Gordon supports this. Gordon looked at the images of women in newspapers, advertising, mass-circulation magazines and the electronic media and concluded that 'The portrayal of women as housewife, male appendages and sex-object is the dominant image of women projected by editorial content and adver-tising' (Gordon 1981, p. 31).

Another study (Royale 1981) which undertook content analysis of all adver-tisements on the Jamaican network JBC-TV during a one-week period rated advertisements for overall message tone and visual impact on a five-point conscious-ness scale of levels of intensity of female roles portrayed. Among the significant findings were:

1 83 per cent of ads used a male voice-over
2 there were no ads showing women in an identifiable professional role
3 older women were not used as 'talent' whereas older men are considered authori-tative and distinguished
4 images of the 'liberated woman' were distorted, for example showing her as sexual hunter
5 the worst ads played on a strong female fear, that of male rejection.

Also notable are the high imported content of the region's media (70 per cent of total transmission on TV) and the under-representation of women in local programmes.

This leads us to question the impact which such gender-role stereotyping has on the identity formation and actions of Caribbean females, particularly in their formative years. We can only guess at what the impact might be, in the absence of any research which documents such relationships. But the conclusion can be drawn that the media as agents of socialization are presenting distorted role models. If one were to judge from the Jamaican media, the one consistent role model which is presented is one heavily based on physical beauty and body image (Gloudon 1981). Tied up with the self-image of women, then, is the increasing notion that the female body is a marketable commodity. Thus 'beauty' as an image is consis-tently promoted over 'brains', to judge by the media coverage accorded female achievement in each sphere. Women most frequently promoted in the media are beauty queens, fashion models and half-naked photographic models. The heavy emphasis on the physical self is not peculiar to these societies, indeed is promoted as an objective of the billion-dollar cosmetics and fashion industries of the Western world. But the ideal physical beauty that has been projected over the centuries has been a Caucasian ideal or a close approximation, while racially the majority of the region's people fall at the other end of the colour spectrum.

It is therefore not surprising that the question of body image looms large in the self-concept of at least the Jamaican adolescent, with the physical self and skin colour of greatest concern (see, for example, Miller 1967, 1969; Phillips 1973). Miller (1969) found that dissatisfaction with colour was greatest among girls and that 'a hankering after a white or Caucasian ideal' was very prevalent in the society.

This discrepancy between 'ideal woman' and 'real woman' and the implied racial dimension are part of what Merle Hodge has identified as the 'tension' between official and 'real' culture, tension which is a permanent feature of Caribbean life. Hodge articulates it as 'The discrepancy between school and home, between the culture of books, newspapers and religious instruction and the culture practiced by the adults with whom the child is most intimately involved and who are responsible for transmitting to the child the mores of the tribe: mother, grandmother, aunt' (Hodge WICP 1982, p. viii). While we catch very few glimpses of the 'real' woman in history books, the media or school textbooks, we can find ample evidence in contemporary Caribbean literature, which, as Hodge reminds us, is highly expressive of this cultural tension. So are drama and manifestations of popular culture, especially music. In chapter 9 we will look at how this tension is expressed in the popular idiom of the calypso.

The image of womanhood that a young girl carries in her head is one of the vital forces that will shape her sense of identity and self-concept and will therefore determine to a great extent her life choices.

In the next chapter, we will look at women's experiences in the educational system and examine how gender-role stereotyping affects female performance and achievements in that sphere.

3 *Education*
& Gender-Role Stereotyping

Education is a key to woman's empowerment, to the acquisition of power and status both within the society and in her domestic life. A woman's educational level will affect her job opportunities and her exercise of legal and other rights, and will influence factors such as contraceptive use, number of children she has, age she commences childbearing — in short, her life style and options.

Caribbean women display a keen awareness of the potential value of education. Because education is perceived and actually functions as a route to upward social mobility and improved socio-economic status, parental aspirations for children are high, especially among parents of lower socio-economic status, who will make tremendous sacrifices to send their children to school and invest in the grooming of 'the bright one'.

While in earlier times boys were the ones selected for educating if family resources were limited (and even if they were not), with the changing perceptions of the role of women and consequently of female education, there has been increasing emphasis on equality of access to education with the emphasis being on 'the bright one' of either sex. Parents nowadays do not discriminate between boys and girls in educational matters to the extent they once did. Although Blake (1961) found 'an ideal of sexual equality in educational and opportunity rights' in her study of Jamaicans, about one-quarter of her respondents (male and female) felt that boys should get a larger share of educational resources. The WICP survey in three eastern Caribbean countries more than two decades later showed there was no noticeable difference in women's aspirations regarding their sons and their daughters. Over 50 per cent said they would not wish to have to choose between educating a son and educating a daughter. Slightly more younger women in the survey were willing to educate daughters over sons, if they had to choose.

Caribbean girls are strongly encouraged to get an education, especially by their mothers. Part of this pressure on girls is ascribed to the fact that working-class mothers know there is no guarantee of male support for their daughters when they become adults. (Durant-Gonzalez WICP 1982). Thus mothers 'interpret education as expanding life options for their daughters. They are concerned that their daughters obtain as much education as possible, and go to great lengths to see that they do, often . . . postponing their own gratification' (Justus 1981, p. 438). Mothers also know that they can count more on their daughters than their sons to care for and support them in their old age.

This drive towards education has yielded remarkable results. In a recent report on the status of women in 99 countries (representing 92% of the world's female population), a Caribbean country, Jamaica, ranked second highest (behind the United States) in educational status of women and another, Barbados, ranked nineteenth. Women's educational status was measured by four variables — primary and secondary education, women secondary schoolteachers, university enrolment and the gender gap (i.e. differential literacy rates for men and women). Jamaica is one of the countries where women's literacy is significantly higher than men's (Population Crisis Committee 1988).

Despite the quantitative achievement of women in education throughout the Caribbean, the qualitative nature of this education and its end results present us with a paradox. Educational opportunities for women have increased dramatically over the last few decades so that women now have *de facto* equality with men in terms of access to virtually all aspects of the formal educational system and in some areas are performing better than men. At the individual level, women are achieving breakthroughs and in some cases approaching numerical equality in some of the formerly 'male' professions. Yet, for the broad masses of women, educational advances have so far not been reflected in substantial improvement in their status in the world beyond school. The majority of women are still to be found in domestic labour, or in white-collar jobs such as teaching and nursing, both low-paid occupations. Women, especially young women, still have the highest rates of unemployment and given that early and frequent childbearing is still the pattern (chapter 4) the linkages between education and life options have clearly not yet been realized. The WICP survey data showed that women on the whole still fail to make a connection between educational choices and earning power and value the socializing aspects of education over the material (see McKenzie WICP 1986). Education has not so far freed Caribbean women from the trap of a family system which places undue emphasis on childbearing and female familial responsibilities, yet continues to emphasize patriarchic structures and values (chapters 4 and 5).

What explanations can we find for this lag between the drive to achieve education and the failure to harness the power of education?

It is true that occupational choices open to girls continue to be much more limited than those open to boys and that women are far from gaining equality in the formal economic sector. But, in making educational and other life choices, do girls limit their own horizons because of their perceptions of the options open to them? Because the most significant influences in their lives — parents, guardians, teachers — are females who steer them along conventional female paths? Because of the limits imposed by gender-role stereotyping? How far does the educational system provide viable alternatives to early childbearing and reduction of the serious role conflict which affects the educational attainment and performance of girls? How far does the system prepare girls for the real role most of them will play as adults — that of breadwinner?

The evidence that is available does not permit us to draw any definitive conclusions regarding any of these issues. The time factor could be crucial: women's unimpeded access to education spans only one or two generations and, while external barriers have fallen, the internal barrier — the 'psychic landcape' — might still be intact. Women — and their societies — might still be bound by past conditioning. There is no doubt that the peculiar history and culture of the Caribbean have been significant elements in shaping the role that education and other teaching agents have played in female socialization and identity formation. Though the educational status of women, educational structures and curricula have been changing dramatically over the past 30 years or so, we will see that the legacies of the past are still influential.

In this chapter we will look, first, at the educational system itself: the historical legacy which has shaped Caribbean education, including the ideology of female education. We will also look at some social and cultural factors which will inhibit or advance access to education and progress in school, especially as these relate to women. Secondly, we will look at attainment and performance of Caribbean women in the school system and their occupational choices. Finally, we will examine briefly the role that female socialization and gender-role learning might play in influencing women's educational performance and occupational choices.

Historical and cultural processes

Historical background

Though standards of education and facilities vary from one Caribbean country to another, the structure imported mainly from Britain is similar in all the countries in terms of educational provisions and philosophy, curriculum, methodology, textbooks and certification. All the territories share a common history of education (though traces of French practice and philosophy might still be found in some systems) and continue to move along the same paths.

Although there are individual schools of some antiquity in the Caribbean, a formalized system of education dates only to 1835 when a system of national education at primary level was established throughout the colonies. Through the Negro Education Grant, the newly freed slaves were the main beneficiaries. Up to that time, elementary schooling was provided either by small private schools for blacks established through the generosity of plantation owners or efforts of Christian missionaries. The earliest public primary schools were located mainly in the towns and were attended by adults as well as children, so great was the thirst for knowledge among the newly freed. They provided the most rudimentary of education, usually the three Rs plus religious instruction. Limited secondary education was available through endowed schools; these were virtually all schools for white boys established through charitable bequests of wealthy benefactors. Most children of the white plantocracy were in fact sent back to England for their schooling, though this was far more the case for boys than for girls, who, at best, might be provided with governesses at home.

For a long time, education served mainly to reinforce the class and sexist biases of colonial society. Upper-class men were to be educated to be leaders, upper-class women to be 'good wives and good mothers'. Once secondary girls' schools began to be established in the late nineteenth century, separation of girls and boys for their education became an entrenched part of the educational system. Up to recently, few coeducational schools existed at secondary level, and even many primary schools were, and still are, divided into boys' and girls' schools.

Where the great masses — men and women — were educated at all, the purpose of such education was to 'civilize' and render them good and faithful servants — a pliable and largely undifferentiated labour force. Although a great deal of lip-service was paid to education for the masses in the post-emancipation era, until well into the twentieth century there was little money assigned. A visitor to Jamaica in 1861, for instance, found that, for the 65,000 children between the ages of 5 and 15 in that country, the vote for education worked out at less than a shilling per child per year (Augier and Gordon 1962, p. 176). The churches were far more active in the creation and running of schools, and the division of education between secular and religious authorities persisted in all the territories until recent times.

The secondary grammar schools continued to cater to the white and, later, brown elite until well into the twentieth century. The fact that these schools were fee-paying effectively excluded the majority of the population until well into the 1960s; so did the fact that, up to a certain time, illegitimate children were often not accepted. These schools were academic in orientation and artificial in structure, based as they were on the structure and curricula of English grammar schools. Students sat external examinations of Oxford and Cambridge Universities set by English examiners who in all likelihood had never had first-hand contact with the West Indies.

The curricula of all the schools, borrowed from England and subject to little reform, continued to be irrelevant, an irrelevance reinforced by imported textbooks and alien imagery and concepts. An education commission of 1931 noted that 'The time-table of the average school is littered with subjects or with fragments of subjects that bear no relation to the lives of the pupils or the qualifications and ability of the teachers' (Williams 1973, p. 150).

In the post-war years, educational reforms went hand in hand with the expansion of the economic and political systems of the West Indian territories, which began to move to greater autonomy from Britain. The year 1939 marked the start of a revision of curricula and the introduction of textbooks written and prepared especially for Caribbean schools. Another significant development was the establishment of the University College of the West Indies in 1948. In 1962, full political independence was attained by the two largest territories, to be followed in subsequent years by political decolonization of all the territories. Pat Mohammed notes that the newly emergent states adopted a manpower-planning approach which was applied to the development of education. While the five-year plans which became the new blueprints for state policies might have contained no explicit references to female education, they implicitly conveyed the idea of equality between the sexes (Mohammed WICP 1982).

The ideology of female education

Until a few decades ago, female education was explicitly shaped by the ideology based on gender-role stereotyping which had its origins in Victorian England — that the female is a dependent being whose true locus is the home and whose vocation is that of wife and mother (see Cole WICP 1982a; Mohammed WICP 1982).

Although small private schools undoubtedly existed to train 'young ladies', the first established girls' school seems to have been the Catholic St Joseph's Convent School in Trinidad, founded in 1836. Thereafter, the churches of all denominations were to play a major role in the education of both males and females. This would have some significance for female education especially, since religious denominations generally tend to support patriarchic structures and would have a vested interest in reinforcing conservative women's roles.

But there does not seem to have been any real public concern with female education as such until the late nineteenth century. In examining the situation in Barbados, Joyce Cole notes that the Barbados House of Assembly established a Commission on Education, which found, among other things, that few girls were educated beyond infant school. The Mitchinson Report of 1875 which resulted, devoted only one paragraph to the education of girls. This paragraph is nevertheless most instructive for it shows the kinds of questions about female education that were exercising men's minds in far-off England (from which the commissioners came) as in the remotest colonies: 'Whether girls should receive identically, the same education as boys, whether their capacities are precisely the same, and if not, what ought to be the subjects on which their studies should be concentrated, are still unsettled questions.'

Commissioner Mitchinson was nevertheless clear on one thing, the socializing function of the educated female:

> if female education here is unsound and flimsy, narrow in range, and wanting in thoroughness; if, moreover, the most valuable part of a young child's education, including the formation of its task, and the development of its mental capacities depends mainly on early maternal teaching, it is idle to expect the boys in our first and second grade schools to go there well prepared and receptive of culture till this defect is remedied. So that after all, perhaps the key to the problem of education really is to be found in the establishment, if possible, of thoroughly sound female education in the colony.
>
> (Quoted in Cole WICP 1982a, p. 7)

It should be reiterated that what Mitchinson was discussing was not the education of all women but of women of higher social status; women of the lower orders, like their menfolk, would for a long time continue to be 'hewers of wood and drawers of water'. Thus, at primary school level until the late nineteenth century, there was no distinction in subjects taught to boys and girls. This in fact reflected the reality of the lives of working-class women, who were not confined to the home and domestic activity but performed hard manual labour alongside their men until relatively recent times (see chapter 6). As women moved out of the fields and into the kitchens, the emphasis on vocational training centred around domesticity took shape and women's education more and more thrust them into the stereotyped female mould. In time, the ideology based on the concept of women as housebound 'civilizing agents' would explicitly come to inform the education of all females.

Subsequent reports continued to emphasize this function of female education. As late as 1940, a senior education commissioner could be found expressing much the same sentiment concerning women's role even as he championed female education. Hammond argued that: 'If it were necessary to choose between them, it would be better to provide more of this kind of education [i.e. secondary] for girls, giving them as wide a range of interest, domestic, social, and artistic as possible and the influence of teachers of the best obtainable quality.' This generosity was rooted in the same beliefs as those expressed by Mitchinson 60 years earlier. As Hammond saw it:

> Women set the tone of social intercourse, and women make the homes and the mental climate in which children are raised. A boy brought up in a cultivated home will not lack cultivated interests even if his schooling is less generous than could be wished, and his interests are likely to be stimulated further if he wishes to marry an intelligently educated girl.
>
> (Cole WICP 1982a, p. 21)

Girls' schools were to be the training-ground to prepare women to be 'good wives and good mothers'.

Between the late nineteenth and early twentieth centuries, increasing attention was paid to the establishment of girls' schools. However, while girls had started out having equal access to primary education, from the late nineteenth century, when secondary grammar schools for girls began to be established, the principle of the single-sex school became an entrenched part of the school system at all levels and persisted until recent times. Joyce Cole argues that such segregation led to a relatively inferior education for girls. Girls' schools were effectively discriminated against on three main grounds: (i) most of the funds for academic education were spent on boys' scholarships and boys' schools; (ii) there were important differences in curricula; (iii) there were important differences in standards (Cole WICP 1982a).

Although the sex ratio of the West Indian population as a whole slightly favoured females, more secondary schools were provided for boys than for girls and for a long time scholarships to secondary schools and to universities were available to boys only. The differential expenditure on boys' versus girls' schools also reflected the official ideology. Thus, in Trinidad and Tobago at the end of the nineteenth century, while government expenditure on the three boys' schools totalled $6,800, the one girls' school received no financial contribution from the state. In Barbados, in 1899 Queens College (for girls), which had 106 on roll, received a grant of $200 per annum while $1,000 was allotted to Harrison College (for boys) for 160 students (Barbados 1978; Cole WICP 1982a).

The prevailing ideology also ensured that, up to a certain time, lower standards were expected from girl pupils and female teachers since they were believed to be intellectually inferior. Curricular differences applied from the earliest grades in school. While in primary school a basic education was provided by a common curriculum, specialization occurred as early as grade one, when needlework was offered to girls only; at grade three, agriculture and drawing were offered to boys only. The vocational emphasis for boys was different from that for girls; girls' education was largely domestic and aesthetic; for instance, in Barbados singing and recitation were provided as subjects for girls only. Where vocational training for lower-class girls was proposed, it centred around housecraft: laundering, dressmaking, basketry, millinery and child management. Commercial training was to a limited extent offered in secondary schools. After the 1920s the concern with 'female education' at the lower level expressed itself mainly in the teaching of needlework and domestic science (Cole WICP 1982a).

The curricular differences were emphasized at higher levels in the school system so that for a long time science was not regarded as a subject to be taught in girls' schools at all (Cole WICP 1982a). Even today, girls' schools are generally less well equipped for science teaching than boys' schools (see Hamilton 1976). At a time when secondary schools for girls did not offer Latin or Greek as did the boys' schools, they provided drill and drawing exercises.

The treatment of female teachers also reflected these biases. At the end of the nineteenth century in Barbados, female teachers were allowed by the examiners to omit English and algebra but were examined in a subject called 'thrift'. Arithmetic examinations for male teachers were more difficult than for females. All of this reflected and served to reinforce the notion that women were the intellectual antithesis of men (Cole WICP 1982a) and also to justify inferior pay. Thus, while from the start of a system of public education women played a significant role as teachers, they were assigned a subordinate role in keeping with their perceived status as the 'weaker sex'.

With the establishment from the late nineteenth century of schools specifically for girls, women came to play a prominent role as educators, especially through their connections with religious orders, though in public schools for a long time male teachers far outnumbered female since married women were not allowed in teaching. Over time, barriers against female teachers fell and their influence came to pervade schools of both sexes to the extent that education today is regarded as a largely 'female' occupation. However, until recently, women continued to be severely discriminated against in the matter of salaries. The Education Ordinance of 1855 in Guyana set the following salary scales for teachers of different classes, the classes referring to the grade of their certificate:

To male teachers (1st class) 720 dollars per annum
To female teachers (1st class) 540 dollars per annum

To male teachers (2nd class) 400 dollars per annum
To female teachers (2nd class) 320 dollars per annum

To male teachers (3rd class) 200 dollars per annum
To female teachers (3rd class) 160 dollars per annum

There was no sexual distinction in the qualification of teachers of the second and third class. Men and women of the first class were required to possess qualifications in reading, writing, arithmetic, grammar, composition, geography, history and science. Females of the first class were exempted from knowledge in book-keeping and geometry, which men were expected to have; but all female teachers of whatever grade were expected to teach needlework (Gordon 1963, pp. 190–1).

A watershed in education as in other areas of socio-economic life was the West India Royal Commission, headed by Lord Moyne, which examined conditions in the West Indies in the year following the widespread riots of 1937–8 (but whose report was suppressed during the war years and not published until 1945). Yet even as the commissioners advocated the education of girls — in fact equality of educational opportunity — they also revealed the same ambivalences regarding women's roles which characterized earlier reports: 'The present low status of women in the West Indies makes it the more important to secure essential equality of educational opportunity between the sexes. If there are to be happy marriages girls must be able to be companions to their husbands and therefore need every opportunity for as wide a cultural education as possible'. (GB: West India Royal Commission 1945, p. 130).

What the commission recommended was that, at lower levels of the school system, vocational training for girls should begin at an earlier age than for boys, to be supplemented by employing girls of school-leaving age as assistants in infants' play centres, which they recommended should be attached to primary schools. Discussing secondary education, the commissioners noted that fewer girls were enrolled in secondary schools and that government provision for girls' secondary education was lower than for boys; there were no government secondary school for girls in Guyana or Trinidad and only one such school in the whole of the Windward and Leeward Islands. A significant recommendation of the commissioners also gives some idea of the quality of female education then existing:

It is also essential that girls anxious to enter the professions and capable of doing so should not be denied the necessary preliminary education. Complaints were made to us in evidence . . . of the difficulty of obtaining girls with the education necessary to enable them to enter the nursing profession. Further, many girls find it very difficult to obtain the teaching in subjects such as mathematics, Latin, physics and chemistry demanded by the scholarship regulations: in justice either the regulations should be so modified as not to discriminate against girls, or the appropriate teaching should be made as readily available to them as to boys.

The commissioners also suggested improvement in vocational training for girls.

Factors affecting education today

Women have benefited greatly from the phenomenal expansion in education which has taken place over the past few decades. From the 1960s, secondary education in the larger territories began to be expanded and the base of entry broadened through competitive scholarship exams for so-called 'free places' in schools. More girls than boys are successful at this level. The new emphasis also recognized for the first time equality of education between the sexes and coeducation became the norm for new government schools built after that time, although single-sex grammar schools existing before in many of the territories have been maintained, and a grammar school education is still regarded as the most desirable, though this is available to only a small portion of children.

Despite the official ideology of the democratization of education, the fact that only some children of school age are able to gain access to various levels of the educational system because of the shortage of school places, coupled with the poverty of so many parents, ensures that the hierarchical elitist structure on which colonial education was based continues to the present. Some sexist barriers might have fallen, but boys and girls alike continue to suffer from the inadequacies of the system.

The quality of education provided also varies greatly down to the level of the individual school. Critics of the system continue to find much in the curricula that is largely irrelevant to the lives of Caribbean children (see Eric Williams 1973; Drayton WICP 1982) and therefore a demotivating force. If examinations are used as a measure of achievement, then the high level of examination failure might be cited as one example of the irrelevance of the system to children's lives (see Gordon 1963; Drayton WICP 1982).

The Caribbean Examinations Council (CXC), introduced in 1979, is charged with developing a new Caribbean-based curriculum and with new certification as examinations tied to the English school system will be gradually phased out; it is still too early to tell what the full effects of the CXC will be, but it is looked on with hope as a potential source of cultural transformation.

Socio-economic factors   Despite the improvements in education over the last few decades including widespread access, race, class and ethnic and social origins do continue to play a significant role in the extent and quality of education a child receives and in progress through the system. It is true that theoretically post-primary education is open to all who are able — there is no discrimination against any child capable of succeeding. But the child from the poor home will start out with severe handicaps and hurdles to be overcome at all levels.

There are far more students than school places, especially in the larger countries and even at the lowest levels. Children who cannot afford to go to elite private schools are severely disadvantaged by inadequate or non-existent pre-primary facilities and overcrowded and physically poor primary schools, many located long distances from the child's home with poor transportation facilities. Secondary school places are so short that children are subjected to an '11-plus' examination which determines which of them will gain entry to prestigious grammar schools and which will have to be content with other forms of education perceived to be inferior.

Even though secondary education is theoretically 'free' to those children who succeed in gaining entry, tuition is the only thing that is free in most cases. The cost of finding uniforms, books, lunch money, transportation and other fees can severely tax the resources of lower-income families; education of any sort requires a relatively substantial cash outlay.

Opportunities for vocational and continuing education are generally inadequate or non-existent, especially for rural dwellers. In societies where the school drop-out and examination failure rates are high, few or no avenues exist to recover lost educational opportunities. This is especially crucial for women, since so many drop out of school to have children, with no hope of continuing.

Yet it is these very unschooled women, conscious perhaps of their own unrealized ambitions, who will become the primary motivating force behind their children to secure and maintain a place in school. Many of the daughters will fall by the wayside — as their mothers did. But more and more will succeed in the system, against all social and economic odds, as the rising number of professional females from all socio-economic backgrounds can attest.

Because of the prevalence of female household heads (see chapter 5), the mother's sacrifice for her children is often greatest. Working-class mothers especially are known to undergo severe deprivation in order to further their children's education. One 32-year-old Antiguan, a teacher's college graduate, described the nature of her mother's sacrifice:

> She did without food many times. She had to pay my school fees, buy uniforms and books; that took a lot. She wasn't working, she had to stay home to look after the children because she started having children very young; she had me when she was fifteen. All he [her father] did was just to bring that money and you had to make it do however you can. She make sure that her husband and children are taken care of; whatever is left in the pot, whatever scraping there is, that's what she took for her[self]. Many times she would sit down and she would tell us about certain things. She said that sometimes no food is left and she just have to make lemonade, not even lemonade, sugar water and drink it and be satisfied. She went without dresses you know, underwear, few, all for her children.

Another Antiguan woman of 49, who worked mainly as a domestic helper, was proud of the fact that as a single parent she had sent six of her eight children through high school:

I. Were you both mother and father to your children?

R. Both.

I. How did you manage that?

R. Well, I went out working. Whatever little I got, I leave myself and I give to them. I see that they come up with something to wear and something to eat. If I feel it's not enough I prefer to do without and give it to them.

I. Did you have to do without often so that they could have?

R. Sometimes.

I. What kept you going?

R. Just strength. Because I remember sometime I would drink a little tea in the mornings and at lunch time whatever I get I will give it to them and I would do without. Sometimes the pay was very small you have to meet so much demands with that small pay and so you have to make a sacrifice.

I. And you prefer to sacrifice self.

R. Yes. For them.

Despite the high level of sacrifice, poor economic status of parents can contribute to school absenteeism and a high drop-out rate. Poverty has been a significant handicap to the educational advancement of women especially. In large families it is common for the eldest or successive girls to be kept at home to handle domestic chores and care for younger children while the mother goes out to work. Thus the mother's, and daughter's, aspirations are defeated at the very start. Even if girls do not actually drop out of school for these reasons, they might result in such poor attendance and performance that the effect might be as devastating as no school at all. One 35-year-old woman who helped to raise nine brothers and sisters described such an experience and its impact on her own life:

> We were poor and she [her mother] used to have children very fast. Because I was the eldest I had to stay home most of the time. Sometimes on mornings I had to get up and help. Go to the river, wash the clothes and come back. And she would leave and she would go to the mountain and I am at home. I have to bathe them and provide feed for them and things like that. Sometimes when I did go to school, might be once in a week, sometimes twice in a week, when I go the other children call me 'visitor' and things like that. It was very embarrassing. So I said, 'Mommy, look, I can't take this thing any more.'

Her poor attendance at school and its expected effects on her learning, combined with an unsympathetic teacher, led to her leaving school at 14.

> Sometimes they would do new subjects and I wasn't there. I could remember one time the teacher did give me some lash, plenty plenty licks because I got the subject wrong because I wasn't there to do it. I was about twelve at that time. So I go home and I said, 'Mommy, look at my hands, blue, licks up to here.'

But her mother kept on encouraging her to stay on in school:

> That time I was in class one. Then I rally until I reach in three. I was about fourteen and she said you have another year and you're yet young and you must try. I said, 'Mommy, what is the use I going? I have to go today, stop tomorrow, go today, stop tomorrow. You can't catch up anything so.' So I just make up my mind and I didn't go back.

This woman looked back with regret on her missed chances: 'Well I coming up now and I see many opportunities come to me and because of the lowness of education I couldn't stand it you see.' Her educational opportunities were frustrated at every turn because she also fell into the trap of early pregnancy: 'I could have gone into nursing, you know, because I was so intelligent and trying to think very big I wrote in for nursing and I got a reply from them and at the same time, when I had to go for the exam, I got pregnant with my first daughter.' Her first job was in domestic service, but she later married a fundamentalist minister and is now president of the women's group in her church.

A Vincentian recalled how her schooling was truncated at the age of 11 by the need to help her mother: 'I didn't finish the whole six class. I just had a few months in six. My mother had a baby and she was very sick and the Doctor said she wasn't to leave the bed so I had to stay home and take care of this little one for her.'

The way in which a whole family's education can sometimes become subordinate to the demands of the domestic situation is illustrated by another woman's story. Her mother had six children and, by going to school on 'shift', they were able to help in domestic and economic activities — cultivating and chocolate-making.

> Most of the time we weren't able to go to school. Sometimes my mother have it and sometimes she don't have it. We have to stay home from school. And after she start working, when we reach a certain class we had to stay off. One go this morning and one go this afternoon and who go in the afternoon will go next day in the morning. So we had to do it so as to take care of a little one that she had. We had to prepare our own meals before we leave to go to school. When very young, my sister came out from school and start to work. I now start to take over all these things. I had to go to town, take messages, come back, hustle and cook

lunch before I go to school. Sometimes I reach to school very late because part of the lesson gone, so that was why I didn't catch up with the first subjects.

This woman dropped out of school at the age of 14 to start working. She ended up raising eight of her own children and several 'adoptions', earning a living principally as a domestic. But, by dint of hard work and struggle, she was able to send six of her children through high school. She is the woman whose 'sacrifice' of self in order to school her children was quoted earlier.

The wounds to one's self-esteem caused by not being able to learn in school are incalculable. Another informant recalled:

When I was small I didn't get the firm foundation at the beginning of school. When I was going junior school I couldn't read. We had this book, B'rer Rabbit, West Indian Reader. And you take a stick and you go up to the board and you point and I could only call the word 'the'. To call other things I start to tremble you know, because I know I'm going to get licks.

Again, part of her problem was having to stay away from school to help her mother: 'I used to have to stay home with the children and didn't get that firm foundation in school. I not really blaming my mother, you know, because she had it hard with us.' This woman, 23 years old at the time of the interview, was the eighth of 13 children. She nevertheless managed to get secondary schooling as she was taken to live with relatives while still young.

Even where there might be no domestic responsibilities involved, just sheer poverty itself has been a factor in keeping many out of school. One informant who left school at sixteen explained:

We were having financial problems at home. My father was in the States and my mother was in England and we weren't getting any money from them and my grandmother and my grandfather was a little old and they couldn't do anything. And I just couldn't see them suffer, you know, and in spite of it all she was trying to tell me not to stop from school but she couldn't convince me because I just can't see people suffer. That's why I left school.

The nature of the educational experience All the women quoted above are explicit not only about the way the home environment can limit educational opportunities but also about the negative aspects of the educational experience itself, especially for those who have problems keeping up. We know that attitudes towards school affect not only performance and behaviour but perceptions and beliefs. For the child, the total school experience will be coloured by many things, beginning with the firm foundation provided in early childhood and a love of learning inculcated at primary school level.

A significant element in forming negative or positive perceptions of the school experience lies in the interaction with teachers. The teacher's attitudes, beliefs, social philosophy and teaching methodology will also have profound effects on the child's performance. Obviously many children do have a positive school experience and form warm and lasting relationships with their teachers. But, for these and many other women who took part in the WICP survey (1,600 women who went to school in the 50-year period from roughly 1920 to 1970), school is too often a memory associated with punishment and humiliation, as a 54-year-old Vincentian woman of Indian ancestry recalled of her last day in school at the age of 11:

If you don't have your homework correct or you have a blot, he give you no reason, he would just beat for blind. I was very much afraid of the strap, of getting flogged. So when he called you up to call the words, one hundred hard words, you really don't know which one he is going to give you to spell, you began getting nervous that you might make a mistake. For instance, he'll ask you to spell 'weather', meaning the rain, and if you spelled it right, then he would ask you to spell 'wether' meaning a goat that was castrated. That day when I left school was when he gave this to write out and I made so much mistakes because of fear. He said, 'I don't know whether the wether was killed in the weather or not' and I had it all puzzled up. I knew it if he had asked me, you know. But when I came to write, because of fear, I didn't know what I was doing. He began calling us to spell it and he wasn't explaining, he was just saying, 'Spell out: "I don't know whether the wether was killed in the weather or not." ' And I made the mistake the first time and he held me here and he spanked me across my back with a strap and my back was blistered. Held me across my neck, my dress neck and he gave me about three lashes across my back and then he threw the book to me and then I went home and Mummy could not get me to go back to school. I was frightened and I never went back to school.

The use of corporal punishment in Caribbean schools has diminished and, indeed, is no longer used in girls' schools or most boys' schools, but mental cruelty, indifference or an impersonal approach still remain and prevent many children from identifying with their teachers. Phillips in his study of *Adolescence in Jamaica* (1973) noted that 'the area of pupil–teacher relationship proved to be one of the least satisfactory school experiences as viewed by the adolescents themselves'.

Although working-class parents might display high aspirations for their children, parental influence is not enough to ensure the child's success; parents' own lack of education, inability to help children with homework and lack of time to spend with children are some of the factors which will work against their effort. While lower-class families can provide the incentive for mobility, children from these families are still disadvantaged in terms of career choices and aspirations since such families can provide role models for only a narrow range of occupations (Rubin and Zavalloni 1969) and, even today, few schools offer career counselling.

Cultural factors   Other cultural factors deriving from socio-economic status, race and class are found to be significant variables in the motivation and academic achievement of boys and girls. It has been demonstrated that children from poorer homes generally grow up in atmospheres that are deprived and unstimulating and have access to the worst schools. Correlation between socio-economic status and cognitive and intellectual development, educational success and achievement has been demonstrated by a number of studies. Nevertheless, since the home and school environments do interact, they can work together harmoniously or can provide contradictory models for the child. A good school environment can help to counteract the effect of a bad home life while poor schools can have ill effects on children from any type of home. Other studies suggest that parental guidance and encouragement are more useful predictors of school achievement than social class. It has also been tentatively suggested that females more than males need positive home environments and teacher attitudes to perform well (Leo-Rhynie 1978, p. 283).

A study by Rubin and Zavalloni of social aspirations among secondary school youths in Trinidad found significant differences among children from different social classes and racial and ethnic groups and between boys and girls. The authors found that 'White and coloured students come from families and from a social milieu which provides middle-class role models and standards that are implicitly absorbed in the process of socialization. Lower class students may need to draw their role models from distant sources . . . Their long-range goals tend to assume heroic qualities in contrast to those of other students' (Rubin and Zavalloni 1969, p. 66).

Ethnicity, class and socio-economic status also have a bearing on the way in which girls mediate the conflict between educational and familial roles, between school attendance and childbearing. In societies like the Caribbean, such conflicts are acute. Girls are pushed to get an education so that they can be economically independent; the same girls are also pushed to 'prove themselves' by early childbearing.

In their study in Trinidad in the late 1950s, Rubin and Zavalloni (1969) found that racial and class backgrounds of girls significantly affected the resolution of role conflicts. All girls in their sample overwhelmingly desired marriage and saw a career as a 'modern' role for a woman, one which should antedate marriage or be an interlude from full-time family responsibilities. Nevertheless, while a large number of white girls (about 23 per cent) could envisage careers only as wives and mothers, only 4 per cent of girls in other racial groups (black, East Indian, coloured) did so. Although over half the girls expressed conflicts over marriage and a career, there was less conflict among black girls because, the authors concluded, it is customary for women they know to work for wages and to be economically independent. White girls had the greatest conflict over the traditional vs. modern role for women, probably because, at the time, there would have been few white women workers as role models. For the East Indian girl, the choice revolved around one of two alternatives: either to become a full-time housewife or to have a career and avoid marriage entirely. Within this culture, the combination of marriage–career was at the time untenable.

These findings might now be dated as women of all classes, races and ethnic groups have forged new social and economic roles in the ensuing decades. But they do reflect an important historical process, the fact that women of different races and ethnic groups have performed different roles in the labour market (see chapter 6) and that female education has been geared to such role performance. This in turn would have influenced each woman's perception of the opportunity structure and how far a female of her race and class could expect to go. As we have seen, for a long time the education of white upper-class women was of the 'finishing school' type to prepare them to be 'good wives and good mothers', a status to be realized only by this group. Brown girls aspired to this status too, but the economic circumstances of many were such that they were forced to earn a living — at least until they found a husband. With the broadening of the economic base, they found a niche in commerce since for a long time throughout the West Indies black girls did not have access to front office jobs in banks and other institutions such as hotels, large department stores or commercial establishments; it was the policy to hire white or near white. For black girls, therefore, education has been the route to upward mobility through occupations such as teaching, nursing and social work, while, for 'modern' East Indian girls, education provided the means of escaping from 'tradition and unwanted marriages' (Mohammed WICP 1982). In traditional East Indian families, girls were not allowed to take on low-status jobs, so, at first, a professional career was the only option.

We will now turn to look at how far women have progressed in the educational system since gaining equality of access, and the uses to which they have put this education. While we can make no direct linkages between attainment and performance and the economic, social and cultural context so far described, we should bear these factors in mind. Evidence from other countries has identified such external factors, together with internal factors such as gender-role stereotyping, as influencing educational performance and choices.

Attainment and performance

From the 1960s onwards there has been increasing equality of educational opportunities between the sexes. And Caribbean girls have taken full advantage of this. Indeed, the high level of female educational participation is surprising to some observers. Cross and Schwartzbaum (1969, p. 194) in their study of social mobility and secondary school selection in Trinidad in the 1960s found girls marginally over-represented in the secondary school population, a situation they found 'in curious contrast to the evidence from other "developing" countries and even Western industrialized societies'. Over the last few decades, girls' educational participation and attainment have equalled and in some cases surpassed those of boys at various levels of the systems.

But, despite their high level of performance and examination success rate *vis-à-vis* boys, there is, for reasons not yet explained, progressive drop-out of girls as they proceed upwards. There is also considerable sex differentiation in the subjects and courses pursued.

The proportion of girls and boys in primary school approaches equality. At the age of 11 or thereabouts all Caribbean children sit a common entrance or 11-plus examination, which determines which children will gain entry to the very limited spaces available in secondary grammar schools. Those who fail to gain entry can go on to less prestigious institutions such as senior schools, junior secondary, secondary or technical high schools. In some countries, children who fail the 11-plus can sit the grade nine achievement test to gain entry to other schools. The secondary grammar schools prepare children for careers and white-collar jobs, the secondary, vocational and technical schools for blue-collar jobs and the senior schools for low-ranking occupations. Both socio-economic status of parents and urban or rural origins are found to be factors that influence children's performance and thus final placement in the school system, though this is not to suggest that there is not a great deal of mobility through educational achievement.

At both common entrance and grade nine achievement level, girls perform better than boys; however, in Jamaica at least, a 50–50 ratio between the sexes is maintained in allocating places in the schools. The argument which justifies this policy is that it is recognized that boys mature later than girls. Despite this, at secondary school levels throughout the region, there are more girls than boys in every country. What is significant, however, is the fact that female enrolment is likely to be higher than male in junior, independent and newer secondary schools — those very schools which in some countries, such as Jamaica, offer a more restricted range of subject options, provide no opportunities for sixth-form work and are regarded as less prestigious than the traditional grammar schools. Enrolment figures for fifth and sixth forms of grammar schools confirm lower enrolment figures for girls at the higher secondary levels though female enrolment has been undoubtedly increasing (Cole WICP 1982b).

Girls also perform better in high school examinations at all levels, though they are only just now approaching numerical equality in enrolment. In the higher grades in grammar schools, we find more boys than girls enrolled. Fewer girls than boys will sit the O-level examination, which is equivalent to a secondary school-leaving certificate, but their performance in the examinations outranks that of boys, even in such traditional 'male' subjects as maths, advanced maths, physics and chemistry — though fewer girls sit these particular subjects. Fewer girls also move on to A-level, which prepares students for entrance to university and prestigious careers, and fewer still will elect science subjects. Those who do perform better than boys in the A-level examinations (Cole WICP 1982b). The situation is somewhat different at the other secondary institutions; more girls than boys seem to persevere through the system. Nevertheless, at these levels as well as in non-formal and continuing education, educational choice to a great extent continues to be gender-differentiated.

By the time girls reach tertiary or university level, the gender biases evident in educational choices are full-blown. From a certain age in high school when children begin to be groomed for higher forms, they are encouraged towards 'arts' or 'science' subjects. In most cases the girls opt for or are pushed into 'arts', the boys into 'science'. An even stronger gender bias is reported for vocational training in other types of schools. Boys learn woodwork, mechanics and other 'masculine' subjects, girls are offered beauty culture, domestic science and secretarial training (see, for example, Mohammed WICP 1982; Hodge 1985).

In examining the data available for vocational, post-secondary and higher education, Cole confirmed the concentration of girls in traditional sex-linked courses. For instance, in Barbados only 1 per cent of technology students in the Community College were girls compared with 76.7 per cent in fine arts and 67.4 in liberal arts. To take another example, in St Kitts/Nevis, enrolment figures of the government's Training Institute showed girls participating in only two courses, a commercial/secretarial course or training in hotel work. Similar trends have been observed in Trinidad and 'Tobago, where in vocational training girls are found to be concentrated in home economics, dressmaking and design and secretarial courses while boys predominate in areas such as building construction, welding and mechanics (Cole WICP 1982b).

A case-study of Jamaica by Elsa Leo-Rhynie also highlights the differences existing in educational choices. She looked at the status of women in that country in 1980–1, the midway point of the UN decade of women, using as a frame of reference Article 10 of the United Nations Convention on Elimination of All Forms of Discrimination Against Women. This article identifies eight measures by which countries could ensure for women the same rights as men in education. She noted that girls are disadvantaged regarding access to secondary education since the system maintains a male bias regardless of girls' performance. In teacher training colleges, women students predominate (80 per cent). Yet, while only one-third of all secondary school teachers are male, two-thirds of all schools have male principals. Occupational and vocational choices at the tertiary level also reveal a sex bias. For instance, the Jamaica College of Agriculture had an enrolment of only one-third female in 1980. At the College of Arts, Science and Technology, engineering remains the province of males while institutional management (including home economics, catering, etc.) is largely attended by females. Subjects grouped under 'science' were 'female' but these include occupations such as medical technology, pharmacy and hospital records (Leo-Rhynie 1984).

At the University of the West Indies similar trends were observed. Female enrolment had increased substantially over the last two decades so that, while in 1960–1 the sex ratio throughout the university system was 2 : 1 in favour of males, by 1980–1 the ratio wàs 1 : 1. But the faculties were still largely sexually stratified. Engineering, agriculture and medicine were all still largely male, arts and general studies and education significantly female. Only in the faculties of law and social sciences were the sexes fairly evenly distributed. Women outnumbered men at undergraduate level in all traditional disciplines; men outnumbered women in all graduate programmes except the diploma in education.

Leo-Rhynie found that, in Jamaica, women 'are not explicitly discriminated against at any level of the educational system' or in areas such as sports, or grants or scholarships for study. Nevertheless, she concluded that 'there are still forces operating in the school and the society which influence girls to perpetuate the stereotypes of women through the choices they make in terms of school subjects, vocational areas and occupational roles'.

Occupational choice

The creation of equal educational opportunities for women has not created an equal thirst for the same career opportunities as men although change is undoubtedly occurring — and at a very rapid rate. A number of studies done over different times and in different Caribbean countries reveal a great deal of similarity in the occupational choices of women, regardless of their level of schooling and socio-economic background. First choice is for traditionally 'female' occupations — teaching, nursing, secretarial or clerical work. And, it seems, if women who have already passed through the system had a chance to go back to school, they would make the same choices. As we shall see below, even while older women in the WICP survey expressed dissatisfaction with many aspects of the schooling they had received, they 'continued to express their desires for more schooling along conventional paths' (McKenzie WICP 1986).

One of the earliest studies of occupational preferences was done by M.G. Smith, based on research in rural Jamaica in 1957–9. Nursing, teaching and dressmaking were the overwhelming occupational choices of these peasant girls (Smith 1960). In St Vincent some 25 years later, girls were making the same choices. A question-naire administered to all students aged 11–15 years in a primary school to test occupational aspirations found that nursing ranked highest for girls (45.3 per cent), followed by shop work (22.7 per cent), teaching (18.7 per cent) and clerical work (Rubenstein 1984, Table 1).

Other studies in Jamaica reveal a similar pattern of female choice, though they were conducted in different levels of the school system, in both rural and urban areas, among different socio-economic groups, and using different methodologies. What is perhaps most revealing is that, in all the studies done, girls' choices were found to be not only predictable and limited but also far more realistic and attainable than those of boys. While children generally romanticize their futures, it has been noted that boys do so far more than girls. Thus one study showed that well over 50 per cent of boys whose formal education would end at 15 aspired to jobs in the higher professional range which required university or a good high school education, while only a fraction (7 per cent) of girls in the study showed similar 'unrealistic' aspirations (see Phillips 1973).

The Rubin and Zavalloni study of Trinidadian high school students showed a similarity of 'female' occupational choices by girls. Most of the careers envisaged did not require university training although these girls were among the elite of the educa-tional system and in forms which groom students for university entry. The percent-age of girls who had plans for entering university was considerably lower than boys. Many, like their less well-educated sisters, were in fact planning to seek careers as teachers and nurses and to continue their careers after marriage — the ultimate goal of the majority. The researchers found that, while there were significant differences in aspirations and occupational choices according to socio-economic status, class and race, girls expressed more limited horizons than boys for all groupings. This was found to be the case in the drive for achievement as well as educational and occupational aspirations. The students were asked to write essays giving sponta-neous descriptions of their future goals. It was found that 'Fantasies of heroic deeds and great accomplishments were found to occur almost exclusively among the boys' (Rubin and Zavalloni 1969, p. 104). Girls on the whole expressed 'modest sentiments' and did 'not match the intensity of the desire for recognition expressed by boys'. The authors suggested that a lack of role models might provide one explanation:

> Social and cultural, as well as educational factors, tend to limit women's roles to the traditional, and there are few other feminine role models in their society for girls to emulate, even in fantasy. The Hollywood star image is apparently too race-bound to provide even a fictional role, and in 1957, very few women had emerged on the national scene to capture the imagination of young girls.
>
> (Rubin and Zavalloni 1969, pp. 104–5)

Florence Nightingale was the only female figure 'of historic or international fame' selected as a role model by these girls.

Although access to education for girls has improved dramatically in the decades between the earliest studies cited and the latest, we see that occupational choices for women remain strangely rigid; that choices might, however, vary according to socio-economic status of parents and ethnic group; and that girls exposed to the higher levels of secondary education (sixth-form grammar school), which is taken as pre-training for professional roles, do not always opt for these roles. However, the fact that most of the studies cited were done between the 1950s and the 1970s should be borne in mind. A more recent study of professional women in Jamaica showed that, although the ratio of professional women to men has been improving, women are still predominantly represented in teaching and health-related occupations (Leo-Rhynie and Hamilton 1982).

When we come to look at the actual employment status of the region's women (chapter 6), we will see that the choices made conform closely to the occupational structure and it might be that the occupational structure influences the choices made. But, even if this is so, the way in which people perceive the opportunities which are open to them is only one of the factors which will influence their occupa-tional and other life choices. Such influences include both an external dimension and an internal or subjective dimension.

We have already mentioned some of the external factors — race, class and socio-economic status, the school experience itself, and the historically determined opportunity structure. The influence of significant others, especially the strong presence of females in the society, should also not be overlooked.

In the WICP study, female influences generally were found to be significant contributors to the motivation of female students. When asked who had assisted them with their schooling, just under 70 per cent of all respondents reported 'no help from male relatives' and 75 per cent reported 'no help from male teachers'. The main type of help received from female relatives was economic assistance and motivation; help received from teachers consisted almost equally of academic assistance and motivation (McKenzie WICP 1986).

It can be assumed, then, that the female influence on career choices will be strong. Since female role models are themselves largely in occupations nowadays perceived as 'female' — as teachers, nurses, secretaries, etc. — they might encourage girls to opt for safe career choices — as teachers, nurses, etc. — discouraging careers in which there are few or no female role models and which are therefore untested and risky.

One researcher on occupational choice in Jamaica took note of the fact that the Jamaican rural family pattern is daughter-oriented: 'Thus parents, particularly mothers, are more likely to lavish their highest ambitions on their daughters.' Daughters, he says, are regarded as more stable, more capable of benefiting from study, and more likely to achieve parental ambitions than boys (quoted in Phillips 1973).

The nature of the Caribbean social system ensures that certain factors are more conducive to girls achieving their goals than boys — as long as their aspirations remain modest and goals limited. In the Caribbean context, the limits — self-imposed or external — on girls might in fact work to their advantage. Within these societies of unemployment and blighted hopes, ambitions are not easily realizable and it is the careful, plodding, patient girls who might find it easier to succeed in their modest career goals.

It is those girls who opt for more challenging careers or occupations, those invading hitherto male-dominated areas, who will have to learn how to break out of gender-role stereotyping and assume a more challenging mode of behaviour.

Gender-role stereotyping and education

The patterns followed by Caribbean women in terms of school attainment and performance, occupational choices and aspirations, are similar to those followed by women in other Western societies. A body of literature on the subject suggests that, in general:

1 Girls perform academically better than boys from primary school to adolescence, when girls start to drop out of the system.
2 Girls and boys perform differently; for instance, girls appear to be 'arts' oriented and boys to be 'science' oriented.
3 Girls make different occupational and career choices from boys; in general, girls' choices are less ambitious.

It is now generally accepted that gender-role socialization and the development of stereotypically 'male' or 'female' behaviour plays a major role in determining and influencing the respective performances and choices made by males and females as they proceed through the school system and gear themselves for the assumption of adult responsibilities.

Research in the Caribbean confirms findings from elsewhere about gender-stereotyped behaviour — girls 'are encouraged to be unassertive . . . and dependent', in keeping with the perceptions of the idealized feminine image, while boys 'learn early in life that self-assertion will not meet with negative reprisals' (Henry and Wilson 1975, p. 166). Thus the stage is set for the enactment of behaviours associated with gender-role stereotypes: conforming girls, challenging boys.

Romer (1981) points out that while girls from an early age are encouraged to achieve, they are expected to do so in an 'obedient, conforming, and other-oriented fashion' and while they get better grades than boys throughout school and their performance tends to be stable and good, they do not think of themselves as so good and their expectations for future success are 'significantly lower' than boys. Girls, Romer says, often shrink from real challenges and competition and tend to underestimate how capable they are.

Part of the reason might be that girls subconsciously conspire with the agents of socialization to limit their own horizons. History books focus on male achievement; readers for even young children show boys having adventures, girls as supportive aides; people in high-powered jobs, in politics, in leadership roles are generally males. These perceptions of real life, it is argued, put pressures on male students to achieve, on female students to hold back. Additionally, as we have seen, the female models projected in the wider society — in agencies such as the media and the church and in manifestations of popular culture — are also projecting the traditional female stereotypes (see Cuthbert 1981; Brodber WICP 1982; Hodge WICP 1982).

Differential treatment of children from an early age also influences the development of different types of skills, which will carry over into school and adult roles (Astin 1982).

One example often cited is the approach to mathematics. Many high-status jobs are scientific in orientation; access to them is based on the possession of spatial and analytical skills. Many of these jobs are held by men. This to a certain extent reflects the fact that males show a bias towards the sciences, females towards the arts. Research has also suggested differences in cognitive ability between boys and girls. Girls on the whole are found to excel in fluency, rote memory and reasoning; boys excel in spatial and quantitative ability. Such differences might help to explain why, for instance, mathematics has been traditionally regarded as a 'male' subject. But are the differences biological, or do they result from gender-role stereotyping? Are boys better at mathematics because from an early age they are engaged in play that will develop spatial, manipulative and scientific skills, action and physical ability and are generally made to feel that 'boys must learn maths' because boys grow up to be engineers, architects, scientists, etc,. professions which rest on a maths–science base?

Girls, on the other hand, are usually given toys such as dolls and encouraged to 'play house', activities that encourage sedentary occupations and from an early age are groomed to behave and select courses of study that are in keeping with the perceptions of the idealized feminine image. Parents and teachers, and the educational structure itself, conspire to steer girls and boys in gender-typed directions. While these 'feminine traits' and 'feminine skills' are appropriate for the traditional female role of homemaker, they do not necessarily gear girls for income-earning activities. The world of work demands from women a different set of postures. The extent to which a woman is successful in a 'man's world', i.e. the world of work, might depend on how well she develops these.

Secondly, as we have already mentioned, there is for women severe role conflict between the world of home and the world of school. If females are socialized to see motherhood as woman's primary role, then a career might be regarded as secondary and even bright girls with good academic records will opt for 'safe' careers such as teaching or secretarial training that they can fall back on if the more desirable alternative, wifehood and motherhood, falls through.

This conflict might also help to explain why the academic performance of a girl falls off as she reaches the upper levels of secondary school; she might be becoming more conscious of the choices facing her. Another explanation suggested is that, while at earlier ages girls progress better than boys in the school system because it stresses conformity, rote-learning, etc., by mid-adolescence achievement becomes a more acceptable male virtue and female behaviour becomes less compatible (Jackson 1979, pp. 47–8). Also related might be one aspect of the female self-concept, that certain elements in our cultures still encourage women to 'play dumb'.

Thus some women might underachieve because they do not want to appear too bright in case it makes them less attractive to males, less 'marketable' in the courtship and marriage game or, increasingly, in the 'body-marketing' game.

Within the Caribbean school system itself, whether in single-sex or coeducational schools, gender-appropriate behaviour learnt at home is encouraged. In the process, girls might be encouraged to emphasize 'expressive traits', i.e. charm, manners, kindness, etc., while boys are encouraged in the 'performance dimension', i.e. the realm of achievement, professional aspiration, etc., where a mix of both might be more appropriate to steer one through the realities of everyday life. The curricula of most schools are often to a certain extent gender-differentiated, with the differences being particularly acute in vocational and continuing education.

The way the school itself functions, i.e. its structure, teaching methodology, the nature and structure of the curricula and the content and presentation of textbooks and other learning material have also been found to reinforce gender-role stereotyping, though we can present little evidence from the Caribbean.

However, the WICP survey throws some light on the topic. Hermione McKenzie, who analysed the data relating to education, found that, when the women were asked to reflect on their educational experience, all emphasized the socializing aspects as the greatest benefits derived by them and only a few indicated any practical benefits. Personal development and self-respect were the predominant effects which school was said to have had on their adult lives, followed by the ability to communicate. Schooling as a help with their livelihood was low in their ranking. McKenzie concludes that, in general, 'the instrumental uses of education, such as developing cognitive skills and earning a living, rank below the value for personal development and socialization into female roles' (McKenzie WICP 1986, p. 96).

From her analysis of the WICP sample, McKenzie concluded that two basic themes emerge: (i) the role that education plays in socializing women into passivity and acceptance of a conventional female role, and (ii) the emphasis by respondents themselves on education for intrinsic results, such as personal development, as an alternative to perceiving education as a path to material power and occupational mobility.

Nevertheless, we should not overlook the fact that women in the study feel that they have been cheated in their education and that they continue to persistently strive for the opportunities they feel they have been denied, if only through their children. This does not suggest that women are passively accepting the roles they have ended up playing, or their status in life.

We might conclude that, although it is more than likely that women will have to assume a major role as breadwinners, this consciousness does not yet articulate with the education provided or desired. Women's attitudes to education as well as their educational choices are still largely preparations for the traditional role of women, but not for the demands of a sophisticated job market or for the real world that Caribbean women inhabit. Female socialization, identity formation and lack of role models in some spheres all seem to be strengthening rather than weakening the traditional female role (McKenzie WICP 1986).

Yet, when the survey results are differentiated into age-groups, the responses of women of different ages can perhaps be taken as an indication that rapid changes are taking place. The educational levels of the women in the survey were in large part related to age levels and reflected the increasing educational opportunities for women. Most of the older women in the study had only a primary-level education but a substantial minority, particularly younger women, had attended secondary school; between 40 and 50 per cent of these had attained O-level educational standard. About 10 per cent of the sample had post-school training and 1.7 per cent had been to university.

McKenzie concludes that most of the women in the sample appear to have had 'a substantial modicum of education', though its effectiveness in terms of certification and vocational relevance might be questioned.

These women's views about their education reflect in part changing perceptions and attitudes, with greater levels of dissatisfaction being expressed by the younger and better-educated women. Women over 40 generally expressed satisfaction with the way school had prepared them for adult life. Those with better education were dissatisfied with the way school had prepared them for adult life; those with tertiary education were the least satisfied; generally, younger women were better educated and less satisfied. McKenzie found that, on the one hand, there was heavy resignation to or acceptance of whatever education had been gained; on the other hand, there was frustration that education did not do more for them.

Although women on the whole accepted their level of education, many had unfulfilled aspirations centring mainly round the desire to use education more effectively to earn a livelihood. But, when their wishes as to further education are analysed in terms of what they would like to have studied, these women reveal nothing beyond traditional aspirations. Among women who had already been through secondary school, the subjects desired were for educational enrichment such as foreign languages, sciences and commercial subjects. Older women stated a desire for more basic educational subjects such as English and mathematics. Women did have unfulfilled aspirations regarding education mainly for further study of the traditional type and to find a traditional job. Thus McKenzie concluded, 'these conventional paths are the target of their strivings' (McKenzie WICP 1986, p. 100). They are nevertheless dissatisfied •by the lack of vocational and practical relevance in education. Their aspirations for their own children, boys and girls, concentrate on secondary and university education for better earning capacity, increased knowledge and, not unnaturally, a better education than their own.

II *Family & Household*

Edna Manley, *Hills of Papine*, 1949 (Mahogany, height 23″)
A.D. Scott Collection, National Gallery of Jamaica, used with permission of
   A.D. Scott and the National Gallery
Photographer: Jacqueline Gannie

4 *The Concept of Motherhood*

Attitudes to childbearing

Childbearing is one of the few areas in the lives of Caribbean women that is not surrounded by ambivalences. There is an almost universal impulse to mothering:

I. There are a lot of girls who have children early, a lot of young girls that have children?

R. Oh yes, you know that is the only product we have here.

I. Children?

R. Yes, that's our product.

Although women today have greater options through education than their mothers and grandmothers ever dreamed of, the view persists that the real vocation for women is motherhood: 'It's the natural thing. If a woman don't bear a child, your district call you all sort of things. Man feel 'fraid of you.' Girls are socialized from an early age into this role.

Dorian Powell, who examined the WICP responses to childbearing, noted that high value and status are attached to the mothering role. For most women, it is more important than wifehood. It is through childbearing that women realize their self-image: there is the conviction that women ought to have children (Powell WICP 1986). 'I never had no children and now I feel like a johncrow,' one WICP informant exclaimed. The reasons are complex but may be categorized generally in terms of destiny, physical effects, self-identity and self-fulfilment, emotional satisfaction and cultural factors.

There is, for instance, widespread belief in the biblical injunction to be 'fruitful and multiply' and in the many myths that surround childbearing or childlessness. Each woman, it is believed, is destined to have a set number of children and to bear out her 'lot'. Many physical and mental disorders are attributed to childlessness. The most common belief is that a woman who does not have children will be sickly and subject to numerous disorders ranging from headaches to madness. Such beliefs reported in the 1950s by Kerr (1952) of Jamaican women still find currency in the Caribbean today (see Durant-Gonzalez WICP 1982).

These beliefs are not only widely held by women themselves but are reinforced by the arguments advanced by men, who see 'fathering' a child — as opposed to parenting — as the true sign of manhood. 'Making a baby' is how he asks a woman to prove herself to him. Where he is in a steady relationship with a woman, he might also see repeated childbearing as a means of keeping her at home.

Regardless of what external pressures are applied, the fact is that women themselves do want children. Nine out of ten women surveyed by the WICP saw childbearing as a fundamental role for women. First, children are seen in relation to family life. One woman simply stated: 'a child completes the family'. Secondly, children are perceived as an essential part of female identity. 'It's a good thing to do, it makes you feel like a woman,' a WICP respondent said of childbearing. Many women cite the emotional satisfaction to be derived. 'I was just very happy, I was excited, thinking now is the time I am going to have a baby of my own, somebody to call me mummy,' a woman who got married at 20 said of her reaction to her first pregnancy. Another who had had two children and a break of 15 years said of her late pregnancy,

> I just felt that the home would be too lonely without somebody. I began getting lonely for another person around me. I started seeing the boys getting big. My neighbours would always bring their kids to me so I more or less became a baby-sitter. I used to say, instead of minding another person's child, it's best I have one, I just had a craving for another child.

Yet there are more than emotional or sentimental reasons for having children. A pragmatic element is sometimes involved. Children are perceived by women as not only an emotional investment but a material one — as minders in their old age. Fully 90 per cent of parents in a study by Blake (1961) expected that their children would help them out later.

Children are also seen by women as part of the resources they can call their own, a reason for being as well as doing. This is especially significant in societies where relationships with men are frequently frustrating and insecure (see chapter 9). Women derive psychic satisfaction from the mothering role, especially in the absence of satisfactory alternatives to childbearing. While men traditionally derive 'power and authority, prestige and status, from direct links with the economy, women derive theirs from the family, mainly through children' (Powell WICP 1982). This is probably more so for women who lack other types of resources such as education. The correlations between educational levels and fertility, and education and contraceptive use, bear this out (see Durant-Gonzalez WICP 1982; McKenzie WICP 1986).

A young Antiguan woman in a visiting union explained the role that her child plays in her life:

> He ask me how I feel because I have this child for him and he's married. I tell him I don't really feel any different because I know you was a married man, right. I wanted a child. I'm in the house, I'm lonely, sit down, do something, cook, make fudge, make anything. I use to be on the stove nearly every day doing something. I said, having a child makes a good difference in life. You can at least say if you work who you working for. If I work every day and I don't know who I working for, what the hell I'm going out to work for?

A child can refocus a woman's world, as this mother noted: 'I would go to a dance. I wouldn't come home till morning. When you come you drunk you tired you weary. Nobody say, "Mamie me want me tea." Nobody there to stretch your sleep. You bathe, you eat, you go back to sleep. A child takes up a lot of your energy and a lot of time.' Children help to reduce the loneliness of women when their men are not around (Powell WICP 1986); 'looking after the children' gives a woman something to do: 'It makes a big difference in the home. When a man and a woman are married and he's going out and might have to leave her alone, this could result in bickering. If children are home to keep her company and she is reasonable, she wouldn't mind so much. She would be looking after the children.'

Women derive power and status from the act of successful child-rearing. As Victoria Durant-Gonzalez points out, in many Caribbean villages such women are regarded as 'good mumma'. Thus childbearing is a cultural expectation which enables women to gain social rewards and social recognition — sometimes the only route open to them (Durant-Gonzalez WICP 1982, p. 15).

Of course there are women who do not believe that childbearing is woman's inescapable destiny. One woman said, 'It is not a priority. You can live without them. If you think you won't be able to have them and raise them the way you want, that's no good.' But the conventional attitude towards a childless woman is that she is a 'mule', i.e. barren and beyond the pale of society. Girls in the Caribbean are presented with few if any alternative role models to childbearing. Durant-Gonzalez (WICP 1982, p. 14) argues that 'the role of childless adult female is an empty role in the sense that it lacks role models, and is unclear and ill-defined within Caribbean societies'.

Merle Hodge scathingly observed that:

> At both levels of the society — the respectable upper class which marries, and the deemed-not-so-respectable lower class which does not consider marriage compulsory — the image of womanhood is strangely rigid. Girls are still borne along, as on a conveyor belt, into what is presented to them as the only possible fulfilment for a woman — marriage and/or child-bearing.

According to Hodge:

> One section of our young womanhood is taught that they are not to go out and fetch illegitimate babies like their 'common', 'low-class' counterparts, but to groom and prepare themselves for the Husband, while the other section, the 'common', 'low-class' counterparts, acquire the knowledge that the way to hold down the man of the moment for a little longer is to 'make baby' for him; and at any rate the childless woman is an abomination, a pitiable creature.   (Hodge 1977, p. 11)

Virtually all the women in the WICP survey were mothers: 96 per cent in St Vincent, 89 per cent in Antigua and Barbados. In these territories, family size was six children per mother (St Vincent 6, Antigua 6.1, Barbados 5.4). But, when women in the survey were asked the ideal number of children women should have, most of them said four.

Despite the desire to have children, birth-rates in recent years have been falling and the Caribbean is now among the low-fertility regions of the world. Contraceptive use is reasonably high.

The WICP research confirmed earlier findings and research elsewhere that there is high correlation between education and employment and fertility (for example, Roberts 1975). The more education a woman has, the fewer children she is likely to have and the more likely she is to be employed. Women in married and common-law unions were found to have the largest number of children, those in visiting unions the lowest. This might be accounted for by findings elsewhere that after the first union which results in a child, women in visiting unions tend to pass through long periods in a single state, and this usually corresponds to the highest period of female fertility (see, for example, Roberts and Sinclair 1978).

Learning the facts of life

Although the premium placed on motherhood is so high, one of the contradictions in the region is that girls grow up receiving little or no formal preparation for the role. From the time the Caribbean girl reaches puberty, the greatest worry of adults is to keep her constantly watched to prevent her having relations with the opposite sex and getting pregnant. A woman who was 49 at the time she was interviewed recalled of her adolescence: 'You know how old people used to behave in those days, I guess not in the States but in the West Indies, as soon as you start having your period they start looking out and as soon as you're talking to boys, they think the world of things going on.'

The authoritarian climate in the home reaches its full force during adolescence. This is the time when the mother especially is engaged in a struggle to protect daughters from 'potentially harmful contacts'. She usually has the support of other females in the yard or the community to support this. 'Daughter-watching' becomes a pastime. But how do they go about this? Principally by warning girls from the minute they reach puberty to stay away from men. They do not usually tell them why. Indeed, some mothers argue that telling a girl the facts of life will put ideas into her head and make her 'force ripe' or 'big before her time', i.e. sexually precocious. The 'social distance' which exists between parents and children leads to difficulties in transmitting information on the facts of life (see, for example, Braithwaite 1953; Clarke 1957; Brodber 1968, 1975; Phillips 1973).

Only a generation or two ago, boys and girls were usually provided with no sex education whatever. Nowadays children are exposed to some form of sex education in schools and matters affecting sex are discussed in the media. Population control programmes in some countries aim their messages directly at youngsters and include a sex education component; contraceptives are also easily available in most countries. Thus some young people, particularly those in urban areas in the larger territories, are now better informed about these matters than their parents. But, in rural areas and more conservative parts of the Caribbean, boys and girls still grow up knowing little or nothing about their bodies, the opposite sex or the mechanics of sexual relations. This ignorance about their bodies and its functioning sometimes persists through life. There are women who have borne several children who still fail to see causation between sexual activity and childbearing. Roberts and Sinclair's study of Jamaican women (1978) found that one-third of their sample (of 500 women) had no knowledge of reproductive processes; another one-third knew only that sexual intercourse was involved but not how. Only 10 per cent were found to have 'adequate knowledge' on the subject. There was equally widespread ignorance of the menstrual cycle among most groups of women — 82 per cent of the sample had no knowledge of the subject (Roberts and Sinclair 1978, p. 112) and only 5 per cent indicated 'satisfactory knowledge' (p. 245).

Discussion about menstruation and sex is still taboo in many homes. A Guyanese East Indian farm woman in the WICP study remarked of her 10-year-old daughter's approaching puberty: 'Me no know wha gon happen. Me and she daddy notice this thing, but how me go tell me lil baby about wickedness?' (Odie-Ali WICP 1986, p. 276).

One WICP informant in her forties, who grew up in a household where the children had an otherwise open relationship with their parents, said, 'We could talk about school, right, religion. We were forbidden to read certain books because they were immoral, we couldn't hold a conversation on sex and we couldn't gossip about our neighbours or anybody with them.'

In former times — and in some cases still today — girls were not taught about menstruation until the event occurred. Thus a natural process in the transition to womanhood becomes a frightening experience. Mothers in turn transmit knowledge to their daughters in terms of a painful secret experience. The immediate connection between the menses, sexual experience and inevitable consequences is heavily underscored, as these examples show:

She never told me anything. The day that happen to me I was so scared I didn't know what to do. I say, oh my, what am I going to tell her now, she might beat me or something. I stood there in the bathroom. She kept calling me. Well, my father was alive at the time but he was living in England and he came to visit us that Saturday. That very day I was sixteen years old, you wouldn't believe that. It was my birthday. I could remember as if it happen yesterday. I knew he was out there but I didn't want to come out. They keep calling me and I do as if I don't hear them and in the end one of my sisters came in the bathroom. She called my mother and Mum came. All she said to me, 'so you in there and this thing happen and you wouldn't come out'. She sent me to have a bath and all she told me [is] if I go and have anything to do with any boy I would get pregnant.

This same woman, now the 50-year-old mother of six sons and one daughter, was asked if she had told her daughter anything: 'Yes, I explained certain things to her. I didn't in any details you know, but I give her a few instances and I told her exactly what happened. But she always tell me, the way how I explain it to her, if she was following me she would be afraid of men until she die.'

A 54-year-old East Indian in St Vincent recalled:

I wasn't told the facts of life at all. I was fifteen. One girl friend said, 'I became a young lady last week' and I said, 'What is it all about?' She said, 'You don't know?' I said 'no'. She said 'I bled and my mother did this to me and that and the other.' I went home and it was bothering me because I always talk to her and I said, 'E. said that she became a young lady last week, Mummy, what's that?' And she had already told me what I wanted to know and she said, 'Well that's the time when a girl becomes a young woman and that's the time when she would have a baby if she's not married and do anything that's wrong.' Two or three weeks after that I became a woman. She said that I have to have it every month and I'm not supposed to go in the water and physically I have to take care of myself. And she never say to me that is the way babies come or nothing, she just kept it like that. It wasn't until I got married that I got books and knew about what used to take place.

This woman was also told by her mother to keep the subject a strict secret and always look out for the date — 'it would always be on the same date and I must always be dressed accordingly, prepared for it even for two days before'.

A woman in her sixties explained how and what she told her granddaughter, whom she raised, when her first period came: 'I got the Modess. I said, "well you know what this is". She said no. I told her, "this is what would make you have children, you know. It wouldn't be easy, you'll have to feel some pain, so the further you keep from boys it will be much better for you."' Her education of her granddaughter over a period of time consisted mainly of discouragement of sexual activity:

I kept on telling her [at] different times what happen to other girls, you know. If I hear another little one make a baby I will call her and say 'you hear so and so make a baby? You know what will come from that? She'll have to be mashed to pieces, you know, because nobody say yes, is mine. And if you go to get one, it will come the same, and then how would you bring it? Where would you bring it? I won't be able to mind it.' And I kept on telling her . . . so she didn't make any.

The fact that their daughters have now entered a 'dangerous' age is constantly emphasized by mothers:

> **R.** My mother said 'well madam, you are a young lady now. But I'm just telling you, you must not play with boys or else you become pregnant,' and she showed me what to do and that was that. She said nothing more.
> **I.** Did she ever give you any books or . . . ?
> **R.** Nothing. Those things were not allowed in our home, she felt that they were immoral.
> **I.** You went to a Catholic school, did you have sex education in school?
> **R.** No, never.

This woman (now a teacher in her forties) was in turn responsible for transmitting information to a younger sister:

> One day she came in the bedroom and she saw me and she said, 'what's that I see you putting on there?' So I said, 'girl, I am having my menses'.
> She said, 'What is menses now?'
> I said, I don't know myself more than every month a set of blood does run down, run down out of me, somehow I don't know.' Then one day she came home and said, 'girl, whew, if Mummy knew this she would kill me dead'.
> So I say, 'What you saying?'
> 'They had one talk in school about boys and period and this and that.' Now she was in high school by then.
> I said, 'well, listen to me, the next time they are having this kind of talk you better stay out of it you hear, because that is not in our training and our upbringing and if you go and join with them you are just as bad as them'.

Some mothers do not impart information to their daughters at all:

> **I.** So your mother didn't tell you anything about your period?
> **R.** My mother never tell me. No ma'am, I never had any discussion with my mother about none of that.

There are cases, however, when girls are given some form of sex education by their mothers. One woman said that her mother

> always gave us a lot of books when we were growing up and changing into puberty. She was always free, you know, there was never any hiding or anything of the sort. She would teach us about sex and changing and boyfriends and what was expected and what was normal and things like that. She brought us a lot of books. We had *Becoming a Woman*. I remember that.

Preparations for motherhood

Sexual attitudes and behaviour represent a particularly conflict-ridden area of socialization. Agents of socialization — school, church and home — all uphold the ideals of virginity, chastity and sex only after marriage and, in former years, used to deny even the existence of sex for women: the childless 'spinster' was the only female who could hope to secure and keep a government job. Married women could not be employed permanently in the public service — a rule which in some countries has only recently been changed. In other countries, females in certain jobs, for instance postmistresses, could not marry and keep their jobs since cohabitation was not allowed on the government premises on which they had to reside. In other areas, female public servants such as teachers had to resign if they got pregnant. Married women were not permitted to be principals of schools.

Nevertheless, this 'Christian ideal of the monogamous society' (Phillips 1973, p. 68) is not accepted by everyone. Persons of different classes uphold different mores of sexual behaviour and have different aspirations and means of fulfilling them. Mothers' aspirations for middle- and upper-class girls, internalized by the girls themselves, in the 1960s was for an education leading to a profession and/or a husband (see Rubin and Zavalloni 1969). During the same time period, a survey of pre-marital sex in Jamaica revealed different attitudes to the subject among working-class and middle-class girls. Three-quarters (75.5 per cent) of girls in a working-class sample saw nothing wrong with pre-marital sex while in another sample of middle-class adolescents (both sexes) more than half (55 per cent) were against it, with girls contributing a higher proportion than boys against (cited in Phillips 1973). This suggests that girls of different classes adhere to different standards of behaviour, or at least did up to the time of these surveys. Yet the working-class mother's vigorous protection of her daughter from the age of puberty and the continual verbal and sometimes physical chastisement of those who transgress the admonition to keep away from men suggest that she would want her daughter to uphold middle-class standards.

However, this would be a very simplistic explanation of a very complex and seemingly contradictory process. A more likely explanation advanced by Braithwaite (1953), Brodber (1968) and others suggests an economic motive — that mothers are really projecting their own unrealized ambitions on to their daughters and would like them to become viable before entering the childbearing stage. From her study of this process at work in Kingston yards, Brodber (1975, pp. 58–9) concluded that:

> Yard dwellers, like the rest of the . . . community, desire that they and their daughters defer sex and child-bearing until it is socially acceptable, until they have gained certification and can enter the labour market at a point other than that of casual labour. But they themselves are convinced that sexual activity is natural and they know that in the circumstances of their lives, sex is one of their most marketable attributes and one which would facilitate their social mobility. They know that unless skillfully used, it can invalidate their goals so they continue to guard their girls against involvement in sexual activity by their militant stand against social intercourse with the opposite sex. The energy which they put into it and the failure which they see as endemic to this plan must create great frustrations.

But the mother's motivations are never explained to the daughter and the potent combination of sexual ignorance and early sexual experimentation leads for most to early pregnancy. In any event, the working-class girl usually does not have to move outside her home to find models of behaviour which are contrary to the ideals which are being projected. Her mother — usually the unwed mother of several children and who defied her own mother and had her first baby as an adolescent — represents the most concrete role model. Grandmothers, older sisters, cousins, aunts, neighbours — virtually all the female sex around her — are, or have been, engaged in the same process. For these reasons, the behaviour of the West Indian girl who enters into early childbearing is seen by some as part of a cycle repeating itself (for example, Blake 1961). There is also considerable peer-group and cultural pressure on the young girl to 'prove herself' a woman by having a baby.

On the whole there is for the Caribbean adolescent very little preparation at home or at school for this emotionally turbulent period. In rural areas especially, there are few outlets for social and creative activity. The level of teenage frustration is high and, as Kerr noted (1952, p. 81), in these circumstances 'the only activity is sexual activity'. There are few approved avenues for healthy mingling between the sexes and meetings are clandestine. The girl especially has so far spent her entire life under the strict control of others; and has not learned any healthy way of curbing her natural sexual impulses (Blake 1961). The transition to adulthood is abrupt and — for the girl — usually occurs when she finds herself pregnant.

One final factor is that many girls grow up in households with no adult male present; we do not know how this affects a girl's socialization but, from studies in other countries, we know that it might make her awkward in her dealings with the opposite sex when she enters adolescence (Romer 1981). Where there is no adult male present in the household, there is also no adult male protection and girls from these households might be more vulnerable to physical advances and suggestions from males of all age-groups, though the incidence of incest and sexual abuse by older males suggests that she might also be at risk in her own household.

Generally, in matters relating to the opposite sex, girls might find their social-ization ambivalent and contradictory. One 41-year-old Antiguan woman, who described herself as 'well brought up', who had her first child in the socially approved manner — in wedlock — and then, when the marriage failed, several children by different fathers, was sufficiently steeped in her early conditioning that, many years and many experiences later, she was unable to see the dysfunctionality of how she had been socialized to think and how she had performed:

R. Things I used to hear about them, misfortune happening to them, some would get pregnant and you hear a group of girls in school talking and they laughing and chatting and they'll be saying, 'oh, you know who's pregnant?' and 'you don't hear the latest?' and I never used to like it, you know.

I. Do you think because your mother had you at fourteen that maybe this . . . ?

R. That has a lot to do with it because I always keep in my mind that I would never like what happen to my mother to happen to me. I always felt after a boy gets you into trouble and he knows . . . if a girl gets pregnant and she's not married, that boy lowers her prestige, you know, he lowers the girl, she drops down.

I. Why is that?

R. Because it's not proper for a girl to have a child and she's not married. It's no disgrace you know because we all make mistakes, we're not perfect. There is a lot of temptation and some girls are very nice girls, well brought up, but they're just tempted you know, and they yield and you fall. You land up with a child.

But 'misfortune' and 'disgrace' happen only to the female. While adolescent girls are being watched and confined, threatened and warned against having relations with the opposite sex, their brothers are usually given no instruction regarding their relations with girls or the possibilities of and responsibilities of paternity. Indeed, in the upbringing of the sexes as in other areas of Caribbean life, a strong double standard exists: 'The male's pursuit of sexual favours during "dating/courtship" is acceptable evidence of his masculinity — no one seems to worry too much if the boy "comes home late". On the other hand, the female's acquiescence to such favours usually leads to "she spoil herself" or "she give way herself"' (Grant 1984).

Or, as one young West Indian woman expressed this phenomenon: 'Boys have very little experience of fatherhood to learn from, since their fathers are largely absent or ineffective, but in addition their mothers openly condone the same kind of irresponsibility in their sons which accounts for their fatherlessness' (Hodge 1977, p. 43).

Not surprisingly, a great many first pregnancies, especially, arise from 'accidents' — not the result of promiscuity but of a first and single event. A 22-year-old tells of her first pregnancy:

> **I.** Your pregnancy, did it happen because you wanted it to happen, or it just happened to you by accident?
>
> **R.** By accident. I tell you, I was too young to get a child at that time, I feel I was too young for it. There was nothing I could do because I was a bit scared so I aint tell nobody nothing; I just keep it to myself.
>
> **I.** So when did you tell somebody?
>
> **R.** Well afterwards they see me start acting funny and strange and looking kind of fatty. I then decide to tell.

Roberts and Sinclair's study in Jamaica (1978) confirms that in that country many first births result from a single sexual contact at an early age for the woman. This has led them to formulate a subtype of visiting union called a 'casual relationship'; it is designated a union only because pregnancy has resulted; often the man is not seen again.

Of course, pregnancy as causality can settle into a pattern and can result in several children, as was the case with a young woman who at the time of the interview was working the 'clubs' in Barbados on and off as a prostitute:

> **I.** You said that the first pregnancy was a mishap, it wasn't a real steady relationship with anybody?
>
> **R.** It was just a guy that I meet at football so me and he talk for a couple of weeks and then . . . It wasn't no love or anything like that.
>
> **I.** And then the miscarriage. Who were you pregnant for at that time?
>
> **R.** A hotel fellow.
>
> **I.** So this was a steady relationship?
>
> **R.** Well no. He was just a mad guy I was attracted to.
>
> **I.** How long were you going together?
>
> **R.** Me and he use to talk and thing, so I just get pregnant and you know he got problems. I got problems. He got problems because he is married.
>
> **I.** Okay, your son that you had at twenty, who is this for?
>
> **R.** A fisherman fellow.
>
> **I.** So this was a relationship?
>
> **R.** Yes, I knew him from '75.
>
> **I.** And your daughter that you had at twenty-two, your daughter that you had recently, this relationship was a steady relationship?
>
> **R.** Yes.
>
> **I.** It was visiting too. He didn't live with you?
>
> **R.** He sleep.
>
> **I.** He slept there?
>
> **R.** Yes.
>
> **I.** He ate at your house as well?
>
> **R.** Yes.
>
> **I.** But he didn't really live there as such, have all his clothes there?
>
> **R.** No, only some.
>
> **I.** Did he sleep there most nights?
>
> **R.** All night till a year and then the two of us disagree.

As we have seen, there is very little in the upbringing of the West Indian girl to prepare her for normal relationships with men. One Antiguan mother's complex feelings about her teenage daughter's sexual activities are revealed in the extract below. A former domestic worker turned cultivator, she was 38 at the time of the interview. She herself has always lived with her own mother and is in a visiting relationship with the father of six of her seven children:

I. How did you feel about your daughter getting pregnant?
R. Well me nearly go crazy. I curse plenty. When she get pregnant I really didn't know. But my mother was so strict she find out because she had more dealing with her because she look after her. I didn't know. I were blind.

Her own mother took the girl to a doctor and the pregnancy was confirmed. On hearing the news, our informant started to cry:

My mother tell me tek it easy. Me didn't know she friendly with the boy cause she nah talk much so I don't know something hideable. And after I get to find out, me tell she, 'Well let me tell you something: Me nah walk behind no man fa tell them you with child. So you just go and find that pickney pappa.'

Her mother took the girl to the baby's father the same night and asked him, 'you know me daughter so?' He acknowledged that he was the father. He stayed with the girl and baby for a while until, according to our informant, he turned into a Rastafarian, which she disapproved of. She pressured the daughter to break off the relationship and the daughter eventually did so. She was asked if she would want her daughter to get pregnant again: 'If she have a boyfriend I wouldn't mind if she get pregnant, so long as he's a good person, like, he can sustain the child.' She was asked what she was telling her other daughters about life.

R. I telling them them must live up and try to get their schooling, get education first. A child is not a job. Easy to get fall [i.e. pregnant]. Have a boyfriend they get fall and they can't sustain the children to give them education. All that me a tell them.
I. Are you telling them anything about family planning?
R. No, never.
I. Why not?
R. Me nah really want for open their experience but me sister, the one that nursing, always told them, and told me mother, that when the girl come sixteen must let her use family planning. But me never, me never tell her that, me feel kind of funny, delicate you know, to tell them about that. So I really don't tell them but me mother will tell them.

Despite the strictness which they observe in rearing daughters, parents are anxious that the girl should by a certain age 'prove herself' by commencing childbearing. For most black working-class families, marriage is not a prerequisite to childbearing but a steady, acceptable 'baby father' is hoped for. If a girl is allowed to go out with a male, her parents are not usually surprised when pregnancy results. A Vincentian woman in her mid-thirties recalled that her mother did not react in her case because, as she explains, 'The fella went home and speak to them so they expect anything. Because if somebody come home and you allow that child to go out with that person, you expect anything to happen.' In other words, if they allow the girl to go out with a boy they are tacitly acknowledging that she is a woman and ripe for womanly experience. However, if she continues to live in the parental home after childbearing, parents expect to continue to exert strict control over her movements, even to punishing her physically. Our informant's second pregnancy, for a different man, made her father so angry 'he put some licks on me. Up to the time I have children I use to get licks, I wasn't on my own.' Another stated of her mother's reaction to her first 'baby father':

> She didn't like him at all. She used to beat me for him. And I still go and get this child and when I get it she threw me outside, so I meet hardship with it. I had to mind it, me alone. I go and live with one of my family and when it time for me to get the child, my mother take me back home and I had my child by her home. And after the child start to get big I start to give she rudeness and she throw me back outside.

In another case, the woman's parents accepted her first child but three years later, when she got pregnant again, her father beat her so badly that she had to be hospitalized.

In her constant exposure to conflict between what she is being told and what she perceives around her, the young girl is also being subjected to strong pressures in a society which presents her with few alternatives to childbearing. We noted the pressures on a girl to 'prove herself' a woman by having a baby as soon as possible, lest she be given the greatest social condemnation, that of being a 'mule' or childless woman. Peer-group pressure is also strong from girls who have already 'proved' themselves, and from boys — or older men — who are busily exploiting her ignorance and superstition. Men and society at large exploit the girl's ignorance of the process of conception itself ('If you don't have sex you won't keep well'; 'Sex settles your menses') as well as the means of preventing conception ('Have sex standing'; 'Have sex in the sea'; 'Urinate immediately after sex').

Reactions to first pregnancy

The sexual revolution has ushered in changes to many parts of the Caribbean and parental influence is loosening, especially in urban areas. But, in many cases, the old behaviours still apply. Researchers have noted that, when the unmarried girl becomes pregnant with her first child, it becomes a traumatic event, and the reaction of her mother — and father — is almost ritualized. Announcement of, or discovery of, the pregnancy is a crisis event in the family. There is a great deal of quarrelling and often violence towards the girl. She is frequently turned out of the house, and seeks shelter with kin, neighbours or family friends. Usually they set out to effect a *rapprochement* between the girl and her parents so that, before the birth of her child, she is taken back into the family home and the baby is literally born into its grandmother's hands.

One scholar (Blake 1961) does take issue with the notion that the mother's behaviour is merely ritualized, arguing that her anger is genuine since the girl's behaviour represents flagrant disobedience. By beating the daughter and turning her out, the mother establishes that she is a good (strict) mother and that the disgrace is none of her doing. When the girl has suffered and is suitably contrite, she will be forgiven.

The experiences of many women who were asked to recount their parents' reaction to their first pregnancy confirm that a standard response to this event is still widespread. The Antiguan cultivator referred to above was asked about her first pregnancy:

I. How did your mother feel about it?
R. Well, she feel funny. She went on bad with the first but after she take it good for she love grandchildren plenty.

I. So the first baby she got upset, the second baby she didn't say anything and the third she said nothing?

R. Nothing.

I. So by now she's looking at you being a big woman?

R. Yes.

This woman was asked to relate the circumstances of her first pregnancy:

I. Did you tell her that you were pregnant?

R. She just saw it for herself.

I. How did she find out?

R. When time come to see my period, she just check on that.

I. She used to check your period?

R. Yes.

I. Your mother's good. How did she do that?

R. She know the time and she just look around and she don't see anything and she just call me up. I would just 'chups' and go about my business. Only to find out really you sleeping, sleeping, sleeping. And she say, 'hmm hmm a what mek yu a sleep so?'

I. So then she fussed?

R. Yes.

I. Did she fuss all during the pregnancy?

R. Yes. She was very strict.

The dynamics of a situation involving girl, boy, parents and relatives is more fully explored by a 35-year-old businesswoman who is in a visiting union and now has several children. She was a 17-year-old schoolgirl at the time she recalls:

R. I remember when he [her father] found out, when my mother told him. It was about midnight. He woke me up and told me I had to leave home. I can't forget that. I cried but that didn't help. Just about everybody in the house was awake by that time because he spoke so loud the neighbours could hear. So my mother told my brother she would take me to her family, so we went down that night.

I. And what did your mother say?

R. She was so annoyed with the way he went about it. She isn't saying that he shouldn't feel hurt. But to wake me up and tell me those things!

She was asked how she had told her mother of her pregnancy. She replied that her mother had observed certain signs — her behaviour at dinner, the tightness of her dress — and merely needed to have her deduction confirmed: 'She asked me who is the father and I told her. She sent my brother to call him so he came and he talk. That was quite alright you know, but she kind of scold us, like a good mother.' The boy was a schoolmate, one year older than she was:

What really bothered my mother, she said that I was living with my father and if he was paying more attention to us he would have found out. She wouldn't have to come and find things out. [Her mother was working on another island and had come home on vacation.] The noise my father made the night, the boy stayed at his house and heard. So his sister came up to find out what was going on. We told her what was happening and she too was disappointed seeing we had to take exams. So she said her little piece too, but she talked about marriage. I said no. I mean, we were kids, we didn't know anything. So my mother asked me what I think. I said, 'no way, mum, I'm not going to play no dolly house'. Because I didn't know nothing about thinking of a family and whatnot. I didn't think it was the best thing to do and I am very satisfied that I made that decision, up to now.

The unwed girl also has to face community reaction. A 23-year-old white-collar worker explained the reactions to her teenage pregnancy:

I. In terms of your middle-class status was it expected that you would get pregnant?

R. No.

I. How did the community react?

R. Everybody was like my father, they said: 'What!' You know that kind of reaction. Actually I was afraid to face a lot of the family friends because you know that is what they are going to say and you feel funny when they say it like that. But then it pass off, you know, as they grow accustomed to it.

I. And what about your own personal friends your age?

R. Most of my friends my age had already had their baby.

I. You were late . . . ?

R. Late is something. I was nearly the last. The people who were having babies with me were my juniors in school.

Response to children

Whether their pregnancy is 'accidental' or not, most young mothers seem to feel positive about the birth of their child. As one recalled, 'I felt good. I love children and I felt real nice to know that I can have one of my own.'

When a girl becomes pregnant it is important that the father be known, and be named, otherwise the situation is regarded as disgraceful. If the father acknowledges and supports the child, so much the better. When support is not forthcoming, then the girl's parents resign themselves to taking the child:

I. So you were a young girl having a child and you were working at the estate. How did your mother feel about you having a child?

R. She didn't feel so well but afterwards she took me. We mothers always be fretful when these things come, especially if nobody comes and say it is mine. You know how hard it is. So she was angry but afterwards she came back good and she treated me well.

I. So the father didn't come and say it was his?

R. No, he didn't come.

I. Why not?

R. I don't know.

I. How did you feel about him not coming to your mother?

R. Well I didn't feel so well but it happened already.

The greatest disgrace is if the father cannot be named:

R. It's terrible, one of the worst things in life, it's a shame you having sexual intercourse with so many men and next thing you get pregnant and you don't even know who the father.

I. Do you know girls like that?

R. Yes, we have one like that. She has two children and she don't know who the father for both of them.

I. So she didn't call any names?

R. Yes, she called names. Names! A child can't have names. Somebody got to be father.

I. So what happens when she calls names and no one comes forth?

R. Well her parents have to take the child.

The young mother is more than likely to have been born into a large family herself and would have had experience in the caring of her siblings, which she can apply to the caring of her own child:

I. Who helped you with the care of your own child? Who told you what to do?

R. Nobody really because being around my mother when she had hers, I was more or less pre-educated to having children. I didn't know how to have them but to make their meals and how to bathe them and things like that.

Another woman who had been working as a domestic was asked how she had learned to care for her child.

Working with other people, I see how they look after their babies and they have to go out and you have to take care of it. My bigger sisters have them children, I see how them wash their skin, comb their hair, breast feed their child and they give them bottle. I learn from my bigger sisters too, and my mother.

Some women seem to be born to mothering. One woman told how she acquired the knowledge to care for her own baby: 'I was always taking care of babies all around the neighbourhood because where I grew up we always had younger children and growing up as a teenager we would help and have them spending the day with us and so on. We always had babies taking care of.'

But probably the single most important fact about childbearing and child-rearing in the Caribbean is that the girl is more than likely to have a wide network of family, friends or neighbours to assist her:

I. You went from marrying right into mothering. Where was he born, in the hospital or at your house?

R. At home.

I. With a midwife?

R. Yes.

I. Now you're 17 and you have a baby. What was your reaction to this whole business?

R. To me it was a burden because at 17 you're supposed to be enjoying life and here I am all saddled with a child and a husband to see about. It wasn't easy, but his aunt who was living near was very helpful. She used to assist me with washing and things like that and helped me with the child because I didn't know anything about taking care of a baby.

Kinship support

Even if a female relative is not present for the birth, for the first few years of the child's life at least, the young mother can often count on a wide kinship network for moral and more tangible forms of support. Kinship networks have long been recognized as an important means of enabling Caribbean females especially to cope with their family responsibilities. However, the whole process of networking has been little studied. Preliminary research done by Dorian Powell for the WICP does confirm the importance of family networks. The dynamics of networking is revealed, for instance, in the case of Jennifer, a single mother who was one of Powell's informants:

> Jennifer gave birth to twins. One she says looks like the father, the other does not. So he takes the former and says the latter is not his child. Jennifer has six children in all and has no job. How does she cope? She gives one child to her mother, one to a paternal [grand]mother, the father takes one and she manages with three. A cousin assists with food, and Jennifer . . . struggles on. Her mother is her main tower of strength. Her brothers and sisters would assist, but as she is the eldest child for her mother, she hesitates to accept help from her younger siblings.
>
> (Powell *et al.* WICP 1982, p. 36)

Powell's exploratory research has revealed that 'kin relations bear a significant portion of the child-care burden of urban women . . . Most often fathers are absent from the network of individuals who assist with child care' (Powell *et al.* WICP 1982). Assistance not only is provided at childbirth but continues during illness, financial distress, school holidays and with baby-sitting. Powell's informants referred to some of their sources of assistance:

> 'My brother stands a lot of expenses for my daughter who is with him in the United States going to school.'
>
> 'Mother looked after the children while I worked so I used to take them over to her during my work hours.'
>
> 'My sister cared for the baby while I worked.'
>
> 'When my children were near to be born my grandmother came and stayed with us. She usually stayed for about six months after each child was born.'
>
> 'My mother comes up from the country to help out. She brings meat, fruit, vegetables and normally I have to force her to take the money for the meat.'
>
> 'Sister abroad sends money and parcels with rice, sugar, soap, flour and my brother sometimes drops by with vegetables and provisions.'
>
> (Powell *et al.* WICP 1982, p. 37)

We should nevertheless not overestimate the strength of such network assistance available to women, for certain trends in the region might be working to undermine these very traditional means of enabling them to cope with their child-caring responsibilities. One of these is increased urbanization, combined with the tendency to commence childbearing at earlier ages. Not only first but sometimes second and third children are being born to teenage mothers. These trends have great implications for the future of the mother and child. The physical and mental risks to teenage mothers and their children have been well documented. So have the social and economic consequences which usually follow. The chances are that the teenage mother will have to terminate her schooling. Unschooled and unskilled, she will then join the ranks of the unemployed, which are already highest for her sex and age-group.

The situation in which her child will be raised will probably be less advantageous than was her own situation as a child. Part of the reason is that increasingly younger mothers are leading to increasingly younger grandmothers. Some grandmothers in urban Jamaica, for instance, are now under 30 (Grant 1984), still in their reproductive years and also in their prime years of activity in the labour market, and unprepared or unable to assume the traditional grandmother role. The grandmother in urban areas especially is less able than before to lend a hand in caring for her daughter's children. The young mother herself is likely to stay at home to 'mind baby', which means that her own access to jobs and to skill training and her exposure to the world of work are severely curtailed. Most vulnerable of all is the young woman in the city who for one reason or another finds herself totally isolated from kin and friendship networks.

Increasing abandonment of their children might be one index of the pressures on these young mothers. A study of abandonment in Jamaica has confirmed that, where new babies are involved, in some cases there is no social unit awaiting the child's arrival, and abandonment is usually by single mothers who are 'socially isolated', that is, they have no identifiable kin or friendship networks, no contacts and no fixed address. In some cases, no one knew of their pregnancy. Many of these women were themselves abandoned by their 'baby fathers' as soon as they heard of the expected child. Of 208 women in one ward at Jamaica's maternity hospital, Victoria Jubilee, only 55.2 per cent were found to have some form of support from the baby's father during pregnancy — roughly the same percentage as the women who were living in a union. This means that 45 per cent of the women expecting babies would probably have to fend for themselves — with no male support — after the child's arrival. In 20 per cent of cases, the mothers indicated that they were disappointed with the father's reaction to the announcement of pregnancy; in many instances he was not heard from again (Brodber 1974).

As Lucille Mathurin Mair has observed of this type of mother, 'single-handed, she is unable to control the forces that circumscribe her life and that of her children. She turns more and more to new paterfamilias, the state, admitting her powerlessness to deal with the one meaningful role the society leaves to her, the role she traditionally values most of all, that of mother' (Mathurin 1977, p. 6).

And yet, while there is undoubtedly a substantial number of mothers who are unable to cope with their responsibilities — and this number might be increasing — Caribbean women who end up with sole responsibility do find the means of coping with the children they so eagerly — and sometimes thoughtlessly — have. In chapter 7, we will look more closely at some of the strategies the region's women have devised to ensure the survival of themselves and their children.

5 Family & Household

Having a baby is only the first step in a woman's transition from girlhood to full-fledged womanhood and the assumption of familial responsibilities. The chances are that first children will be born to a young single mother who is still living at home. But sooner or later she will move on to the next stage: some form of union with a man and the setting up of her own household. While for some the first union might result in permanence and conformity to a nuclear family ideal, most women will pass through several types of unions before settling down in one. There is a 50–50 chance that by the age of 40 she might find herself single once again and, as the head of a large household, forced to rely on her own resources to ensure its survival. Early childbearing would have truncated her own schooling and left her ill-equipped to compete with males on the job market. In a majority of cases, she will have to settle for the only jobs open to her — domestic labour or other forms of service occupations — or else develop other, unorthodox strategies for survival. The power she wields in the domestic sphere will depend on whether or not there is a resident male who contributes to household upkeep. If there is, then she will yield family headship and decision-making on critical issues to him, or at least play down her own role outside child-rearing, which is universally acknowledged as her responsibility. This scenario describes the life cycle of large numbers of Caribbean women.

In this chapter, we are concerned with looking at the various types of domestic unions, women's status in the household, and the special characteristics of female-headed households and female household heads.

Family forms

The pattern of family formation in the Caribbean has attracted considerable attention from scholars over the last 50 years or so and moralists for some centuries. For the pattern is characterized by a high level of non-legal unions, the prevalence of 'household' over 'family' units and a high level of households headed by women. Early observers condemned the 'promiscuity' of West Indians who cohabited without benefit of marriage, with resultant 'illegitimacy'. A great deal of the efforts of early missionaries — and later governors' wives — was directed at increasing the marriage rate and decreasing the illegitimacy rate, which is around 70–75 per cent in Jamaica and St Vincent, with a range in other islands of between 40 and 60 per cent (Roberts 1975, chapter 4).

Since only a small proportion of women conform to the ideal of marriage before family, the maternal role is often fulfilled before the conjugal, indeed is regarded as more important. One WICP informant explained, 'You can have the motherhood without the marriage.' As we saw in chapter 4, a woman doesn't have to get married but she must have children. Furthermore, in many subgroups within the culture, a woman has to prove herself by having children before a man will consider her a suitable candidate for marriage. For her part, a woman might live with a man for many years and bear children for him, but will only consider marriage if certain conditions, mainly economic, can be fulfilled.

Throughout the Caribbean, the marriage rate, in comparison with that in Europe, is low. There is, however, great variation between territories and among classes and ethnic groups. The middle and upper classes tend to conform to traditional European views of the family and family formation and thus to early marriage before childbearing, as do Chinese and East Indians of all classes. Lower-income groups tend to other forms of union, which may or may not culminate in marriage. Thus marriage rates are comparatively much higher for Trinidad and Guyana, the countries with significant East Indian populations, and Belize, with a significant Amerindian population. At the other end of the scale, the marriage rate in Jamaica, which is largely Afro-Caribbean, has remained steady at no more than 3-4 per thousand and has exceeded 5 per thousand only on rare occasions over the past 150 years (see Roberts 1975, chapter 4).

The low tendency to marry in all countries of the region is one that seems to have been least affected by historical and sociological change, as demographer George Roberts reminds us. This lack of fundamental change in familial forms since emancipation contrasts sharply with the other changes — economic, political, social — which have transformed these societies over the 150 years since then (Roberts and Sinclair 1978, p. 6).

Despite the statistics, marriage is regarded as a desirable role for women, as we shall see below. But, in Caribbean culture, the age at which a woman gets married, and if she gets married at all, will vary according to class, race and ethnicity, among other factors. The alternatives to marriage are other forms of union, which are recognized by the culture, if not yet by law. The regional population census recognizes that a woman might also live with a man in a common-law union, i.e. share a common residence, or she might engage with a steady partner in a visiting union, i.e. one in which they have a steady sexual relationship which has resulted in a child or children but are not living together.

The divisions of visiting, common-law and married unions represent characteristics identified by many scholars but first described by R.T. Smith in the 1950s and still found to be persistent. It has been found that, basically, Caribbean women progress from one type of union to another in a sequence of visiting, common-law, marriage. Thus women of different ages will generally be found in different stages of union. Of course, the concept of a progression from one union to another is a typology developed for convenience. Throughout her lifetime, an individual might move back and forth from one type of union to another or might stay within one form of union all her life.

The WICP set out to confirm whether this type of union formation (first described 50 years ago) still persists, and to extract from women themselves their views of these unions. The researchers found that, in the eastern Caribbean countries examined, there has been little change in this area of family life since the earliest descriptions. Censual and other information confirms that this might be true for other parts of the region. Generally, women see marriage as the ideal to which they aspire but there is no rush to get there. A study of women in Jamaica found that over half of the women interviewed had attained marriage by the end of the childbearing period (Roberts and Sinclair 1978, p. 16).

Types of union

Visiting A visiting union is regarded as the first stage in mating, the 'getting to know you' stage, a training-ground for more permanent relationships (see Powell WICP 1986). About one-quarter of Caribbean women are found in visiting unions, most of them younger women. Women tend to move out of visiting into a more stable form of union in their mid-thirties so that in only 10 per cent of cases in the WICP study were women in these unions found to be aged 45 and older.

In a visiting relationship, a man and woman meet for sexual and social intercourse but do not live together. Meetings may take place at his place, her place or her family home, if parents are agreeable. The man's obligations are not clearly defined but it is expected that he will contribute financially to the upkeep of the home and of the children of the relationship.

Powell's analysis of the WICP survey showed that over two-thirds of women in visiting relationships expressed themselves as comfortable with their relationships. More than 80 per cent felt that their unions presented no barriers to personal desires. A sizeable group had no specific expectations regarding these relationships, though they appear to be viewed as transitory. The majority hoped that their unions would develop into a permanent one: in answer to a question as to what kind of union, if any, they would like to be in five years' time, they answered overwhelmingly: married (87 per cent in Antigua, 84 per cent in St Vincent and 77 per cent in Barbados) (Powell WICP 1986).

A great deal of attention has been focused on women in this visiting group as they are raising families without resident partners. Most are found in multi-family households but some are household heads, managing single-handed. Statistics for stress-related illness, behavioural disorders in children, cases before juvenile court, female crime and resort to court for assistance with children are found to be highest for this latter group of women — those raising children on their own. Child-shifting is also highest for this group, as is abandonment of children (Brodber 1974; Barbados 1978, p. 680; Roberts and Sinclair 1978; Jackson WICP 1982; Bell 1985).

Society provides legal protection for women and children in the marriage relationship and most recent family legislation is also tending to include common-law spouses and children. The vulnerability of mothers in visiting unions is underscored by the fact that they are offered no protection by the law. While visiting relationships have in the past been class-based, a recent phenomenon is that of middle-class and professional women opting to have children outside marriage and for visiting relationships.

Visiting is a status preferred by women over common-law unions, mainly for the freedom it ostensibly affords, especially in household management (Powell WICP 1986). Roberts and Sinclair (1978, p. 249) concluded of women in visiting unions that 'economically they do not consider their position unduly difficult; such financial assistance as they receive from their partners has not to be spent in partial support of the latter, as would be the case in residential unions. Such funds serve solely for their own support and for the upkeep of their children.'

Common-law Very young women do not usually enter common-law unions. Such unions are more likely in the age group 25–44, among those who have borne several children in one or more visiting unions and have consolidated their relationship with one man. In a common-law union the couple live together. It is regarded as a stage more permanent than visiting but lacking the legal sanction of marriage — hence the old phrases 'married but not parsoned' or 'married but not churched' to describe such couples.

As in legally sanctioned marriage, the woman is expected to play the housewife role — cleaning, washing, preparing food and taking care of the house — while the man is expected to support the household. Common-law unions are regarded by women as lowest on their scale of values (Powell WICP 1986). Women in such unions have tended to be of the lowest educational and socio-economic status (although, as in visiting, more higher-income women are now opting for this way of life). Although a common-law union is regarded as binding, it is less prestigious than marriage and harder to get out of than visiting. In a visiting relationship, a man might feel that he has no right to chastise a woman since his hold over her is so tenuous, while in a common-law union he can and does play the husband role. His discipline can include ill-treatment and curtailment of the woman's activities.

Common-law living has traditionally been disapproved of on both moral and religious grounds. Many religions regard 'living together out of wedlock' as 'living in sin' and might even ban church members who engage in such unions. Mothers too disapprove on moral grounds of their daughters participating in common-law unions.

Up to recently, common-law unions had no legal status. Recent legislation in a number of countries now gives some recognition to children of common-law unions and, in one country, of partners. Up to 1981, legislation in five countries (Dominica, Grenada, Guyana, Jamaica, St Vincent) provided for legal maintenance of children born in or out of wedlock, once paternity is proved. But no provision is made for the partner. Thus 'the childless woman living in a common-law union has no claim for financial assistance should she need it' and no recourse to the courts even when a relationship of long standing breaks up (Forde WICP 1981, p. 59). Barbados was the only country to give common-law relationships some legal recognition. The 1981 reform legislation includes in the definition of 'spouse' not only legally married couples but those parties in a common-law union who have been living together for five years at least. The parties to such unions have 'a legal responsibility to maintain each other if the need arises and the relevant party is reasonably able to provide such maintenance'. Parents in such unions are also liable, consistent with their means, to maintain the unmarried minor children of that union (Forde WICP 1981, p. 59).

In other countries, the parties in a common-law union are bound by no legal obligations where property rights are concerned and the woman can end up the disadvantaged party in the event that property acquired by the pooling of effort has to be shared out on the breakup of the relationship. This can come about because the man is the one who generally handles business transactions and whose name appears on legal documents. But, as we shall see below, a legal wife might herself end up in an even more disadvantaged position than a common-law spouse.

Except in Barbados, a common-law partner also cannot benefit if the other dies leaving no will. If a will is made, the surviving partner can only benefit if he or she is named as a beneficiary. The new Barbados law gives common-law partners who have been living together for five years immediately prior to death the same rights as legal partners. Under the old legislation, which obtains in most countries, out-of-wedlock children will benefit only if actually named in a will (Forde WICP 1981, p. 83). However, Status of Children legislation in Barbados, Belize, Jamaica and St Vincent gives equality under the law to all children so that children of either parent can benefit equally with children of a marriage (Forde WICP 1981, p. 85) as long as paternity has been established.

It is too early to tell whether the new legislative trends will upgrade the status of common-law unions. Victoria Durant-Gonzalez has identified some negative perceptions of women to the new legislation. One is that married women see it as a threat to their status and that of their children since formerly they were the only ones who had legal claims to the man's property. Where previously, she argues, married women would be tolerant of 'outside' children and lackadaisical about establishing their own legal standing, because they felt they were protected by the title 'Mrs' ('she has the man but I have the ring' is a common attitude towards a husband's extramarital affairs), alert married women are now beginning to examine their legal status within the family. On the other hand, unmarried mothers express concern that Status of Children legislation has removed from the mother the privilege she once exclusively had of automatic legal custody of her children; acknowledged fathers now having parental rights as well (Durant-Gonzalez WICP 1982).

While common-law unions do not represent the ideal for everyone, such unions are frequent (ranging from 11 per cent to just under 20 per cent in the survey countries). Women in common-law relationships cited both quality-of-life benefits and emotional support as their expectations from the union (Powell WICP 1986) but a very large number in the survey countries (as high as 83 per cent in Barbados) said their unions represented blockages to personal desires.

Married Quite often common-law residence serves as a final step in the consolidation of a relationship that leads to marriage. The fact that marriage comes to older women is borne out by the fact that while one-third of the married women in the sample were in the age group 25–34, most fell in the 35–54 age range, in the WICP survey. Approximately four out of every ten married women in Barbados and St Vincent and three out of ten in Antigua had lived with their partners in a common-law union prior to legal marriage. Some of these pre-marital friendships were of long duration, most were over one year and over one-third had lasted five years and more.

These women had positive responses to their marriages. For instance, 87 per cent of Antiguans said their marriage had worked out for them the way they would have wanted it. When asked if marriage had blocked their pursuit of desired activities, social activities were most frequently cited as thwarted, followed by work/career desires and education.

Single According to the regional census definition and common usage, 'single' does not refer to conjugal but to union status; thus a single woman is one who is not in any form of union. This ranged between 20.7 and 23.3 per cent in the sample territories. In the WICP survey, such women were generally found to be an older group who have come out of partnerships. For two of the WICP sample countries — Antigua and St Vincent — more than half of the women aged 56–64 are single. The WICP sample of single women showed that most were in common-law unions immediately prior to their current single state. In the Caribbean, a very small number of women are in the category 'never been in a union', in the sample territories ranging between 2 and 3.2 per cent.

The WICP survey included questions designed to gain insight into how women perceive their involvements, and their answers revealed a general acceptance of partnerships in whatever form of union they happen to be (Powell WICP 1986 — but see our discussion in chapter 9). In a sense this explodes the universal myth that women see marriage *per se* as the sole road to happiness and fulfilment. As Edith Clarke (1957) points out, marriage and concubinage are not perceived as alternative forms, either one might be perceived as 'right' at a particular stage in a woman's life. Each stage is part of a course in the development of her relationships with and expectations of men. Women have different expectations as they enter each stage. Nevertheless, it is clear from the WICP and other evidence that Caribbean women do in the long run wish to marry and regard their other relationships as transitory.

Attitudes to marriage

Certain views of marriage are persistent, men in general taking the cynical view that, for instance, woman's sole ambition is marriage not for love but for financial security and that women judge potential husbands accordingly (Barrow WICP 1986b). This view also gets support in calypsos, which are regarded as significant commentaries on these societies, especially of male–female relationships. In many calypsos, women are projected as 'scheming' to capture men in marriage, with money and status, not love, the ultimate goal (see chapter 9).

Many women do in fact express themselves as perceiving marriage as a means to status and security, especially for their children. Thus they view marriage as a state to be reached — eventually — when the male is able to satisfy certain economic requirements. Indeed, few cite love as the sole basis or condition for marriage, though a considerable number of women of all classes grow up absorbing idealized images of love and romance from foreign films, imported radio romance serials and TV programmes, and foreign books, including 'Mills and Boon', a genre of romantic fiction, published by an English publishing house of that name, which is avidly consumed throughout the Caribbean.

The 'respectability' associated with marriage is also a desirable factor since it is regarded by all sectors as the 'ideal' status. Not only is marriage associated with class, but also religious pressures and moral considerations confer this respectability. Established religions have always upheld marriage as the ideal, some actively discouraging non-marital relations as 'living in sin'. 'Christian' mothers might be more likely than others to push daughters into an early marriage on the 'better to marry than burn' principle. A fundamentalist pastor's wife was asked:

I. How would you feel if your daughter got married at seventeen?

R. Since she can handle it, if it's a Christian person I'll put the two of them to sit down and I'll talk to them and if they are willing I'll stand up with it. Because if I say no, these are two people and they like each other and they can . . . you know things can happen and before I come to shame and our house come down to shame, I'll let her get married.

Nevertheless, there are more significant imperatives that propel women towards or against marriage.

For women who are actively religious, especially those who describe themselves as 'Christians', i.e. fundamentalists or 'born-again' converts, and this is a considerable number, marriage would be in keeping with the expectations of their religious group, and a determinant of their status within that group. A study of Jamaican women, for example, showed that religion is an important factor in the woman's desire to marry (Roberts and Sinclair 1978). The fact that a potential husband is also a 'Christian' would in these cases far outweigh more material considerations:

I. In your religion, under what conditions can you have a boyfriend?
R. When you're saved you ought to look for somebody who are saved just as you are and then instead of going into sexual attitude of living, you decide, well, the better move to take, which is matrimony. Then you get married as long as this is the Lord's will.

One woman, whose unwed mother had her at the age of 14, was expressive of the 'prestige' value of marriage. The experience of her own mother was an object lesson: 'I always keep in mind that I would never like what happen to my mother to happen to me . . . if a girl gets pregnant and she's not married, that boy lowers her prestige.'

Nevertheless the 'respectability' and 'prestige' that marriage brings are not enough to propel some women into marriage with men perceived as unsuitable. Many women prefer their freedom to an ill-advised marriage for they know that 'marriage have teeth', as the proverb says, or as the children's wedding-game song from Tobago advises:

Married sweet-ee
Bam-bye you go see-umee
Horsewhip and supple-jack
Go talk a' you backee
Tra la la   (Elder 1973)

And as women themselves sing in the folk song 'Mango Tree':

Before me marry and go hug up mango tree
Me wi' live so. Me one.

Two women described how they terminated unsatisfactory engagements. The first, now at the age of 35 a 'respectable' married woman, left school at 14 and started work as a domestic to augment the family income:

He see me and he said that he likes me. So I tell him, I have a mother. Because I never stand up in the streets and talk to nobody. I tell him, I have a mother and I will not stand up. He see that I was the type he couldn't fool around with. So he went home to my parents and they accept him.

However, she didn't like certain aspects of his behaviour: 'If you ain't married to that person and they start like that well later on what will become of you? So I find that his ways wasn't very nice and I call it off.'

The other described how she refused an offer of marriage from the father of her two children, with whom she had a visiting relationship:

When I got the second child, when I was about three or four months, he offered to get married to me. We printed invitations and things like that. His parents went all out to help. But he wanted the whole world of women and one day, I got so mad! I used to put up with a lot of things with he and girls but this day I was at home and I heard this woman's voice calling and I look out and I saw . . . well I knew the girl. And he went and spoke to her and went his way with her and I never saw him again until about two days after. Well, you can imagine how you would feel. So when he came I told him, 'look, let us call it off, right'. I tell him, 'let's just forget everything'. It was hard for me to do it but at that time I was angry and when I am angry I just make up my mind one time. I'm a person if you see I'm finish with something I'm definitely finish. I don't like to go back to things that's been put down so I just forget him.

As Madeline Kerr noted nearly forty years ago, 'Women coming from homes where men are irregular inhabitants or non-existent know that life is possible without a male as an economic help and are proportionately haughty.' One woman she quoted as saying, 'as soon as they put the ring on your finger they start treating you as they like; before that they behave themselves' (Kerr 1952, p. 86), a view held, incidentally, by the male of woman's behaviour on getting married (Barrow WICP 1986b) and one of the reasons cited by males for staying out of marriage in the first place (Rodman 1971).

But economic factors are of paramount importance, especially in lower-income groups. The ability to support a wife financially is a prerequisite for marriage and, while this might be available to middle-and upper-class males, it is not often possible for the lower-class male. A number of studies on the West Indian family over the past 50 years point to this as a significant element in the low level of working-class marriages. As one observed, 'lower-class people, faced by the conditions of poverty . . . seem to be more attuned to the legal advantages and disadvantages to marriage than to moral considerations' (Rodman 1971, p. 69).

Yolanda Moses, in a more recent study of a community on the island of Montserrat, emphasizes the importance of economic factors:

> Marriage is perceived by the majority of working-class women in my study as undesirable because it restricts their alternatives. If they married, they would have to be economically dependent upon and loyal to one man. While this may work for middle-class married women whose husbands have more steady jobs and incomes to help support a family, it would be a 'dead end' for most young working-class women. They would not be able to form 'friending' relationships with other men nor would they be able to expect a great deal of assistance from their kin groups.   (Moses 1981, p. 509)

Assuming that conditions are present for marriage, the event might not take place until certain status symbols associated with the married state are achievable, even among poor people. Hence marriage between a stable common-law couple with children might be delayed for many years until they feel they can 'afford' it. This might take so long that the grandchildren can serve as wedding attendants. Primary among the symbols noted by researchers in former years were (i) the wedding itself, which should be as lavish as possible, (ii) provision of a house, (iii) ability to provide for the wife so she need not work. While an unwed partner could work without loss of prestige either to herself or to the man, a wife who was forced to work, especially at a low-status occupation, entailed loss of face since it declared to the world that her mate was unable to maintain her in a higher status than before.

Though the force of these attitudes might have become somewhat muted under economic pressures, this view of marriage as altering one's economic and social status still persists, as is shown, for example, in this quotation from a WICP informant, a washerwoman from St Vincent who has four children with the man she has lived with for 12 years:

I. Are you married to the Mister?
R. No, me ain't marry.
I. You want to get married?
R. No, me don't want to get married.
I. Why not?

R. He not going to marry me, he don't make up he mind and say marry. Me want somewhere to go and live a happy life, me wouldn't marry and live in this, eh Miss.

I. Why not?

R. Me want somewhere better to make the children them comfortable, man. Remember these child them coming up big and they want their own room for private and everything because the other one going for young woman just now. No, me not going to marry in this state here.

I. So if he would put you in a better place you would get married?

R. Yes. If he would make up his mind to make me happy in a decent little house and everything and he say we go marry, I will marry.

At least some of these earlier criteria for marriage still hold true and are applicable to all status groups. Women interviewed in the WICP cited the provision of a home, care of children and good behaviour on the part of the man as preconditions for marriage. However, in today's economic situation, a home is regarded as something that a couple can jointly work to acquire and both men and women of all classes recognize the need for wives to work to augment the family income. Indeed, the working wife is increasingly being accepted as the norm for all status groups, though low-status jobs will be avoided if possible.

Up to the 1950s and 1960s the ideal in the Caribbean was full-time mothering and housekeeping and women almost automatically gave up their jobs on marriage, if they could afford to do so. This increased the woman's status in the eyes of her neighbours and enhanced the prestige of her husband. The 1960s and beyond have seen a reversal of this trend and married women now form a significant part of the workforce of the region. Some WICP respondents were in fact scornful of the notion of the non-working wife, feeling that women should never under any circumstances be completely dependent on men. As one woman described her sister-in-law's position, 'that's why he is treating her that way because she sits down and depends on his dollar before she get up and go get some work'. This same woman, a teacher in her forties, described the situation in her own household. She was asked, 'How does your husband feel about you working?'

R. It's just something normal.

I. Is that usual in the Caribbean for men to feel that it is just normal that their wives work?

R. Some men really want their wives to work so that they can get the money to go spreeing, right. So they don't care whether the woman work yes or no. But with my husband and my work there is an understanding.

She explained that once her husband stopped her from working since it was felt that she was 'overworking' herself:

He said that he married me to take care of me, not to destroy me before I don't stop working. But he thinks a woman going to work is an advantage to the woman. Not for the money, but she happens to meet people, she happens to learn and to educate and so women keep track of life, right. But when the woman is put aside just at home, and she has to be a maid for the man, he doesn't like this style, you know. I don't like it either.

She was asked about how her friends' husbands felt:

R. I know several of my friends who have to work and take their salary to their husbands. And they don't know whether it is spent on cigarettes, liquor or food because after they work for their salary, the dollar is left out to them by the week to go to the grocery. I think it is very wrong because if you're working and I'm working and both of us suppose to have equal status, it's best for us to put our salaries together, sit down and work it out, our budget. Most of my friends' husbands don't look at it that way.

I. Now what about husbands who just don't want their wives working?

R. I think they are no kind of husband at all.

Two groups of men in Barbados who were interviewed regarding attitudes to women felt that female partners, married or not, should become gainfully employed outside the home in order to contribute to household finances (Barrow WICP 1986b).

And yet, because much of the legislation in the region is still based on patriarchic structures and values, working wives are legally disadvantaged in many areas and in fact might be in more disadvantaged positions than unmarried women. We will therefore look briefly at some of the legal advantages and disadvantages of marriage for women.

Legal status of wives While conjugal rights are to some extent reciprocal, as Norma Monica Forde points out, 'the strong proprietary overtones of the period when the rights were the prerogative of the husband and the duties were imposed on the wife, linger on in many areas' (Forde WICP 1981). Although it is officially accepted that the husband is the head of the household and therefore determines its location, the modern law allows a wife to live apart from her husband for health or work reasons without being regarded as a deserter. A wife has no legal compunction to take her husband's name but not doing so is difficult because custom and administrative procedure have 'given this practice a legal quality that is generally recognised'. Both parties have a duty to consummate the marriage (failure can lead to nullity) and sexual intercourse is regarded as a 'mutual right' — provided that it is reasonably exercised. Four countries (Dominica, St Lucia, St Vincent, and Trinidad and Tobago) have abolished the right to bring action for the restitution of conjugal rights. In other countries, while in theory it can be enforced by the courts, in practice it is unlikely to be. But refusal to comply with a court order may be taken as evidence of desertion (Forde WICP 1981).

The law pertaining to divorce is very complex and varied throughout the region, consisting of both 'old' and 'new' legislation. The main feature of the old law is that it is predicated on a 'fault' concept. The basic features of this concept are that 'One party petitions for termination of the marriage, on the grounds of specified "matrimonial fault". One party holds that the other party is responsible for the marriage breakdown, one party is guilty and the other is innocent. Ancillary dealings such as maintenance and custody of children are related to the blameworthiness or otherwise of the parties' (Forde WICP 1981, p. 38). The 'old' legislation continues to apply in a number of countries. Under the old laws, either party can petition on the grounds of adultery, desertion, cruelty or insanity. In addition, the wife can bring a petition if her husband since the marriage has been guilty of rape, sodomy or bestiality.

Up to the time of writing, Barbados had the most progressive new legislation. The 'fault' concept is de-emphasized in favour of counselling to rebuild the broken marriage. The sole ground for divorce is that the marriage has broken down irretrievably. The old clause that a petition for divorce could not be brought in under three years of marriage has been maintained.

It is in terms of her contractual capacity and joint property ownership that the married woman's rights are most limited; indeed her contractual capacity is more limited than a single woman's (Forde WICP 1981). Until the end of the nine- teenth century, a married woman, along with infants and lunatics, was presumed to be incapable of managing her own affairs (Cumper and Daly 1979) and, unless specially allocated, her property was automatically passed to her husband on marriage. By Married Women's Property Acts passed in the various territories from the late nineteenth century, a married woman became capable of acquiring, holding or disposing by will or otherwise of any real or personal property as if she were a single woman (Cumper and Daly 1979). But, while the law throughout the terri- tories is clear on the issue of separate property owned by married women, it is not so on communal property.

Despite the increasing number of working wives, including many who have worked to maintain husbands while they obtained educational or professional qualifications, the woman's financial contribution to the family is not legally recog- nized. There is no legislation directing a method by which ownership of matrimonial property can be determined on divorce. An evaluation of the monetary contribution of each spouse has to be made, and no certain rule has been evolved. It is usually the husband who handles business transactions and is regarded as principal bread- winner, and property such as the house is usually conveyed to him. Where the wife has been able to make a monetary contribution, the rule is that property rights are determined on the basis of money alone. As the law stands, the wife is therefore disadvantaged when consideration is given to the ownership of a home. The wife who has never been gainfully employed but who has functioned as a housewife is in a worse position. In the absence of a formal agreement, she has no real right to a share in the matrimonial home.

Nor does the law take into consideration the thrift and industry of the wife who manages to save something from the housekeeping money given her by her husband. In the case of death, half goes to the surviving spouse and half to the wife's estate. The general rule is the same regarding other matrimonial property. Unless the wife can show that she has made a direct contribution, she is not entitled to a share of this property. Even where she has made such a contribution she cannot be sure of the extent of the interest which will be awarded her by the court.

Except in Barbados, a wife can be written out of her husband's will, since in most countries a man or woman is free to leave property to anyone. If a husband or wife dies without making a will, the surviving spouse is automatically entitled to all personal property but only one-tenth of the value of the estate. The wife can obtain a life-interest on only half of the rest of the estate, only one-quarter if there are children. By family inheritance provisions in the laws of Belize, and Trinidad and Tobago, surviving dependents can apply to the court for maintenance from an estate if no provision has been made for them. According to new family legislation in Barbados, a wife is entitled to one-half of her husband's estate if there is no child, and one-quarter otherwise (Forde WICP 1981).

The disadvantaged legal position of wives is underscored in several other ways. For instance, in the income tax legislation which still prevails in most countries, the wife's income is automatically added to the husband's and he submits a joint return. Usually income tax is collected from the wife although she is not separately assessed. Where the husband is the sole earner he is permitted to claim a wife allowance; where the wife is earning, the value of her earned income or a stipulated amount may be claimed, the choice depending on which of the two totals is lesser (Forde WICP 1981).

The operation of citizenship laws is another area in which there is discriminatory treatment. While some countries have now equalized the right to transmit citizenship through either or both parents by birth and through registration, in many countries citizenship by descent depends on the male partner where the parties are married. Thus, if a man marries a non-national, she automatically qualifies for registration as a citizen. The reverse does not occur. A foreigner who marries a female citizen does not automatically have any rights in her country and must obtain a work permit if he wishes to live and work there, a situation which has placed severe stresses on some marriages.

Reasons for not marrying It is unlikely that legal disadvantages would deter a woman from marrying since few are conscious of the legal aspects of marriage. Many do advance other reasons for not marrying. Women in the WICP survey placed a great deal of emphasis on their freedom and independence. 'I except that eventually I might consider marriage,' said one informant. 'I want to be married one of these days but I like my freedom,' said another. One woman underscored the need to first gain experience of the world before settling down:

I. What do you think would be a good age to marry?

R. About when you are in your forties because right now me couldn't really get married. A couple years, they would chop off me head.

I. Why is that?

R. Cause me really want to go this place and see how the world look, right. See how other people live. Sometimes because we don't see how other people live, we get ticklish.

Another young woman expressed a great deal of ambivalence on the subject:

R. In five years time, I would like to be married. You don't always young, you know. The things that you could do when you are young you can't do when you are old, right. You will have to change your ways.

I. So how does being married affect this particularly?

R. Well I would say it's just the same when you are single because you can't stop a man from talking to a woman when he's married, you can't stop them from talking when they're single. So it's the same.

I. You mean it's all the same to you, married or single?

R. Yes, it's the same.

I. What would you expect from marriage?

R. Marriage is security and all sorts of things. I don't know.

I. You think you would be more secure if you got married?

R. You can be secure single too.

I. So which is it, married or single?

R. Well if you married or you single, and you do a man anything, you still get a good beating the same way.

Of course, a woman's view of the married state will be coloured by her own experience. A 31-year-old domestic, mother of 10 children, stated vehemently:

R. If I were born again I would never get marry.

I. Never get married, why?

R. That life is like keeping down life, a worrisome life. With all my problems is just . . . if I was to born again I wouldn't marry.

I. You said your problems stemmed from being married. Before you were married he didn't abuse you?

R. He used to drink a little bit. Since he married he do it worse.

I. But why did marriage do that?

R. Not because of marriage doing that but you know seeing as we get married he feel it's a bigger tie.

Another woman regretted not heeding her mother's advice:

I. How did your mother feel about you getting married to him?

R. She didn't want him at all.

I. Why not?

R. She said she don't like him. So even to the time we marry she put in her appearance as a mother and she do what she could for me, but she never like him, never never like him.

I. Who did she want you to marry?

R. She didn't have any plans of somebody but it's just that she don't want these people [from a certain area]. She didn't want them for they were cruel people, she said, so she never love him.

I. Was she right?

R. Righter. If I had known I would have obeyed her.

This same woman, now in her seventies, a former domestic and agricultural worker, describes some of her experiences of married life:

I. He has been gone thirty-two years? You lived together six years?

R. Yes.

I. He went to look for work?

R. He did say that. He went to look work and he would come back to better our position. So it may be that he didn't get it better up to now, because he ain't come back yet.

I. Did he write to you?

R. Two times, two letters only. One he reach safe and one he ain't got no work.

I. The six years you were married, what was your life like with him?

R. It was terrible. His hands wasn't fast but he would sleep there tonight, here tomorrow night, there next week, there next month. Sometimes I ain't see him for the week until when he come. I'll have to get his meals and put it there and he will bring his dirty clothes and put it there and he would fret if I don't do, but to strike, he don't.

I. He didn't strike you?

R. No, he not quick, but he would say all kinds of bad things if I answer him. But he not striking. He would say, 'well I want so and so I want so and so. You already married and you stay home here.' That's all he used to say and curse his bad words and things.

As it happens, the informant who gave the most fulsome praise of marriage turned out to have had experiences which were virtually the antithesis of her own expectations and values. She had had a bitterly disappointing first love and marriage, in which she was rejected and sent home by her husband, subsequent unsatisfying partnerships which yielded several children with different fathers, and mental illness during which some of her children were separated from her. Nevertheless, she is still sufficiently steeped in the stereotypes to assert:

I think it is a selfish woman who would not want to get married and have children and look after a man, keep him clean, and if he wants to have her as a wife and he's good, especially if he's religious, a Christian. I think it should be the pride and joy of every girl to be a housewife. That's what we women were made for. To be housewives.

Since the overwhelming majority of women express the desire to marry — eventually — the relatively low marriage rate in the Caribbean might be attributed not only to the reasons already cited but also to the unwillingness of men to marry. Since the low marriage rate is a mainly black lower-class phenomenon, many reasons have been advanced to explain it and, in the process, Caribbean family forms. Both historical and structural explanations are popular — and both stress male marginality as the end result of these processes and as the reason behind casual rather than legally binding relationships.

Structurally, marriage is viewed as impractical for poor black folk, who have therefore adapted their family forms to suit their conditions — hence the prevalence among this group of visiting and common-law unions.

Historically, marriage was virtually impossible under slavery. Chattel slaves torn from their homes in Africa were not permitted to form legally binding relationships in the New World since they themselves were property; in the British colonies slave marriages were not permitted until the late eighteenth century and few actually took place. Slave families did exist, but the male could not carry out his functions as protector and provider and had no real authority in the household since his functions were usurped by the slave-owner. Additionally, under slavery the mother was the only recognized parent. A slave's paternity was of no importance (unless the father happened to be the master, in which case the child could hope to enter the more privileged mulatto group).

These arguments flow together: that the system of slavery created a male marginalized in the domestic and economic spheres, with no responsibilities regarding fatherhood and with consequent wounds to his self-esteem: 'During the days of slavery the master was the child's "sociological father" and the mother was dependent on the system of slavery rather than upon the child's biological father' (Rodman 1971, p. 183). After slavery the responsibility shifted from the slave-owner to the state (through 'welfare' in the United States) or to surrogate parents in the Caribbean (see 'child-shifting' in chapter 1) as coping strategies (Rodman 1971). Even though slavery in the Caribbean was abolished over 150 years ago, economic conditions have continued to reinforce marginality of the black male since he is often unable to carry out his principal economic role, that of provider (see chapter 2). Only males in the upper income groups are able to perform these functions and are therefore able to establish stable family units. Given the correlation between race and income, family 'instability' is frequently described as a black lower-class phenomenon.

These arguments have also given rise to certain stereotyped images of males and females, principally those of the dominant black female/emasculated black male. Feminist scholars are now challenging these stereotypes, arguing like Lucille Mathurin Mair that, far from being 'marginalized' during slavery, the male slave was not only in an economically superior position compared with the female, but played virtually all religious, political and economic leadership roles in slave society; that female subordination was the norm then, and has continued to be a feature of Caribbean society ever since (Mathurin 1977). Additionally, although the system of slavery did serve to give legitimacy to the centrality of the mother role, a notion 'which was firmly entrenched in the kin systems of the West African tribes transported to the New World' (Massiah WICP 1982, p. 62), it did not necessarily introduce or perpetrate the notion of male marginality. Recent scholarship has in fact suggested that the nuclear family was more common during the later years of slavery than was formerly believed (e.g. Higman 1975) though some of the conclusions regarding this have been challenged (see Reddock 1988).

The myth of the dominant black female is perpetuated today in the glib use of concepts such as 'matriarchic society', and in the reciting of statistics which show an increasing trend towards female household headship as if headship *per se* confers power on women. To see how closely her performance matches this alleged dominance and power, in the rest of this chapter we will examine woman's functioning in the domestic sphere, especially in relation to household structure, the determinants of power and status in the household, and the position and status of women who head households.

Power and status in the household

Family vs. household

It is now well established that the nuclear family model is not always applicable to the Caribbean since the household might be the more usual setting for domestic life. The major difference between a 'household' and 'family' is that members of a household share a common residence and at least one daily meal and may or may not be related to one another. A family is regarded as a group of people who are related to one another but who do not necessarily live together (White WICP 1986). We should emphasize that, in many cases, a family and a household are one and the same.

The WICP sought to gather information on the household in order to establish how the woman functions within it. The WICP approach differs from previous ones, which automatically assumed that a man is head of the household. In the WICP survey, a woman was the reference point by which household type and household headship were determined.

Based on female responses, six household types were determined, two 'simple family' and four 'multiple-family' households. According to White's (WICP 1986) analysis, one-third of all households within the sample of 1,600 households were found to be of the 'simple family' type, consisting of woman, partner and their children living together under one roof. In over three-quarters of these 'simple family' households the couple are in a legally married union. There is usually a working male as a breadwinner and, in two-thirds of these homes, the woman is a non-working housewife. Other 'simple' types of households consisted of a woman living alone (under 5 per cent of cases) and of women and children alone (around 10 per cent of cases).

The multiple-family household types reveal the almost endless permutations of Caribbean domestic life. The WICP made three classifications: family links in these households could be vertical (i.e. three- or four-generational); or lateral (including adult siblings living together) or both vertical and lateral together. The three- or four-generational household is far more common than that of adult siblings living together. Where the latter is the case, female siblings were far more likely than males to share a household. Brothers and sisters together were found to be the case in only 7.5 per cent of all households surveyed.

The sixth type of household consists of people who are not necessarily related to one another and might include, for instance, mother, father, children and a friend of either partner.

Defining household headship

Many problems arise in defining who is head of the household. In cultures based on the nuclear family, it is automatically assumed that it is a male. But this might not be a reasonable assumption to make in the Caribbean context. Making such an assumption has led many researchers to introduce a Eurocentric bias in defining and reporting on headship. The regional census itself makes this assumption and assigns headship to the woman only by default, i.e. in the absence of a suitable male. According to the census definition:

> The head of the household is generally the person who is responsible for the upkeep and maintenance of the household — usually the husband or common-law husband. Where the husband or common-law husband is not the head, or where no man lives in the household, the person who claims the position or who is so regarded by other members of the household is treated as head.
>
> (quoted in Massiah WICP 1982)

Massiah has commented on some of the problems inherent in such an approach: 'By leaving the matter to be settled by the respondent, rather than instructing the enumerator to categorize on the basis of a specific criterion — presumably responsibility for upkeep and maintenance of the household — a distinct cultural bias is introduced into the data.' She further argues that:

> In the Caribbean, where matrifocality of the family is stressed but male authoritarianism is the ideal, there may well be a tendency to overstate male headship. By contrast, where the allocation relies on the 'person who claims the position,' it becomes possible for a woman to cite herself as head, in the absence of her husband/partner at the time of enumeration. Whether either of these biases is sufficient to offset the other is impossible to tell.
>
> (Massiah WICP 1982, p. 8)

A woman's perception of household headship might be quite different from a man's. In the WICP survey, which asked women themselves to identify the head of their households, 3.4 per cent who reported themselves as heads also reported that they were living with a male partner.

This points to the fact that the idea of how to define household headship is still unresolved since subjectivity might be involved in reporting this status. As Hermione McKenzie observes:

> To what extent do women appear as household heads because the male partner was simply not present at the census interview? Or, alternatively, is this an accurate indicator of male marginality? On the other hand, to what extent may even more women who were truly heads of households have been omitted simply because a male partner was resident in the household?
>
> (McKenzie WICP 1982, p. 11)

Despite the limitations, the findings from the WICP are useful because they permit us to see how women themselves perceive their role and status in the domestic domain. The WICP did not assume that a male was head but asked the female respondent herself questions that were used to classify household types and define household heads. Gender, property ownership, household responsibility and age seem to be the principal criteria which determine household headship (White WICP 1986).

Gender Some women accept the traditional view that a man has to be head. One respondent remarked 'he is de head as he is de man'. Another explained, 'It is a God-given requirement that the man is the head of the house.'

Property ownership   Ownership of house/land, or both, on which the household group reside was an important determinant of headship. Some women said they were head of the household because 'the house belong to me and I have to take full responsibility for it', or they said that their partner was head because 'the house is his — he built it'.

Household responsibility   Some women saw their partner as head because 'he brings in the money and looks after everything', or they cited themselves as head because 'I run the affairs of the house.' In one case the respondent's husband had been overseas for 25 years but she maintained that he is the head of the household because 'we correspond and he supports me'.

Age   Age was also a factor though this might be a reflection of status gained with age. In households with siblings and their offspring, the eldest usually claimed the position of head; this appeared to be generally accepted by other members (White WICP 1986).

Characteristics of households

Nearly half (48.8 per cent) of households in the WICP survey were headed by women. However, while close to 50 per cent in Barbados and Antigua were headed by females, male-headed households predominated in St Vincent, the least developed of the territories.

In about 3.4 per cent of the households headed by women, there was a resident male partner. Although no specific question was asked as to why this situation existed, two reasons were suggested by the responses: (i) temporary absence of the male partner; (ii) ownership by the woman of the house and land on which the family resided. It appears, however, that such situations did not preclude the man from making a significant contribution to the running of the household or from being an important decision-maker in household organization.

In all other cases where a male partner was present, he was generally regarded as household head. In these households there was a clear-cut sexual division of labour with the male performing the income-earning role and the female the domestic and child-rearing roles.

Female heads seem to be more prevalent in multi-family households, especially those which are vertically extended (three- or four-generational). The incidence of joint headship was low in all the territories, with St Vincent recording the highest proportion — 5.5 per cent.

Decision-making in the household

Ultimate authority in the household might not rest with the person identified as the head of that household. To test this, WICP researchers in the three survey counties asked women living with a mate 10 questions concerning the making of major decisions in the household. The questions centred around the following:

1 Purchase of major household items
2 Amount of money spent on food

3 How to spend money saved
4 Whether to borrow money
5 Where to live
6 Whether to have another child
7 Bringing up the children
8 Use of contraception
9 Sharing of household tasks
10 Schooling of the children

This survey (examined in detail in White WICP 1986; Powell WICP 1986) revealed that women figure prominently in domestic decision-making. Although there were variations in pattern from country to country, and between married and common-law unions, generally women function as 'managers' of household affairs and are consulted by their partners on domestic matters. However, there might be a tendency to male or female dominance, depending on the type of decision to be made.

About half of the questions had to do with childbearing and child-caring; the rest were in the area of household management. In household management, women seem to be sole decision-makers in traditional female-dominated areas such as sharing household tasks and the amount of money to be spent on food. Roughly six out of every 10 married women in these territories exercise their rights and so do most of the women in common-law unions. In other areas of household management, however, there was a stronger tendency to joint or male-only decision-making as far as married women were concerned. These decisions relate to: where to live, purchase of major household items, how to spend savings and whether to borrow money. Antiguan and Vincentian married women identify these four areas as involving both partners in decision-making. Barbadian women see 'how to spend savings' as a decision which is most often made by women. A possible reason is that savings are usually spent on domestic emergencies such as illness, things for the children or supplementing the household money, reflecting a concern with day-to-day household affairs, a responsibility which the males seem to leave entirely to the women.

Decisions involving 'where to live' and 'whether to borrow money' are usually either male decisions or jointly made. The fact that the male usually provides housing accommodation for his spouse and offspring, coupled with the social expectation that he is the one who will have the collateral for securing long-term loans, probably accounts for this. But the traditional patterns are changing and women are now being consulted in these once male-dominated areas. This may be in response to economic pressures, which force more women to make a significant contribution to household expenses. It is interesting that 'where to live' is the only area which is not seen as woman-dominated among women in common-law unions in St Vincent and Antigua, though it is so regarded in Barbados. However, many common-law women, like their married counterparts, see borrowing money as an area which is either male-dominated or egalitarian. Few see it as the preserve of women. This might be due to the way in which women perceive the system and the way it functions.

Where decisions relating to childbearing and child-caring are concerned, there is more agreement among women, regardless of their marital status. Decisions on the use of contraceptives seem to be a female prerogative, though a significant number of women do consult their mates. Women overwhelmingly see decisions affecting the upbringing of children as made by themselves, except for decisions affecting schooling, which married women usually make with their husbands. However, common-law women perceive this as an area of female decision-making alone.

These findings regarding female dominance in domestic decision-making are supported by research in other areas. A study of farmers in Guyana (Odie-Ali WICP 1986) showed that the males claimed headship of their households but admitted that their wives made the majority of day-to-day decisions. Of the women interviewed, a little over half named their husbands as household head. Yet the majority of these women (79.1 per cent) claimed responsibility for decisions on expenditure of income in household management. Male farmers perceived child-care activities as definitely female responsibilities, with their role being that of provider and disciplinarian in the home. For instance, male informants saw it as their responsibility to provide clothing and other necessities for schooling but not to see that the children are prepared for school in the morning.

In summary, these surveys show that women tend largely to see their men not as main decision-makers but as partners in the decision-making process. This view is more popular with women in married than in common-law unions. The latter tend more frequently to see women as the main decision-makers. Egalitarian decision-making structures have a slight majority over the woman-dominated structures. Overall, the perception is that women have an input in decision-making in most households, either as main decision-makers or sharing decision-making with their partners.

Powell (WICP 1982) argues that female power is predominant in common-law unions and that this may be linked to the fact that the absence of a formal marriage contract weakens the perceived if not the actual dominance of men over women. So that women in non-legal unions may indeed enjoy more freedom and independence in their familial relationships than do married women. The ability to make decisions could indicate such independence. Indeed, as we have seen, in matters relating to property, married women are legally disadvantaged.

What, however, is of significance is the fact that women in common-law unions do not cite this power and perhaps do not even perceive it. Common-law unions were perceived by women in the survey as the least desirable of the three forms of unions and lowest in status.

The women surveyed certainly did not equate decision-making with power. Regardless of their own functional roles in the household, including their financial contribution, as long as a man was present he was cited as the head, except in very rare cases. This suggests that, although women see themselves as an integral part of household decision-making, they still perceive the male as the symbol of authority in the household. Yet evidence from the WICP and elsewhere strongly suggests that, while the traditional perceptions remain, traditional patterns are changing. Decision-making in shared households is becoming more egalitarian and more and more women are becoming heads of households.

Special position of female household heads

The fact that throughout the developing world more and more households are being headed by women might be taken as a sign of increasing 'woman power' in these countries. What we are really witnessing is an increasing feminization of poverty, since such household heads are usually found to be in the most disadvantaged position in the society as a whole. Caribbean women are no exception. They are disadvantaged in relation to the female population in general and in particular to the population of men who are household heads (see Massiah WICP 1982).

For the region as a whole, an average of 32 per cent of households are headed by women, ranging from a low of 22.4 per cent for Guyana to a high of 46.6 per cent in St Kitts/Nevis. The difference between the highest and lowest might be explained by one demographic fact, that female-headed households are more common in countries with significantly large black populations and correspondingly low in countries with significant East Indian (Guyana and Trinidad) and Amerindian (Belize) populations.

While there is a trend to increasing female household headship in the Caribbean, the phenomenon is not new. Massiah (WICP 1982) attributes this to three main causes:

1 The historical heritage of mating and family forms which are distinct from the conventional nuclear family model.

2 Economic factors, some of which generated an emigration ethic as an integral aspect of the culture (both internal and external migration). To this one might add the inability of the male to assume his socially defined role as household head because of his inability to secure jobs at wage levels which would permit him to maintain a household.

3 Sociological factors relating to increased female independence associated with improved socio-economic conditions. This has led to widespread adoption of the non-residential or visiting union as a 'socially acceptable option rather than a deviant alternative', i.e some women become heads of households by choice.

Many arguments have been advanced to explain the high incidence of female household headships in the Caribbean, including the demographic (a greater surplus of females has led to a higher proportion of female-headed households) or as a phenomenon within the context of the female life cycle (K. Otterbein and R.T. Smith quoted in Massiah WICP 1982).

Characteristics of female-headed households

The phenomenon of female household head describes a wide range of domestic arrangements 'typified mainly by the absence of an adult male in the relation of spouse or partner of the dominant female' (Massiah WICP 1982). The households may be two- or three-generational units; in the latter the dominant female assumes responsibility for self, children and/or grandchildren. The essential criterion is that 'her position as head of the household is recognised and admitted as such by all household members' (Massiah WICP 1982).

Of course some female-headed households contain no children, though households with children predominate. Some women assume headship for obvious reasons such as widowhood, separation or divorce. The rate of widowhood generally is higher than that for divorce in the region. In the territories, widowed females range from a high of 34.1 per cent of the total population (Guyana) to 11.4 per cent (St Vincent). There are nowadays longer life-expectancy rates for both sexes, but females generally outlive males. There is also, throughout the region, a low remarriage rate for both widowed and divorced women.

Widowed, separated or divorced women form a small proportion of female household heads; 50 per cent have never been married, though they have been in some form of union previously. The high median age of household heads (ranging between 44.6 and 54.9 years for all the territories) might be accounted for by the fact that one-third of the female single-person households consist of women over

65 years of age, who might simply have outlived their partners. In some households there might be a residential male (husband/partner) who is unable to function as household head for economic or health reasons. Where the male is unable to sustain his economic role effectively, his status within the household deteriorates and a female-headed household develops.

From the 1970 Caribbean census, Massiah (1982) has developed a profile of the female household head which shows that she has less education than her male counterpart and is less likely to be employed (a mean average of only 42.4 per cent in the labour force compared with 89.2 per cent of male household heads). An average of four persons are dependent on her (compared with 4.8 dependents in male-headed households). Many household heads are older women (median age over 40), 50 per cent of whom have never been married (compared with 25 per cent of males).

Although they are the sole or principal breadwinners, female household heads are particularly ill-equipped to compete in the job market since 88.3 per cent of them have no more than primary schooling. Of the women employed, one-third were in 'service jobs', i.e. were working mainly as domestics. The rest were mainly in low-paying jobs; 8.2 per cent were in professional and administrative positions, 20.9 per cent in clerical and sales, and 18.5 per cent in production and other occupations (Massiah 1982).

The status of female household heads helps to emphasize the difference between myth and reality which permeates many aspects of Caribbean domestic life. For, although family forms greatly differ from the nuclear family ideal, both males and females in all kinds of unions express conformity to the ideals of the sexual division of labour in the domestic sphere and to patriarchic family structure. While the model is not traditional, the ideological position of women is (Powell WICP 1986).

In practice, women do exercise power in the domestic sphere, are major decision-makers in some areas and share decision-making in others. Yet the real decisions which involve interfacing with the outside world are still made largely by men. Women also fail to recognize their own power in the home and continue to defer to men in many areas, despite the changing economic climate which forces more and more women to become breadwinners. Women's status in the household is also disadvantageous according to laws which do not recognize her contribution to homemaking.

The myth of the black matriarch is one of the most pervasive in Caribbean societies. But in what does the matriarch's alleged power and dominance inhere? While some younger, upwardly mobile women nowadays voluntarily choose single parenthood and household headship, for older women there is usually no choice; the role is foisted on them by circumstances. Female household heads on the whole are poor, black, uneducated and in the worst-paid and lowest-status jobs. It is these women who are truly working miracles, in ensuring at least the survival, and sometimes the advancement, of their families.

In the next two chapters, we will examine the strategies that women like these employ to cope with their family responsibilities.

III *Sources of Livelihood*

Edna Manley, *Ghetto Mother*, 1981 (Ciment fondu, height 43″)
Used with permission of Dr Paul Chen-Young
Photographer: Maria La Yacona

6 Working Women

The problems of survival, of maintaining families, of seeking sources of livelihood are not female-centred problems. Indeed, in many societies these are regarded as largely male responsibilities. We have seen that the main expectation of the male in many Caribbean households and families is that he should function as provider. 'The man is expected to work and to earn for his family; his status within the family hinges on how adequately he provides . . . The man's worker-earner role is crucial because it links the work and family worlds, in which the man plays two of the most important roles in his life' (Rodman 1971, pp. 177–8). Yet it is frequently the Caribbean woman who ends up playing the breadwinner role.

Despite the idealized image of male–female roles which persists, the Caribbean woman generally accepts work as her lot. From childhood, most girls are groomed into assuming domestic responsibilities, including care of the home and younger siblings while the mother labours. Up to recently, it was the widespread practice to farm out surplus girls from the very poorest homes to those of the better off, where they became the household drudges euphemistically called 'schoolgirls'. The role model of the mother or grannie who works either in the labour force or on her own as independent cultivator, higgler, washerwoman or whatever is ever-present.

Whereas a few generations ago upper-class girls would have had few examples of women of their own class who went out to work, nowadays the expectation of girls of all classes is that they will earn a living. But, because many girls lack the education and training the labour force requires and begin childbearing early, many will end up having to support their families outside the formal labour force, some in ways that might be 'invisible' to the casual observer.

The WICP took the view that 'work' cannot be conceptualized simply in terms of wage labour. For officially 'unemployed' women still have to perform the miracle of supporting their children — often single-handed. The WICP argued that Caribbean women employ many different strategies to harness the resources they need to sustain themselves and their families and that all of these together constitute what might be called their 'sources of livelihood'. In official measures of 'women's work', only one such source — the formal labour force — is taken into consideration.

The WICP's broad-based concept of 'work' includes not only wage labour but also survival strategies, both of which will be explored in this chapter and the next. The WICP also tried to explore women's attitudes, expectations and values in regard to 'work'. In this chapter, we will begin by looking at what constitutes 'work', the status of women in the labour force and their experiences there. In the next chapter, we will examine women at work in the 'informal' sector and the survival strategies they employ.

The sexual division of labour

The fact that society distinguishes between men's work and women's work is evident from the occupational structure of the region. Caribbean women themselves are socialized to choose training and education which will prepare them for traditional 'female' occupations. Attitudes of both men and women regarding the sexual division of labour are probably most pronounced in the domestic sphere and in the traditional farming sector.

For instance, Guyanese farm women, who were engaged in hard manual labour, still clung to the clear-cut notions of men's work/women's work which obtained in their communities. Weeding, tending seedlings, planting, watering, caring.for the growing plants, reaping and marketing are regarded as women's work. Tasks such as clearing the bush, digging drains and spraying (using large spray packs) are regarded as men's work. But, as in other areas of the Caribbean, women will undertake any of these tasks if no man is available. A male farmer expressed a common viewpoint when he said, 'when there is a push, the woman does work equal and straight with me' (Odie-Ali WICP 1986, p. 273), although the task itself would remain sex-stereotyped. These divisions are encountered throughout the Caribbean. Tasks such as weeding and clearing the ground are regarded as female agricultural tasks, but digging is a male prerogative. One researcher found that historically, in Jamaica, deep digging, which the planting of crops such as yam requires, was taboo to women, as were the implements used for digging, the fork and the pickaxe (Brodber WICP 1986) — though some women of course did break the taboos.

The sexual division of labour is even more pronounced in the household. Domestic tasks remain the almost exclusive preserve of women, since, as we discussed in chapter 2, the Caribbean male is generally not socialized to perform such tasks. The traditional role of the female in serving the male — whether he be father, son, brother or husband, the continued accessibility of cheap domestic labour despite urban trends to apartment living and a 'bachelor' existence, and the traditional expectations of the female all serve to reinforce gender-role stereotyping in the household as in external matters. Males are not expected by either sex to perform certain domestic and other tasks culturally defined as 'women's work', though they might do so in a pinch if big enough girl children are not around.

Historical patterns of women's work

Gender was the significant factor in determining work assignments in the period before European settlement when the role of the Caribbean woman as worker–mother was first established. The indigenous populations (Arawak and Carib) had clear-cut divisions of labour in which women played a significant role outside childbearing and domestic duties. Women's work also included the planting, reaping, maintenance and harvesting of family plots, caring for livestock, weaving, pottery and other tasks. The men were the hunters, food-gatherers, canoe- and house-makers, priests and warriors.

Although the aboriginal populations of the Caribbean islands were virtually exterminated in the century or so following the European conquest starting in the late fifteenth century, those remaining were absorbed into the process of creolization by which new societies were being rapidly created from an amalgam of European, African and aborigine elements. The literature shows that the indigenous populations passed on to the newcomers their knowledge and skills derived from centuries of exploitation of the lands and seas around them; such cultural transmission would be expected to include the sexual divisions associated with the various tasks. These traditions are carried on today by the small populations of indigenous peoples remaining in St Vincent, Trinidad, Guyana and Belize.

Under the system of plantation slavery around which Caribbean societies were organized from the mid-seventeenth to the mid-nineteenth centuries, gender roles were modified by race and class. Colonial society was stratified into white, brown and black, which corresponded to the social and economic power structure.

European females on the plantations were restricted to conjugal and maternal roles since they had an enormous number of black domestic slaves at their disposal to take care of child-rearing and domestic duties. White women of other classes were more active — functioning as independent proprietors of small plantations and businesses. However, because of the low ratio of whites in the total population and the low number of resident white women, such women during the days of slavery must have served as limited role models.

In the middle of the colour–class system were the mulatto or coloured women, born of miscegenation between the races. Mulattos were regarded as useless for plantation labour and were therefore given the higher-status jobs — usually inside the plantation houses. Many were freed by their fathers, contributing to the growing 'free coloured' population of these territories. Mulatto women were able to engage in various activities which enhanced their personal power and independence. Their spheres of influence included the homes of white men, where they frequently functioned as concubines, euphemistically called 'housekeepers'. Such women often benefited from the largesse of the white men who were their fathers, who might free them and give them small legacies, and from the white men who were their keepers, who might also provide them with the means of establishing themselves — usually as petty proprietors. Coloured women established a tradition of being tavern- and hotel-keepers, 'doctresses' or healers, and many, such as Mary Seacole of Jamaica and Rachel Pringle of Barbados, became noted or notorious enough to be cited in the records of their times. In the post-emancipation period, they along with poor white women functioned as teachers, owners of small plantations and petty proprietors of various business enterprises such as hotels, schools or dressmaking establishments.

At the bottom of the economic and social system were the black slave women. Although some were engaged in domestic labour and others in huckstering or petty trading, the majority worked as unskilled labourers on the sugar plantations, the hardest work of all. Field slaves were grouped according to strength and endurance, not according to sex. The evidence so far shows that women contributed the largest proportion of field slaves. For instance, analysis of the work-force on one Jamaican plantation in the late eighteenth century showed that, in 1789, '70 women out of a total female slave population of 162 worked in the fields, in comparison with 28 men out of a possible 177'. Four years later on the same plantation, there were 107 female fieldworkers out of 244, in contrast with 92 men out of 284 (see Mathurin 1977, p. 3). Towards the end of slavery, when Jamaican sugar plantations had an excess of female workers, 'not only were the majority of Jamaican black women labourers in the field, but the majority of Jamaica's labourers in the field were black women'.

Historian Elsa Goveia in her study of the Leewards noted of field slaves, 'No other group . . . was so completely subject to the harsh necessity of slavery as an industrial system. The life of the ordinary slave was characterised by coercion and dependence. The gangs of field slaves were worked for long hours under discipline of the whip' (quoted in Mathurin 1977).

A female slave labourer would have found it difficult to move upwards in the slave hierarchy since she was excluded from jobs which developed the technical and artisanal skills associated with sugar production. While enslaved women were relegated to field and domestic tasks, their men had a much wider range of occupational choices and access to skills, as Lucille Mathurin Mair reminds us. Findings from some Jamaican estates have shown ratios of 25–50 per cent of the men engaged in skilled tasks, while almost 100 per cent of the female labour force was engaged in the unskilled areas of plantation work (Mathurin 1977). From the start of European settlement, women's opportunities and statuses were structurally determined.

After the slaves were freed in the 1830s, the options open to both men and women were: to continue to labour on the plantations for wages; to establish themselves as peasant proprietors; to combine wage labour with own-account work; or to hire themselves out in the towns, mainly in domestic service. The economic situation was such that an independent peasantry was not well established until funds from emigration beginning in the late nineteenth century began to make this possible and land became available for purchase as more and more plantations went out of production. Thus men and women on the whole continued to labour for others, mainly at hard manual tasks. In very few cases were black males economically able to become sole breadwinners and providers for their families.

It was in the immediate post-emancipation period that the image of the independent black female became full-blown. Some of the newly freed women parlayed the skills they had learnt during slavery as vendors of farm produce or 'higglers' to dominate the internal marketing system. However, most women continued to work for wages on the land: 80 per cent of female labour in the immediate post-emancipation period was so engaged, and, from the introduction of wage labour in 1834, wage differentials for men and women doing exactly the same work were established, a pattern that would continue until the present generation.

Despite the structural and institutional handicaps, women, and black women especially, came to establish a reputation for themselves as providers and managers of their own affairs. Contemporary visitors to the Caribbean repeatedly recorded their impressions of black women as the 'workers' of these societies and of their independent attitudes. Typical of the comments were those made by Bacon and Aaron, who visited Jamaica in 1890: 'Women are the workers among the blacks in the neighbourhood of Kingston. They carry the coal on the wharves, load and unload vessels, drive donkeys and mules with produce, break stones on the road, carry stone and other building material for housebuilders, wash, bake, dig in the fields' (Bacon and Aaron 1890 p. 94).

Such a high level of female activity does not necessarily mean that there was a correspondingly low level on the part of the men; women labourers might simply have been more 'visible'. What it does underscore, however, is that the image of the West Indian black woman as 'worker', as an economically independent being, was established early — and is still an image which persists today, despite sex-role stereotyping. In the post-emancipation period, such women continued to undertake hard and arduous work — including manual labour. It was in those countries where the development of a peasantry was greatest, e.g. Jamaica, that the higgler or market-woman became the dominant icon of female independence and assertiveness.

Meanwhile, white women and, increasingly, upwardly mobile 'respectable' women of other races were being tutored by the schools, churches and other agents of socialization to be 'good wives and good mothers'. Until well into the twentieth century, such women did not enter the workplace but engaged in home activities and 'good works', pioneering voluntary activities of all types but especially those concerned with assisting women.

Indentured workers

The ending of slave labour brought new elements into the racial and social matrix of these societies. With emancipation approaching, and the planters' fears of losing control of their labour force, the British government imported into the Caribbean territories indentured workers from India, China and Africa and European settlers from Germany and Portugal. The Europeans became principally small settlers or went into trade, and the Chinese, too, deserted the land early and established themselves primarily in shopkeeping. The bulk of the indentured immigrants were Indian males, who became agricultural labourers. The smaller number of Indian women who did come were also expected to labour in the fields, though, like the black women whom they replaced, they were paid considerably less than men; they nevertheless remained a sizeable portion of the labour force up to the 1960s in Trinidad. As the Indians became better off and accumulated enough to buy their own land, more and more of their women withdrew from estate labour. The poorer ones could look forward for several generations to a life of early marriage and household drudgery, coupled with labour on the family plot, which was a source of household income through production of sugar-cane for sale to the estates and vegetable and food production for the market. Up to a few decades ago, few Indian or Chinese women entered the formal labour force.

Influence of emigration

A key factor in emphasizing and reinforcing black female economic independence has been the role played by heavy external migration from the region as well as internal migration from rural to urban areas. From the latter part of the nineteenth century to the mid-1920s, the menfolk of these territories left their homelands for Latin America, Cuba and the United States of America as migrant labourers on the big construction and agricultural projects then under way. The size of this emigration was substantial — Jamaica experienced a net loss of some 146,000 persons between 1881 and 1921 and Barbados 104,000 persons between 1860 and 1920. These were the countries which supplied the largest number of emigrants.

The sex-selective nature of this emigration is remarkable. For instance, in Jamaica, three years of emigration, 1881–4 (when the French made the first attempt to build the Panama Canal), attracted one-fifth of the male population of reproductive age, and a similarly high outflow continued to the end of the decade. In Barbados, fully 70 per cent of the total net emigration over the period 1861–1921 was of males (Roberts 1955, 1957; Lowenthal 1957). Large-scale emigration from the region again occurred in the late 1950s to 1970s. The emigration of the 1960s and 1970s consisted mainly of able-bodied males while in the 1970s and 1980s more females than males emigrated — mainly well-educated and skilled workers. The earliest period of high emigration (1891–1921), which was mainly of young able-bodied males, saw a substantial increase in women entering the work-force (Massiah WICP 1986a).

Female independence in this period was reinforced by the fact that it was on the women left at home that the burden of maintaining the household and caring for the children fell, arrangements which became permanent when desertion occurred, or when the man died overseas, a frequent situation given the hazardous working conditions. Where the men did remit earnings, it was the women who exercised the responsibility of investing it in land and other assets and of maintaining them (Massiah WICP 1986a).

Up to the middle of this century, wage labour for women continued to be mainly backbreaking, exploitative drudgery. We gain a picture of some aspects of female employment on the eve of the Second World War from the Report of the West India Royal Commission (1945) (Moyne) which visited the various territories after widespread rioting in 1937–8.

The Commissioners took special note of women workers in three spheres — as shop assistants, domestic servants and factory and manual labourers — and the appalling conditions of their employment in each. Their report threw into high relief the significant role played by women in the field of heavy manual labour:

> Women in the West Indies are employed on other manual labour which would often seem to the onlooker unsuitable for women, besides demanding more than their physical strength justifies. For example, when unloading coal and sand barges, women are required to carry very heavy weights; this form of work is particularly undesirable for people who are in a constant state of child-bearing. A load of sand, which is carried in a basket from the hold of a ship to the dock on the head of a woman, may weigh as much as 72 lb. A load of coal may weigh 50 lb.

Women must have taken on this type of work out of sheer necessity, because it was highly unrewarding:

> Work for more than two days or at the most three days, in any week is seldom available . . . the work is poorly paid and the average earnings of the woman . . . after she had paid a percentage of those earnings to the gang-leader who engaged her, amounts to only a few shillings a week. The same comment applies to the carrier of bananas on the docks, who is paid ¼ d. for each stem and is usually under-employed, and to the carrier of stones on the road, who in some places earns as little as 9d. for a day's work.
>
> (GB: West India Royal Commission 1945, p. 219)

It is perhaps the creative artists who have been most perceptive of this aspect of the female role. Sculptors and painters — whether resident or visitors — have consistently shown black and brown women as labourers and manual workers. Writers have celebrated them in novels such as Alvin Bennett's *God the Stonebreaker* (1964). Female manual labourers have also been immortalized in poetic imagery, as in George Campbell's 'History makers' (1981):

Women stone breakers
Hammer and rocks
Tired child makers
Haphazard frocks.
Strong thigh
Rigid head
Bent nigh
Hard white piles

Of stone
Under hot sky
In the gully bed.

But, although there is this long history of female involvement in heavy manual labour, the stereotype persists here as elsewhere that females are too weak to do 'men's work'. Such stereotypes have become prescriptions which are used to justify the payment of smaller wages to women for doing the same manual tasks as men, especially in agriculture.

Thus, the Moyne Commission found that while men too were suffering from poor wages and working conditions — the riots had arisen partly as a result of these conditions — pay differentials exaggerated the plight of women. The Commissioners noted that, for instance, in Barbados, where daily wages for agricultural workers ranged from one shilling to one and six per day, female agricultural workers were paid one shilling; in Guyana, male workers engaged in weeding earned two shillings and two pence, females one shilling and sixpence ha'penny for the same work; in Jamaica, the highest daily wage for women — one shilling and sixpence — was the lowest daily wage paid to men doing the same work (GB: West India Royal Commission 1945, p. 194). They commented that 'The argument that the man is the head of the household and is responsible for the financial upkeep of the family has less force in the West Indies, where . . . the woman so often is the supporter of the home' (p. 220). Women in agriculture, especially, continue to be paid smaller wages than men.

Definitions of women's work

Official definition of work

Virtually all Caribbean women might perceive themselves as working, but only some are officially categorized as 'workers'. The official statistics reveal little of their preoccupation with seeking various sources of livelihood and/or the time-consuming daily round of activities on which they are for the most part engaged. Rather, the statistics suggest something entirely different: that more than half of the region's women are not 'economically active', i.e. they do not work for wages or salaries or are not seeking work (Massiah WICP 1986a). Conventional labour force statistics include as 'work' only those activities which have a monetary exchange value.

Because statistics compiled by censuses and labour force surveys[1] are a critical tool in the formulation of policies by governments and other planners, we need to examine briefly how the official statistics on work are collected and what are the implications of such data collection for women. Basically, the official data are concerned with the concept of a labour force, a concept which was developed in the United States of America in the 1930s and which reflected concern at that time with the effect of the prevailing economic depression on levels of employment

---

1 In the Caribbean, official data for the study of women's economic roles originate from censuses, labour force surveys and business establishment surveys undertaken by the statistics department of each territory. There is considerable variation in the quality and quantity of the data generated. Only in the case of censuses are common definitions and procedures adopted. In the case of surveys, individual territories devise their own procedures. Published material tends to consist only of quantitative data with little or no analysis (Massiah WICP 1986a, p. 7).

Table 6.1 General Worker Rates by Sex in the Commonwealth Caribbean, 1891–1980

Territory	1891		1911		1921		1946		1960		1970		1980	
	M	F	M	F	M	F	M	F	M	F	M	F	M	F
Jamaica	81.3	75.4	78.4	60.0	78.4	64.7	72.5	33.9	86.3	43.3	70.6	25.6	42.0	22.7
Trinidad & Tobago	87.4	73.9	85.8	64.6	85.4	62.7	78.6	26.1	68.9	28.3	63.4	20.0	69.3	26.6
Guyana	88.4	78.2	89.0	89.0	86.0	67.9	79.2	29.4	85.9	24.7	68.7	15.4	72.3	20.3
Belize	n/a	n/a	n/a	n/a	74.1	14.0	78.2	16.6	86.9	18.1	82.5	18.4	84.2	21.4
Barbados	79.1	78.3	78.0	77.1	79.5	76.9	78.1	49.2	80.7	42.2	75.4	39.4	74.4	47.7
Dominica	83.1	81.0	85.0		94.1		75.5	49.2	86.7	52.6	77.8	36.3	68.3	32.4
Grenada	79.1	68.6	75.1	67.5	72.9	69.8	66.1	43.8	77.3	37.1	73.8	35.5	69.7	36.9
St Lucia	90.5		82.1	75.7	84.7	63.5	77.8	50.5	83.8	40.0	76.3	32.3	71.7	36.5
St Vincent	76.8		65.5	61.1	66.9	64.1	67.8	42.1	80.4	39.3	73.2	30.6	69.0	32.0
Antigua	82.0	74.3	n/a		76.3		75.6	49.1	76.7	36.3	—	—	57.1	33.2
British Virgin Is.	71.9	57.3	n/a		n/a		77.7	12.0	86.9	17.4	86.3	38.2	84.0	55.4
Montserrat	69.7	68.6	n/a		74.2		72.8	55.8	80.1	41.5	77.7	33.1	72.7	42.3
St Kitts	80.5	74.1	79.0	64.0	73.5	65.9	75.7	48.2	85.4	43.2	74.8	35.7	76.4	43.2
High	88.4	78.3	89.0	89.0	86.0	67.9	79.2	55.8	86.9	52.6	86.3	39.4	84.0	55.4
Low	69.7	57.3	65.5	60.0	66.9	14.0	66.1	16.6	76.7	17.4	63.4	15.4	57.1	20.3

Source: relevant census reports.

Notes: General Worker Rates refers to the number of males/females in the working force aged 15 and over as a percentage of the total number of males/females aged 15 and over.

1891–1946 refers to population aged 10 years and over and to the gainfully occupied population.

1960–1980 refers to population aged 15 years and over (except Antigua, where the 1960 figure refers to the 14 + population and the 1980 estimate to the 16 + population).

Data for census years 1901 and 1931 have been omitted due to the small number of territories which took censuses.

(Massiah WICP 1986a). The emphasis was on male labour, in keeping with the traditional approach to the sexual division of labour: men ought to work full-time, women ought to stay at home and mind the children. The main divisions are the separation of the 'employed' from the 'unemployed'.[2]

But many developing countries are characterized by widespread job shortages and consequent labour surplus, and seasonal and intermittent employment. The conventional divisions into labour and non-labour, employed and unemployed are of limited value here. These strictures hold with even greater force when applied to women. It has been argued that the activities of women, while constituting work in the literal meaning of the word, are masked partly because many women tend to work intermittently, in the informal sector; partly because such income as they do earn is so meagre that they prefer not to discuss it; and partly because much of this work relates directly to the maintenance of their households (Massiah WICP 1982).

Nevertheless, the census approach does permit us to identify those women whose main activity is home-based but who do engage in paid employment for some period during the year, since this is an important feature of the employment pattern of women. But two other items of importance in assessing female activity cannot be derived from the census or surveys: (i) they do not identify persons engaged in more than one economic activity; (ii) they do not permit identification of an individual's main source of income. Generally, the census and other data collection systems deal effectively with persons whose economic activity can be easily measured in terms of time and money. For persons who may not be so described, e.g. women, the data system is not as effective.

In an effort to surmount some of these problems, the WICP sought to apply other techniques for measuring work and to find out from women themselves how they defined work. These techniques will be discussed below. Another issue derived from the survey, economic sources of livelihood available to women, will be discussed in chapter 7.

The WICP definition of work

The employment statistics of the various Caribbean countries fail to give a true picture of women's work. By the same token, the 'unemployment' figures do not give a true picture of women who might not be in the formal labour force but who nevertheless engage in income-earning activities.

The WICP sought other means of examining women's work and eventually identified 'employment status' based on answers to the simple question, 'How do you make a living?' supplemented by appropriate probing questions. From the responses, the WICP created categories based on income-earning activity at the time of the survey. The categories were intended to separate those who had a

---

2 In general, the regional census or national surveys focus on the individual's main economic activity during a specified period prior to the census/survey. The potential labour force is divided into seven basic categories: (i) Worked — indicating those persons who were engaged in the production of goods and services for most of the 12 months — employers, employees, own-account workers, unpaid workers. (ii) Seeking first job — those persons who spent most of the year seeking their first job. (iii) Others seeking work — those persons who worked previously but who spent most of the year seeking a job. (iv) Wanted work and available — those who needed a job but did not spent most of the year seeking one. (v) Home duties — persons doing household work but receiving no pay. (vi) Student — persons who spent most of the year in school but had left by the time of the census. (vii) Retired/disabled — persons retired for all or most of the year.

regular source of independently earned income from those who did not. The selected WICP categories were as follows:

1 Not employed: for those indicating no income-earning activity and no participation in home service activity.
2 Home service: for those engaged solely in homemaking and child-care activities.
3 Home production: for those who supplemented their home service with income-earning activities conducted in and around the house, activities such as the production and sale of handicraft, agricultural produce, etc., on a regular basis.
4 Employed on own business/farm: for those operating their own business, with or without paid help.
5 Employed by family member: for those receiving wage/salary from family enterprise.
6 Employed by others: for those working for wage/salary for persons other than family members.

It was felt that these categories would provide a more meaningful distinction between the kinds of work that women do and the relative importance of each in their lives. These categories permit identification of those women who engage sometimes in income-earning activities in the informal sector and the many different types of occupations undertaken by women in both the informal and formal sectors. This female-centred approach enabled the WICP to avoid some of the problems created by the conventional approaches. It also made it possible to identify the sources from which women receive monetary support.

To establish those in the not-employed group, the WICP separated women engaged in income-earning activity and those engaged in household work activity from a third group, those engaged in neither activity. These are the women who are classified as unemployed — 'you just sit at home doing nothing', one described it. Thus the unemployed are seen as those literally without any kind of activity, which contrasts with the census definition of the unemployed as those seeking a job within a specified time period. In analysing the WICP data, Massiah concluded that:

> the status 'not employed' seems to be one of choice for a significant number of women either because they genuinely do not wish to become involved in income acquisition or because they have subordinated their wishes to outside factors. In either case, their decision is based on the availability of at least one other household member as a source of income flow into the household.
>
> (Massiah WICP 1986a, p. 222)

Women's definition of work

Women who go out to a job perform a role that is visible and quantifiable. But these represent only a portion of 'working women' and their labour a portion of women's work. In her daily round of activities, a woman often has to fulfil different roles associated with the domestic, maternal and economic demands of her existence. Although a significant portion of the lives of women is devoted to such activities, considerable confusion exists as to what exactly should be classified as 'women's work'.

No such problem is associated with men's work since men and work are regarded as two sides of an equation: 'a man's work is one of the things by which he is judged, and certainly one of the most significant things by which he judges himself. A man's work is one of the more important parts of his social identity' (quoted in Gill WICP 1984, p. 20).

Even in the Caribbean, where there have been historically high levels of female economic activity, the traditional stereotype persists. Everyone here too accepts as natural that men 'work'. But how should we describe the activities of those women who do not put on working clothes every morning and go to factory or office but who nevertheless spend a good part of their waking hours engaged in non-leisure activities?

To identify how women themselves conceptualized work, women in the WICP samples were asked to list their daily round of activities in the 24 hours preceding the survey. The detailed activities were then grouped into major categories identifying household chores, child care, job-related activities, leisure activities and personal care activities. Analysis of these activities demonstrated that most of the women's time is taken up in work activities. To clarify what the women themselves considered to be work, they were then asked, 'which of your activities would you describe as work?' About 40 per cent of the responses cited housework alone; about 20 per cent cited income-earning activities alone; one-quarter cited income-earning activity plus housework. Thus many of the women working outside the home also regard housework as work. One woman who was asked why she considered housework to be work said: 'Because housework is very hard, because every day you got to do some. Some days the same thing what you do today you got to do tomorrow. You got to cook, wash, sweep, dust, cook, clean, scrub.' She was asked why she thought other people did not consider housework to be work: 'It must be because they don't look for you. Because you don't get pay they feel, well, you home, you ain't do nothing.'

On the other hand, the case-study of Guyanese women farmers found that, while all but one (of 62 women) said they spent between 3 and 5 hours per day in home services, less than half (46.7 per cent) said they regarded work done in the home as work. As one woman said, 'housework not wuk, woman born to do housework'. Here women might be fulfilling community social-role expectations, as the researcher Stella Odie-Ali suggests. She quotes one 20-year-old farmer as saying: 'Even though me ah wuk man to man wid he pon de farm, if he come home and he shirt button fall out and de food na ready and to he liking, is war. Not only he does row, but he mother and father does bad talk. Me own father an all does vex' (Odie-Ali WICP 1986, p. 272).

Although many of the WICP respondents do define housework as work, others are ambivalent about the issue. Some regard housework as a duty. Others claim it's not work 'because you're not earning an income'. To examine this issue more deeply, Massiah (WICP 1986a) undertook content analysis of the detailed responses to this question. This revealed four main criteria by which women define housework. These were:

1 Income: 'All [housework] would be work because you get tired just as if you were working for money. Is the same thing.'
2 Time: 'From the time I wake up and start washing down the pig pen, I am working. Everything is work.'
3 Necessity: 'Washing and cooking — you have to get clothes and food for the children so these jobs are the most important.'
4 Energy: 'You're tired when you're finished. So that is work.'

From these findings Massiah concluded that 'women consider work to be anything which is functionally necessary to maintain themselves and their households'

(Massiah WICP 1986a, p. 186). Women's perception of work includes the caring and rearing of children, household chores and related activities. Like a job, these activities consume time and energy. The only difference perceived is that women gain monetary rewards for jobs while they do not do so for housework. The WICP concluded that Caribbean woman's all-embracing perception of work implies that 'except for leisure, all activities which contribute to human welfare is work and not merely those which are linked to a particular form of economic accounting'. In effect, 'women hold a broadly based perception of work which implies that most women are, in fact, workers' (Massiah WICP 1986a, p. 186).

Women's 'independence'

Income-earning activity is important to women — as to men — because it is bound up with a sense of self. Even though many women are engaged exclusively in home-based work, few seem to be content to be entirely supported by others. The desire for economic independence is a strong characteristic of Caribbean woman and a vital component of her self-image. In a Barbados case-study, one informant, who had spent most of her life working, contrasted the time she was earning, when she felt 'proud, real proud, I felt I was the sweetest woman in the whole world', with her present helplessness now that she is blind and unemployed. Another said that, while she was earning and independent, she did not have to take the insults of her partner's family who 'play great'. A third claimed that when she was employed her partner never made demands on her the way he does when she is unemployed. This need for personal income applies even to married women, especially since it is observed that 'The man's authority in the relationship varies directly with the adequacy of his contribution and with the degree of her dependence on him as her sole source of livelihood' (Barrow WICP 1986a, p. 139).

Further, the WICP survey showed that virtually all employed women, regardless of their union status or income level, or their ability to tap other sources of income, saw their wage work as their main source of support. Having their own money, they said, made them feel good, because they did not have to beg a man any more. Interestingly this was also said by the housewives who had only personal savings from money received from children, or who engaged in income-earning home production or received money from being members of a 'sou sou' (see below). Thus, even when they receive money from their partners, women prefer not to feel totally dependent on them for financial support. In the words of one young woman:

> When you have your own you don't have to ask nobody and they don't have to tell you things that you don't like, right. You spend your money how you want and you save whatever you feel like saving. If you want to go any place you go, so long as you have your own money. Sometimes I am going out with my boyfriend and I know he will look after me pretty well. But still I make sure that I have my own money because you never know what might happen. I'm quick to vex, you know. Let's say one night I went to a dance and I don't feel like staying with him, I have my own money. I can go home by bus then.

An older Antiguan was particularly expressive about the connection between female earnings and female self-image. This 63-year-old told an interviewer:

R. Like now everybody can 'cut style'.
I. What do you mean by cutting style?
R. Because the man working the woman working. If he don't give, she don't

I. have to worry herself because she have her own money. But when he come now to get food and give no money, he do without.

I. So you think money makes a woman independent?

R. It make them independent because they can go to the store or to the shop and buy whatever they want. Some of the men would want to say, 'where you get that dress', and so on. If you have your own money now you can buy it, they can't come and ask no question.

I. So you would say that women are better off today?

R. Plenty. Whole heap. Besides, if you want a pair of slippers, you hear, 'Oh you always want something', but if you have the money you can go out and buy it.

Part of the woman's emphasis on her personal financial independence stems from her negative perceptions of male performance and behaviour and attendant risks to the 'dependent' woman, particularly where children are involved. It is extremely significant that Caribbean women frequently assert, 'my children are my responsibility' (see Durant-Gonzalez WICP 1982). Children generally are perceived not as joint heirs in a family situation but as ultimately the responsibility of their mothers.

In the Barbados case-study cited earlier, all the women argued that 'should circumstances warrant, both men and women should have joint responsibility for providing for household and children, particularly when women are not fully pre-occupied with early motherhood. This view they apply particularly to the contemporary situation of a high and escalating cost of living when "one body money can't stretch"' (Barrow WICP 1986a).

Apart from the feeling of independence which it gives them, women's economic activity also provides them with a means of getting out of the house and relieving the boredom of the daily routine (Barrow WICP 1986a, p. 158) and with broadening their social field (Durant-Gonzalez WICP 1982).

Role conflicts: home/job and the allocation of time

Where women are forced to take up heavy economic burdens, there are conflicts between their economic and domestic roles and in trying to define the spectrum of their work. A man's work is usually clear-cut. Even when he engages in occupational multiplicity, such work usually takes place outside the home and ends on the doorstep. Woman's work, on the other hand, is multidimensional, embracing what takes place in the public arena and what takes place in the home, frequently recognizing no set 'working hours', embracing day and night and drawing on all her resources.

A frequently quoted remark by one of the women interviewed by the WICP is that, 'Woman is a donkey, she work at work and then she go home and work again.' The remark embodies not only the reality of woman's situation as breadwinner and as homemaker, but a perception of woman's work as all-embracing and never-ending. A part of woman's daily challenge, then, is how she should manage her time. For some, it is a dizzying race. A domestic worker whose mother stayed at home as child-minder was asked:

I. How did you manage to go out to work and bring up the children?

R. On mornings I would cook and leave [the meal] at home. I wash and so before I leave, then go out to work. After lunch I get a couple of hours and I go back again and I see about them [the children]. Then I go back to work and I would finish around six and I would go back again and see about them.

Detailed probing into the lives of women by the WICP revealed how a woman's day is fragmented to permit her to fulfil her many roles.

A Guyanese farm woman's day showed that, of 16 waking hours, the largest portion (7h.05 min.) was spent on the farm, 2h.45min. were spent in home services, 1 hour in home agriculture (looking after her poultry), 1h.55min. in personal care and 3h.15min. in recreation (talking, listening to radio). A 31-year-old mother of four children, working as a domestic, broke down her 17-hour day as follows: 6h.15min. at work, 3h.50min. in home services (taking care of house and children), 1h.10min. in personal care, 4h.45min. in home handicraft and 1 hour in recreation (chatting with partner, listening to radio). A childless 59-year-old, who was self-employed, spent approximately 10 of her 15 waking hours in work connected with her business. Household chores were taken care of by paid help. Personal care and recreation occupied the rest of her waking hours. A 27-year-old mother of five, engaged in home services, spent 12 of her 16 waking hours in the care of home and children. Personal care and recreation (reading before bed) took up the rest of her time.

The woman with a job and no adult present in the household is absent from her home at least six hours of the day. She spends an almost similar amount of time doing household chores and producing handicrafts as an extra source of income. Little time is available for personal care and recreation. The woman running her own business from her home spends longer hours in activities related to the business and relatively little time on household chores since she is able to employ help for this purpose. The day of the housewife is characterized by frequent shifts from one activity to another, each taking relatively short periods of time. Nevertheless, this process permits a style of task allocation which ensures opportunity for rest and relaxation which is not afforded the other women.

These examples reflect the various accommodations which women have to make in order to fulfil their domestic, maternal and economic roles.

Women in the labour force

When a woman has the option to work out or not (usually if male support or kin support is available), her own perceptions of outside work will determine whether or not she enters the formal labour force. Her ability to 'turn han' or make a living in the informal sector might also significantly affect her decision. In many cases the status of even the employed is perceived by working-class women as marginal and insecure. 'For while the nature of female employment may have changed over the last century, as economic production has shifted from the canefields to the cities, the quality of work available to most women is still characterised by excessive drudgery' (Patricia Anderson WICP 1984, p. xiii). It is not surprising therefore that 'working-class women place a very low evaluation on the paid employment open to them, although they are preoccupied with establishing some degree of economic independence'.

Their jobs in garment factories, assembly plants or hotels are often subject to lay-offs, lack of paid maternity leave, the frustration of 'piece work', low wages and inflexible working hours, compounded by distance from work and transportation difficulties. Many women — like men — are also conscious of class and racial exploitation at the workplace. As one young woman, who became a shop steward, bitterly remarked of her employers of many years:

> These people don't care about black people you know, they want you to work and they make their money, they got you as some sort of machine that they plug in and make money for them . . . sometimes they get angry with the girls and so, the things they say to you, especially one day the wife said 'she sorry that Hitler or something don't wipe us out', I think that's what she said. Sometimes the girls they even get sick on the job and they really don't show much interest you know, so that is why I say they don't care.

Even if seeking employment is a woman's first strategy for survival, the likelihood of her finding a job in the first place is low; lack of education, skills and occupational training limit her options; the jobs available are usually low-paying and perceived as unattractive, and household instability might prevent her from keeping the job for any length of time. For the first-time job-seeker, the experience can be frustrating and pointless, representing a discouraging introduction to the world of work. One young woman in the WICP survey, who on leaving school sent off many job applications, said she 'felt bad', i.e. humiliated, when she had no replies, a common enough situation when employers are flooded with unsolicited job applications.

Because of the small size of island societies and the way limited resources are allocated, many perceive employment as a favour to be handed out by those in power and themselves as powerless unless they have 'pull' or contacts. One woman, who encouraged her daughter to get a job in the public sector, remarked, 'she says she would want to go by the Post Office or do office work but it is so difficult to get in the first place, if you don't back the Party you don't get by'. Another speaks of trying to get a job through a 'good friend' who had political connections. A 41-year-old Antiguan woman with primary education articulated her frustrations in terms of the social structure. Her applications to enter a hospital to study nursing were repeatedly turned down:

> **R.** They all filled-up, they will say the same thing. They say wait and see and they will send and call you. And you will wait and wait and they will never call.
>
> **I.** So from the time you left school at 17 you're applying to the hospital and that didn't come through. What did you do?
>
> **R.** Nothing.
>
> **I.** So you stayed at home? ·
>
> **R.** Yes . . . Well I tried other places to get something else to do but it was so hard in those days to get a job, you know, you will have to be a picked-out person, Mistress-this or Mistress-that daughter and they will push you up that kind of way. You have to have somebody to really push you forward to get a job in those days.

The current employment situation throughout the Caribbean is grim even for high school graduates, and for the uneducated, unskilled young woman sometimes almost hopeless; the highest unemployment rates are among this group. An unemployed 22-year-old Barbadian who had attended secondary school described the frustrations:

> **R.** Sometimes I feel real confuse and miserable and thing and I home every day and ain't got nothing to do. You does get fed up. Everyday just get up and cook and wash. Just days wasting like that. I feel I should be working, man, get up in the mornings and bathe and wash, to work and come back again.

I. Do you think if you had stayed in school and taken the exam you would have gotten through with it? Were you good in school?

R. Yes. But my cousin, she got certificates too, right. And she was home for a long time until she mother got a job for she in a hotel.

Domestic labour

Frequently domestic labour is all that is available to the young school-leaver. The widespread involvement of Caribbean women in this type of labour dates back to emancipation when many women were forced to exchange 'the oppressions of the canefields for those of the city's kitchens' (Mathurin 1977, p. 5). There, as one observer of the 1890s put it, 'the lash of the tongue was exchanged for the lash of the whip' (Livingstone 1899).

The high level of female employment in 'service' occupations has continued unabated; much of this 'service' is domestic labour in private homes and institutions and in the hotel industry. In Jamaica, for instance, in the censuses of 1946, 1960 and 1970, the service industry was consistently the largest employer of female labour — absorbing over 50 per cent. The 'femaleness' of this occupation can be highlighted by the fact that in 1970 in Jamaica, while there were 4,293 men in domestic service, there were more than 10 times as many women — 43,690 (Boland 1974, pp. 75-6).

Part of this condition is structurally determined; an oversupply of female labour ensures that women remain in the most marginalized, lowest-paid occupations. Such occupations require a high degree of labour mobility:

> The availability of jobs as well as the dire need for employment shift women from rural to urban communities, from the smaller to the larger Caribbean islands, and from the Caribbean itself to such countries as the United States and Canada (where female migrants are engaged in domestic service). A significant point about this shift of labour is that it involves many young women between the ages 18 to 25.
>
> (Mohammed 1983, p. 2)

The Moyne Commission highlighted some conditions of the female domestic in 1939:

> The normal working day of the domestic servant is from 6 a.m. to 9 p.m. She depends upon the goodwill of her employer for any sick leave, annual holiday or other time of release from duty. Workmen's Compensation, where it does exist, does not apply to her . . . The wages of the domestic servant range between 6s. and 12s. a week, out of which she has usually to feed and house herself; they are sometimes as low as 1s. 6d. a week in rural districts where food is supplied. The average rent of the poorest room in the city is about 2s. a week . . . it is not surprising that some of them are 'helped' by men, who make a small contribution to the weekly budget and share the room as 'visitors'. For those who, growing old, get no such assistance, undernourishment amounting to starvation is inevitable
>
> (GB: West India Royal Commission 1945, p. 219).

The round of activities associated with domestic labour today was described by a young Antiguan who entered domestic service while she was still a schoolgirl:

I. Where did you work?

R. At teacher house. I would go down six o'clock in the morning, the bell ring at nine for school so I'll work up until that hour. I'll walk with my clothes and I'll bathe down there and then I'll go off to school and the school is just two blocks from where I was working.

I. How much did you get paid?

R. Ten dollars a month.

I. What kinds of things did you do?

R. Wash, cook, iron.

I. You do that every day?

R. Every day because she have a baby and you know people in those days wanted everything to press [ironed]. Regardless of what it is, they want it pressed. So you have to do that. Then you have to get the breakfast ready for him [the husband] to go to work for eight o'clock. And the father has to go down in the shop, the wife has to go to teach so she has to be there at nine. When the bell rings she has to be over at the school.

I. How old were you then?

R. I was about fifteen.

I. How did you feel about this job?

R. Well, they came and ask my mother if I could come and give her some assistance, my mother said yes and I go, I had to go back home, look after my mother business, in the afternoon. When I finish cook at home I'll get down about four o'clock and stay until about seven, half past seven. My mother come and follow me up and then we would go home and sleep until the next morning.

I. So you weren't in school?

R. Yes. I was in school, had to be in school for nine.

I. So you would get there at six, work until nine, then go to school and . . .

R. Well I had to go back over there to prepare the lunch, so we get break at 11 o'clock, I'll take my break, time to go home and finish up the pot, right. If I'm cooking fungie I'll go over and put on the upper pot and by the time the bell going to ring for twelve she will give the sign and I will go over and fix up, and that's how I get through.

She continued in this job till she was 17, when she got another domestic job where she worked from 7 a.m. to 7 p.m., after which she had a long trek home.

A 35-year-old Vincentian described her first job as a teenager some 20 years ago. She worked, she said, every day of the week:

I. Even Sunday?

R. Every day of the week.

I. So you worked Monday through Sunday?

R. Yes.

I. And what time did you have to get there?

R. Six thirty on mornings.

I. Six thirty in the morning and you worked until what time?

R. Six o'clock in the evening, or so.

I. What were your duties?

R. Wash, cook, clean out, iron and see about a little boy, two children.

In many parts of the Caribbean today, the situation of the domestic worker has improved only marginally. In only a few Caribbean countries are domestic workers protected by minimum wage conditions or stipulated working hours (see Mohammed 1983). Over the last decade or so the plight of domestic workers has been highlighted by attempts (largely unsuccessful) to organize them in trade unions (Trinidad) and by making them the special subject of documentary theatre (Sistren Theatre Collective of Jamaica). Public consciousness regarding this type of labour has been raised somewhat through debates which have taken place in the territories where minimum-wage legislation has been enacted.

Nevertheless the situation of domestic workers even in territories which have passed legislation is still precarious. One of the major issues relates to the general negative attitudes towards this type of worker, especially that domestics are 'less deserving of the respect paid to any other worker' and that housework 'comprises non-work' (Mohammed 1983). Minimum wages for domestics are set below minimum wages for other categories of workers; they do not have available support services such as day-care centres for their own children, are excluded from workmen's compensation laws and belong to no union organization.

In an age when 'sisterhood' of all women is projected as an important weapon in the struggle for female equality, antagonisms between the region's women are most fully revealed in the interaction between female employers and their domestic helpers. A study in Trinidad in 1975, one of the few ever done, highlighted some of the complaints, and concluded that 'there exists a strong element of distrust between employer and employee, one which is rooted in the class difference between these women' (Mohammed 1983).

Domestic work does represent the first job for many Caribbean women and for some remains a lifetime occupation. This occupation involves significant migration of labour, especially of young women between 18 and 25 and in situations where supply exceeds demand, creates an easily expendable labour force characterized by low wages and oppressive working conditions.

Export-processing industries

Some of these characteristics also attach to the newest development in terms of large-scale female employment in the 'modern' sector — export-processing industries in 'free production zones' being created in Third World countries, most recently in the Caribbean basin. Export-processing represents a new stage in the international division of labour (Safa 1983) by which labour-intensive assembly plants are located in underdeveloped countries to produce goods solely for export to advanced industrial countries. The attraction of the Third World for these enterprises is cheap labour, particularly female labour, which constitutes approximately 80 per cent of the workforce in these zones (Stone 1985). The export-processing industry seeks out areas of high unemployment where a docile labour force can be obtained; younger women are considered more pliant and manageable. These preferences are revealed in a survey of these operations in the eastern Caribbean (Safa 1983). The study identified other characteristics of this type of employment: 'In some areas workers are forced to serve an apprenticeship, which can last as long as six months, during which they receive only half the normal rate . . . Many women are kept on temporary contracts and are periodically discharged in order to circumvent the fringe benefits due a permanent worker such as sick leave, vacation time, and severance pay.' There is often a high rate of turnover, estimated to run as high as 300 per cent in one eastern Caribbean plant:

> workers may be fired for being unable to meet their production quotas or for frequent absenteeism. Among women workers absenteeism is often due to family reasons such as sickness, yet there are virtually no medical or child-care facilities associated with these industries. They also suffer from lack of transport, cafeterias and lunch-rooms and recreational facilities . . . advancement on the job is limited, since the reduced number of technical or supervisory positions are usually filled by men, who are usually foreigners.
> (Safa 1983, p. 5)

Such situations are leading to new stresses and strains for the region's women. In most areas, these plants represent the women's first introduction to industrialization and its demands, and are leading, some claim, to a dehumanized and alienated workforce. Part of the problem stems from the fact that workers and management start off with different cultural expectations about work. As Victoria Durant-Gonzalez notes (1985): 'Typically, when industrial work is introduced into a formerly non-industrialised economy, companies and governments only make provision for the acquisition of production skills and production knowledge related to these skills. The need for training in work habits and attitudes is not recognised.' The situation as described in Jamaica might bear this out:

These Free Zone enterprises are accustomed to functioning with severe work pressure, highly disciplined labour, long and arduous work hours, docile workers, high production targets, and freedom to dispose of workers whose production or behaviour fall out of line. These are indeed high stress and very exacting work environments that contrast sharply with the casual, easy going, low work norms and low stress environments to be found in most Jamaican-run factories or other work situations.

(Stone 1985)

The actual work usually involves the development of speed and accuracy as women struggle at routine assembly-line tasks to meet daily production targets, prevented by stringent company regulations from talking to co-workers or from taking breaks at other than set times. Additionally, some of the industries, especially electronics, are found to pose specific health hazards.

But women must work, especially in situations where they are forced into the job market by male unemployment or are entirely without male support. The responsibility of motherhood is a critical factor in pressuring women to enter the job market. As a Jamaican newspaper columnist expressed the 'real issue' for the region's women: 'where cheap labour co-exists with very high levels of open unemployment, the real issue is whether such cheap labour jobs are better than the condition of joblessness into which the 3,000 workers would sink if the Free Zone were to be shut down' (Stone 1985). But equally germane issues might be the social and health costs involved and the need by the region's governments and the industries they attract to recognize these and to attempt to ameliorate the negative conditions associated with this form of labour.

When women, especially those at the bottom of the educational ladder, put all these negative perceptions and experiences of wage labour together, the search for a job can appear a meaningless and unattractive exercise. Of course, not all of these work-related problems are women-centred. But a woman's occupational status is often affected by domestic conditions and how far she is able to juggle work/household demands, as well as how she perceives the job market. If conditions for wage labour are perceived by her as unattractive, then she will concentrate on other strategies:

Yes, I stopped working. I worked about eight years or so. I stopped work because I getting to find that you just working for people, you ain't getting any money, so I just sit down and after my husband get a job, I said, look here, let me stay home and take care of the home . . . his work is very small you see, but you have to satisfy.

The widespread lack of day-care facilities for children also affects a woman's ability to get and keep a job and become a productive member of the workforce. A key element will be how far she can rely on kin and friendship networks. If such assistance is not available or arrangements break down, then the job which has been sought for so long and whose acquisition is so precious will not necessarily last.

Unanticipated changes in household arrangements will severely limit women's participation in the workforce — ill-health of partner, birth of baby, eviction and pregnancy are some of the pressing problems that might require immediate attention to the exclusion of wage-earning activities (Barrow WICP 1986a). Despite all of these negative factors, Caribbean women nevertheless form a substantial portion of the working population and the last few decades have seen a remarkable increase in the options open to them.

Occupational status

Up to the Second World War, women had access to a very narrow range of occupations compared with men. There was no demand for women workers outside strictly defined categories. For instance, in Barbados in the 1920s, 80 per cent of the adult female working population was engaged in only three occupations — agricultural labour, domestic service and as milliners and seamstresses. Laundresses, hawkers and peddlers accounted for 15 per cent. Less than 1 per cent of the working women in Barbados at that time were employed as teachers/governesses and 1.06 per cent as clerks (Massiah WICP 1986a).

Following widespread riots in the 1930s and the report of the Moyne Commission, the various territories in the post-war years began to implement many of its recommendations to ameliorate social and economic conditions. This led to a broadening of the economic base and consequent enlargement of the occupational structure, a trend which accelerated as these territories moved increasingly towards greater autonomy from Britain. Such changes included a shift from agriculture to the development of industry and large-scale infrastructural undertakings, a rapid expansion of the public sector and the broadening of the educational base. Women especially have benefited from improved access to education: in Barbados during the 1960s, for instance, the proportion of women exposed to secondary education increased from 15 to 71 per cent (Barrow WICP 1986a). The post-war demand for highly skilled and better-educated labourers coincided with women's greater access to educational opportunities.

Caribbean women have a high rate of participation in the regional labour force and there are indications that this is increasing, although there are still far more male workers. The female labour-force rate[3] ranged from 18 to 55 per cent in 1960 and 18 to 44 per cent in 1970 — well in excess of rates of 15 per cent for Latin America, 24 per cent for Africa and 29 per cent for Asia recorded in 1975. More recent data available for only one country (Barbados) show a female labour force rate of 44.9 per cent. It is possible that similar trends are operating in other countries of the region in view of the economic diversification which is taking place (Massiah WICP 1986a).

A particularly striking trend has been the decline of women agricultural labourers. Throughout the Caribbean, agriculture has ceased to be a major employer of labour, declining overall from around 30 per cent in 1946 to just under 10 per cent in 1980. Women were particularly affected by the mechanization of the labour-intensive tasks in which they predominated. The female decline was from 27.4 to 8.3 per cent. While fewer women are now engaged in agriculture, their participation is still significant in the smaller territories — St Lucia, Grenada, Dominica and St Kitts. In the WICP survey, the highest female worker rate recorded for agriculture (Barbados) was 10.4 per cent. The shift away from agriculture has also been accelerated by the advent of new options, represented by jobs in manufacturing and other 'modern' sectors.

---

3 The labour force includes both the working population and the unemployed.

Table 6.2 Proportion of Women in Working Population, 1891–1980

Territory	1891	1901	1911	1921	1931	1946	1960	1970	1980
Jamaica	50.9	—	46.3	49.5	—	33.8	37.1	32.5	39.2
Trinidad & Tobago	41.5	41.0	40.1	41.0	33.2	24.9	26.2	25.0	30.4
Guyana	41.2	—	44.1	43.1	33.5	27.8	22.7	19.0	22.7
Belize	[ ]	n/a	[ ]	15.9	14.4	18.6	17.9	19.0	19.9
Barbados	57.0	—	61.6	61.4	—	45.5	41.0	39.3	42.6
Dominica	56.7	—	n/a	n/a	—	43.8	43.4	37.2	32.8
Grenada	49.2	50.2	53.6	58.2	—	48.2	39.5	37.8	37.5
St Lucia	n/a	n/a	53.8	42.8	—	43.0	36.4	35.1	37.0
St Vincent	n/a	—	56.3	58.6	51.8	45.1	38.8	35.4	34.5
Antigua	51.5	—	[ ]	n/a	—	45.3	37.2*	—	39.7*
British Virgin Is.	50.2	—	[ ]	[ ]	—	14.1	18.2	26.6	39.1
Montserrat	56.1	—	[ ]	n/a	—	51.1	44.0	34.9	39.0
St Kitts	53.1	—	56.3	61.0	—	44.9	39.7	37.7	39.6
High	57.0	50.2	61.6	61.4	51.8	51.1	44.0	39.3	42.6
Low	41.2	41.0	40.1	15.9	14.4	14.1	17.9	19.0	19.9

Source: relevant census reports.
Notes: Women in Working Population refers to the number of women in the working popu-
lation as a proportion of the total working population.
n/a Data not available by sex.
Blank cells [ ] denote census taken but data not available.
— Census not taken
* See notes to Table 6.1

As women's presence in the fields has declined, their places in offices have
increased, a move facilitated by rising levels of education and an increase in female-
oriented white-collar jobs. Clerical and service occupations are the two areas in
which there are now proportionately more women than men. Fifty-three per cent
of the clerical workers in the region are women, ranging from a high of 80 per cent
in the Cayman Islands to 38 per cent in Guyana. The service sector has also been
increasing steadily and women dominate it. Two-thirds of regional service workers
are women, with a range of 73 per cent (St Kitts) to 48 per cent (Guyana). However,
most regional service workers are in fact 'domestics' — almost three-fifths of such
workers on the island of Barbados — or hotel workers.

Women constitute a large proportion of professional workers — just under half
(47 per cent). But the majority are in low-paid professions which have come to be
regarded as mainly 'female', such as teaching and nursing. While women are
increasingly breaking into the older professions such as medicine and law, they are
still highly under-represented. And women are still such a novelty in some fields
that Caribbean newspapers still feature as 'firsts' women breaking into traditionally
'male' occupations such as engineering, architecture, surveying or motor mechanics.

Nearly half (46 per cent) of those classified as technical and sales workers are also
women. In most territories this category embraces women who function as hawkers
or higglers, peddlers or street vendors, occupations traditionally associated with
females. There is, however, an increase in salespersons — mainly sales assistants
in commercial and industrial enterprises in the formal sector.

Analysis of both censual and WICP data confirms that despite the post-war
breakthroughs and despite individual achievements, the regional labour force still
remains highly sex-stratified and females are still concentrated in marginalized,
low-paid jobs. Although there is legislation in most territories guaranteeing equal

pay for equal work, women are still nevertheless regarded as a source of cheap labour. Their position as household heads places them in a position to be exploited since, for many, the need to feed the children transcends everything — including militant concerns and the defence of 'rights'. For those women at the bottom of the ladder, there is little social mobility or escape from poverty. As described in earlier chapters, in many cases the cycle keeps going from mother to daughter.

Research (see, for example, Gill WICP 1984 for Barbados) has shown that the process of 'modernization' has not worked to the benefit of women at the lower end of the employment spectrum and, indeed, might be contributing to their marginalization. For they do not have the qualifications necessary for the white-collar jobs which are becoming available but enough alternative jobs are not being provided to absorb those displaced from agriculture and other traditional activities by mechanization and other processes associated with modernization.

Jobs which are being created in the modern industrial sector are either male-oriented, that is, require technical skills not yet acquired by women, or are recognizably 'female work', often representing piece work and other forms of sweated labour in, for example, the garment industry and increasingly in offshore export-oriented enclaves.

At the other end of the employment spectrum, the largest number of women are congregated in low-paid but higher-status 'female' occupations. They are teachers and nurses, typists, telephone operators, secretaries and clerks. Women in large numbers are noticeably absent from production and administrative occupations.

Women also have the highest levels of unemployment. For instance, in Jamaica in 1982 while the overall unemployment rate stood at 27.4 per cent, female unemployment was 40.4 per cent, compared with 17 per cent for males. Women in the age group 15–29 constituted 75 per cent of the unemployed.

Although most territories have passed 'equal pay' legislation, it is still recognized that in most occupational categories women are discriminated against in pay and perquisites and promotional opportunities, though these beliefs are hard to verify. Additionally, even leaders of male-dominated trade unions are beginning to speak openly of 'sexual harrassment' at the workplace and the need to combat it (see, for example, Jamaica's *Daily Gleaner* 2 April 1985, p. 1).

These facts might well describe the status of women in many societies. But in the Caribbean they are thrown into high relief because of the inordinate burden of maintaining their families that is placed on women. The high labour-force activity rate is not motivated by the desire to escape domestic boredom or to augment the family income; women's labour often represents the only income, the source of food for the family pot, the roof overhead, clothes on the backs of children — and sometimes of other dependent family members.

As we have seen (chapter 5) female household heads are responsible for maintaining a minimum of four dependants, more if the household contains other kin, as is often the case. Half of the households headed by women have no resident males and women themselves are ill-equipped to cope on the job market: over 88 per cent of them have no more than primary schooling; only one-third are in full-time paid employment and a significant number of these work as domestics, earning the minimum wage in their respective countries. As they are often outside the purview of labour laws and belong to no union organization, they derive few benefits from improved working conditions in the society as a whole.

Gender-role stereotyping in education has contributed to discrimination in the vocational education offered to boys and girls, equipping boys far more than girls for jobs in the modern industrial sector where the demand is for technical and technological skills. This factor, coupled with gender-role stereotyping in the market-place, ensures that the overall status of women workers in the region is still considerably below that of men.

Nevertheless, the overall status of women in the workforce is far superior to what it was 20–30 years ago. Women on the whole have shared in the diversification of occupational status and the shift from rural to urban areas brought about by the process of modernization and from the broadening of educational opportunities. In the larger territories, women are now coming to occupy key roles in business and the higher ranks of the civil service, are becoming active in the professions and play a leading role in cultural organizations (see, for example, Leo-Rhynie and Hamilton 1983).

There are unfortunately very few data available at this stage on some key issues affecting the roles and status of women in the higher levels of the labour force. For instance, we have no information on how women who are in middle and top management positions in their respective countries got there, what factors contributed to their mobility, how far they have gone or will be able to go within the system, and what are the constraints on themselves or other women. We do not know how these women are perceived by employers, employees, male or female co-workers, or by themselves. We do not know the extent of the discrimination against women in matters of wages, promotions and other issues, though we do know that discrimination exists (see Leo-Rhynie and Hamilton 1983).

Characteristics of working women

What are the characteristics of women in the formal labour force? The WICP survey supplemented by censual and other data for all territories enable us to draw a profile of the Caribbean working woman.

Employment status   The woman who works out is most likely to be single and better educated, with fewer children, than the housebound woman. She emerges as a steady and reliable worker. Most are in white-collar jobs — clerical, secretarial, sales — in professions such as nursing and teaching, or in service occupations, mainly domestic labour.

Most women in the labour force work full-time, i.e. for 40 hours or more each week. Between 76 and 90 per cent of the women in the WICP sample were so employed. Most work for others, i.e. for wages and salaries provided either by an employer or a family member. In the 1970 census, paid employment was the status of 81 per cent of all female workers. Own-account workers represented 17 per cent, with the highest proportions — one-fifth — in Jamaica and St Lucia.

The larger the territory, it seems, the larger the bureaucracy and the more likely women will secure government jobs. Thus in the Cayman Islands only 22 per cent of government employees were women compared with 40 per cent in Jamaica.

Education   The most significant finding of the WICP survey is that, in general, the better educated the woman, the more likely she is to be employed. There is also close correlation between educational attainment and type of job. Women with a primary education are heavily concentrated in service and agricultural jobs (Barbados 70.9 per cent, St Vincent 43.5 per cent), and in service and production jobs (76.2 per cent) in Antigua. Women with a secondary education are mainly located in clerical jobs (53.5 per cent in Antigua, 41.2 per cent in St Vincent, 32.4 per cent in Barbados). Women with tertiary education are found mainly in professional jobs such as teaching and nursing (79 per cent in Antigua and over 50 per cent in Barbados and St Vincent).

For the region as a whole, women are educationally slightly better qualified than males. According to census data, the majority of the workforce have no formal educational qualifications — but 87 per cent of males compared with 77 per cent of females are unqualified. Two-fifths of workers with school-leaving certificates and virtually half the workers with four GCE O-level passes (regarded as the minimum entry requirement into the skilled section of the workforce) are women. A small number of the workforce possess GCE A-level certificates; women represent roughly one-third of these. At higher educational levels, women possess two-fifths of the diplomas but only one-fifth of the degrees.

Age The profile of the woman in the workforce which emerged from the WICP sample is that of an older woman. The high participation rate of older women might be a reflection of the difficulty that young women experience in landing their first jobs. It is significant that, except in the case of St Vincent, Caribbean women continue to be actively employed during their prime reproductive years (Roberts 1975).

Union status Women living with men are less likely to work out than women living alone, with lowest rates of worker participation among married women. This pattern holds for both urban and rural workers. Women in residential unions tended to be far more involved in home-based economic activities than women in visiting or single unions. What is significant is the high level of economic activity displayed by women without resident male partners, women who are for the most part household heads.

Motherhood There is also a correlation between motherhood and employment. Over 80 per cent of all women interviewed by the WICP were mothers; the majority of them were found to stay at home and engage in home production or home services. Put another way, 90 per cent of the housebound women in Barbados and 100 per cent in St Vincent were found to be mothers. Of women who worked out, between 75 and 77 per cent had children. The number of children seems to be a determinant of whether or not the mother stays at home. Mothers employed by others had the lowest number of children: 3.3 in Antigua and 4.3 in St Vincent. Mothers engaged in home services and home production had between 4.3 and 4.8 children, though St Vincent women having their own business had an average of 6.1 children. In Barbados there was little difference in the number of children per mother between employed and not employed. These findings might also be taken as indicative of the lowering effect which employment away from home has on fertility levels.

Reliability Women in the sample were generally found to be steady and stable workers. More than half of those with jobs had never been out of a job from the time they first started working. The majority interviewed had been in their present jobs for over 5 years. Twenty per cent of employed women had held their jobs for 5–9 years and 25 per cent for over 10 years.

The length of time in the job varies according to occupation and may be indicative of changing opportunities. Women employed for 10 years and over are located in the professional fields in Antigua and St Vincent, in service (10–19 years) and agriculture (over 20 years) in Barbados. These reflect occupations for which greatest opportunities existed at the time these women entered the labour force. Women in service and clerical occupations employed for less than a year (Barbados: 31.3 per cent, Antigua 45.5 per cent, St Vincent 26.9 per cent) are reflecting a current demand for female labour in these areas, with the growing importance to their economies of the commercial sector.

Measures of job satisfaction

To explore further the female perception and experience of work, the WICP also sought to examine what aspects of a woman's job gave most and least satisfaction. It was found that the things that women like best relate to the nature of the job itself and to social relationships associated with the job. Thus the opportunities the job offered to help others, to increase general knowledge, to meet people and to develop skills were all important. Interpersonal relations account for one-quarter of the responses in all three territories. Thus 'the people you work with' and 'the boss' are important elements in job satisfaction. Only about 10 per cent cited wages/salaries. The reasons for this could be that many women work out of necessity and have no choice as regards salaries, or that women have not yet been socialized to place monetary value on their labour.

Levels of job dissatisfaction were generally low. Only one-quarter to one-third of the respondents said that they disliked their jobs. The level of wages was the greatest source of dissatisfaction and better-educated women in clerical and secretarial positions were most vocal on this point. Dullness of the job, lack of recognition for their efforts and lack of opportunities for advancement were cited by a sizeable group of women: 26 per cent in Barbados, 16 per cent in Antigua and St Vincent. Despite the fact that women in the sample group lived fairly close to their workplace — no more than 2.9 miles at the maximum — fully 10 per cent of women cited job location as an item they disliked most about their work. What these findings show is that, in their work as in other areas of their lives, these women set a high value on the social element.

Generally speaking, Caribbean women place a high value on economic independence, perceive work in positive terms and consider it important to their self-image. Although some women support the sexual division of labour and regard housework as 'woman's lot' rather than work, many feel that whatever they do which contributes to total family welfare should be categorized as work. Caribbean women, like women elsewhere, have in the past had a low evaluation placed on their economic contribution because of the way labour is officially measured with gross national product regarded as the main index of development. The WICP has tested other measures which would give a more accurate rendering of women's status in the labour force and their contribution to economic development.

Although women's ideal is for a 'good job' — preferably white-collar — the work experience of most women is restricted to menial, low-paying jobs or joblessness. Efforts to decrease female unemployment by the introduction of export-processing enclaves to the Caribbean basin are introducing at the same time certain negative conditions as a formerly unsophisticated workforce of mainly very young women struggle without adequate preparation to meet the relentless demands of industrialization.

There are many constraints against women entering the labour-market — inadequate education, skills and training, role conflicts which cannot easily be resolved because of a lack of support systems for women workers such as child-care facilities. But, as we shall see in the next chapter, women's broad-based elaboration of strategies for the survival of themselves and their families goes far beyond the possibilities offered by wage labour.

7 'Making Do'

Survival strategies

Lorna Goodison's poem 'My mother' is quoted as the epigraph to this book because it describes so graphically a familiar Caribbean role model: the woman as miracle worker, an adept at making something from nothing. The first thing about household management that poor Caribbean girls learn from their mothers and grannies is 'making do'. In Caribbean folk culture, the woman who is 'wutless', i.e. unable to cope with her household responsibilities, is derided. The folk song 'Sambo gal' counsels:

> Hand full a ring and she can't do a ting
> Send she back to she mumma-o

Most Caribbean women are faced with problems related to the survival of their households and with developing strategies for coping. As Victoria Durant-Gonzalez expresses it, 'In the English-speaking Caribbean, an overwhelming majority of the female population is in charge of producing, providing, controlling or managing those resources essential to meeting daily needs' (Durant-Gonzalez WICP 1982, p. 3). Their 'sources of livelihood'[1] extend far beyond conventional concepts of 'work' and the 'labour force'.

Women's strategies for survival or 'making do' also include self-employment, 'scuffling', and other sources identified in the WICP study as male support, kin and friendship networks, pooling resources in the family home, support from adult working children and institutional benefits, all of which will be examined in this chapter.

'Making do'

'Making do' expresses a social phenomenon which is widely accepted: that it is a fundamental role of poor women to make do with what they have or, better still, 'make something from nothing' in order to maintain their families. At its simplest level, 'making do' involves 'cutting and carving' or 'cutting and contriving', i.e being resourceful in using whatever is available to maximize its utility to oneself and

---

1 The WICP devised the concept 'sources of livelihood' to better explain the varied sources women tap for support and to extend notions of 'work' and 'labour' beyond wage labour.

family — the challenge to poor women everywhere. In some cases, 'making do' represents personal denial and sacrifice. As an Antiguan woman explained:

> **R.** The West Indian term 'make do' is, if you haven't got food, you have a little cornmeal even if you have to put a little white flour in it, a little butter, and you fix it up nicely for your children, you make do and they eat it and you strengthen their little stomach. Make do. West Indian women have had to learn to make do and if there is one West Indian woman who has learned a lot of making do . . .
>
> **I.** Is you?
>
> **R.** I am telling you in the raw West Indian term, I have learnt to live without a toilet in my yard sometimes, I have to go to the bush, yes. I have a toilet here today but I have had to make do. I bake on my coal pot, yes. Sometimes I have to cook with wood, things that I have not been brought up in.

A Barbadian recalled her early days of hardship:

> **R.** It wasn't very easy. Sometimes my skirts, I would cut them, heavy material — drill and things like that — and turn them into pants for them [her children]. Sometimes they look good, sometimes they don't, but . . .
>
> **I.** You didn't have any choice.
>
> **R.** No choice at all. You know sometimes I sit down and tell them these things and they don't like to hear them at all. Sometimes they make a joke of it and some say I mustn't tell them, they don't like to hear about it and so on. Those days wasn't very easy at all, things you really wanted to give them to eat you couldn't afford it. Many days I used to cry, boy.

In these examples we see that 'making do' at one level involves resourcefulness, endurance and sacrifice. The concept also embodies the ability to earn a 'little something', which is what women call 'turn han' or 'making a dollar bill'. Women who do not have regular jobs will turn to many other ways of earning or supplementing incomes which will contribute to total family welfare. Frequently such activity represents the struggle of the woman to maintain a 'respectable' status for the family by augmenting her partner's contribution. A woman in her fifties, now a successful businesswoman, describes, first, the nature of her mother's struggles, and then something of her own:

> She did selling. She use to do a little sewing too, a little hand machine you know, but it wasn't much and having a lot of children . . . she had seventeen children. She raised ten. So she had to look for something else to do to help look after them. To buy and sell. My father had a little plot of land that he had rented so he planted it up so that she could get the provision to sell to help raise the children. She used to send us to Sunday School every Sunday. Sometimes when she can, take us to church. My father he had opened a little account at Harrisons [a store] for us to get clothing and she would make her clothes. We raised sheep and goats. We were lucky with goats; we would always have some milk. We had a cow, and she had some fowls, and you get eggs and so on. Every Saturday she would go into town to sell and she bring home groceries. You see her with some big baskets with groceries, man. Packed down the larder.

Our informant spent most of her childhood caring for her siblings while her mother worked, and dropped out of school at 12. She spent two years as an apprentice dressmaker and then, until she was 19, worked as a domestic. She left to get married and resumed sewing to augment the family income. Her husband had five children, whom she raised after their mother died. In all, she had 10 children of her own, five of whom survived to adulthood. She speaks of the days of hardship in her early married life:

I. You were doing sewing?

R. Yes. We bought the machine and we had to service the machine, had to pay down twenty-four dollars to get the machine, then to pay eight dollars a month and I tell you, it was hard. Went into town with a bus fare and twenty-four dollars and I didn't get the machine and I was so hurt I stood up next door to the place and I cry.

I. So how did you get it, when did you get it?

R. The same gentleman I used to work with, he helped me to get it then. When I think about it, I just stand and feel funny, you know. Nothing to eat. Hungry. Nothing to eat and in big Bridgetown waiting for an evening bus. You go morning and you didn't have a bus coming back until late evening. I tell you, it was very painful then.

A Vincentian, now in her seventies, an arrowroot estate worker whose son died suddenly in another island, brought home his four infant children and their mother to live with her. She describes some of their strategies for 'making do'. She started out her daughter-in-law in peddling while she continued to work. Their pooled resources maintained the family and, as the children got older, she sought help from relatives overseas. First, she sold a small house belonging to her son and for her daughter-in-law:

I bought a little coal and a little oil and a little matches and a little everything and I tell her she can go ahead turning it over while I work to keep the children. It worked out well because by she turn over this little thing, I'll get a few bags of coal, I'll bring it then she'll sell it by the measure. The oil, the matches, and the like. So that always keep her with a little few cents and then when I work I bring it and put it down there. And so we make a living.

So deeply ingrained is the habit of 'making do' that, when asked what she would do if she could live her life over, a St Vincent washerwoman expressed her desire in this way:

In my new life I will just stop home and work for myself. I would just take up a tray, sell a little ground nuts and little corn curls and every little thing and sit down at home and work for myself that time, don't work for nobody else again. Neither [wash] clothes, go by the road or nothing, sit down home and work for yourself, you see.

An Antiguan cultivator with seven children ranging in age from 4 to 19 was asked what 'making do' meant to her: 'I try to make like, it's really rough sometimes but I try to manage it. I work the farm, go to the town and sell my vegetables and buy me little food and bring back home for them. The father give me the money, [I] take out bus fare and their lunch money [and] that is it.'

We see from these examples that a woman might turn her hand to several different activities at one time. However, the strategies so far described are more or less marginal activities or 'turn han', a turning to whatever opportunity presents itself to 'make a smalls' or earn a little money. Such strategies might involve selling to passers-by fruit or vegetables from the family backyard, making sweets, preserves, cakes or coconut oil for sale, occasional baby-sitting, sewing, providing laundry or other services, making handicrafts in a minor way. These may not necessarily involve cash exchanges but other forms of payment, including reciprocal ones.

Self-employment

Many women engage in self-employment in a more organized and sustained way. The classic archetype is of course the 'higgler' or 'huckster', who supplies the local markets with food. Throughout the Caribbean, the higgler has become a formidable personality, a symbol of female independence. Her life and economic activities have been the subject of several studies (e.g. Mintz 1955, 1971; Katzin 1959, 1960; Durant-Gonzalez 1976, 1983).

The practice of higglering goes back to the days of slavery when in the larger islands slaves were allowed to produce food for their own consumption on back lands not used for sugar cultivation. They were allowed to sell the surplus. The tradition that the men did the cultivation and the women the marketing continued after slavery ended. In time, the market-woman or higgler in the tradition of the 'market mammy' of West Africa became a formidable link in the food distribution chain. In 1975 a Jamaican government minister told parliament that country higglers contributed 80 per cent of the fruits and vegetables consumed in Jamaica. Victoria Durant-Gonzalez, who was engaged in a study of higglers at the time, noted that this was not an over estimation (Durant-Gonzalez WICP 1982).

In her study of the business of higglering, Durant-Gonzalez noted that it is a well-established occupation with its own performance-ranking systems, skills and methods of recruitment, offering special options and rewards to the women who participate in it (Durant-Gonzalez 1976, 1983).

Higglers are entrepreneurs of the informal sector (Bell 1985); they serve a vital function as intermediaries in the internal economic system (see Mintz 1971) and provide a linkage with international trade (e.g. 'informal commercial importers' of Jamaica, 'traffickers' of the eastern Caribbean). Buying or selling or trading in whatever form is an activity which is common to Caribbean women and is a skill which can be traced to the West African ancestry of much of the population.

To examine the dynamics of self-employment, the WICP included in its survey questions relating to such activity. Women in the self-employed group were defined as those who operate a business enterprise within or outside their homes as their main or sole income-earning activity. The WICP regarded the scale of the enterprise and the presence or absence of paid help as irrelevant. What mattered was that the woman was engaged in income-earning activity organized and executed by herself.

Of the total number surveyed, only a few in the three territories were engaged in self-employment: between 6 and 12 per cent of the sample. These women were equally distributed in rural and urban areas, had a higher mean age than women employed by others, had a basic primary education and lived mainly in married unions and simple family households. They also had a relatively large number of children.

What kinds of activities are these women engaged in? The main activity was found to be dressmaking in Barbados and Antigua and farming in St Vincent, with smaller numbers in all three territories engaged in food and beverage production, shop-keeping and petty trading. When their work history is examined we find that few of them had been engaged constantly in these activities for any length of time. Like others in the informal sector, they exhibit a wide range of employment and occupational experiences, of which self-employment is the option at this particular stage of their lives. This differs significantly from the case of the Jamaican market higglers, for whom higglering is a lifetime career (Durant-Gonzalez 1976).

For the women in the survey (see Massiah WICP 1986a for discussion) the overwhelming reason for choosing this type of income-earning activity is the desire to earn their own living or for the independence which such activity brings: 'Instead of depending, I decide to try and help myself.' 'There was nothing else I could do. I could not get a job so I decided to do something on my own'; these were typical of the responses.

The decision to establish their own business venture appears to be generally an individual one — 'want would make you do anything!' One-third of the women received no encouragement from anyone in their venture. Where encouragement and guidance were forthcoming it was generally from kin; one-half of the sample cited relatives such as mother, elder brother or father. One woman said, 'I used to help my mother and she told me it would be nice if I could do it myself.'

Because of the nature and small size of the enterprises, women experienced few problems in establishing their operations, although there is a suggestion that care needs to be exercised in selecting the type of business. One woman said there was no difficulty with food business: 'It will always sell — anything to eat.' Those who cited initial problems mentioned capital and material as their most urgent needs. By far the greatest source of capital was loans from the bank, either commercial or government. Financial assistance was usually from male partners or close relatives. Those sources also provided other kinds of assistance, particularly moral support.

Hardly any of the self-employed women were able to or needed to employ paid help. Where they did there seemed to be no preference for male or female workers, though there is a preference for employing men to do 'heavy' work. Many of the women claim to be 'making something', i.e. some profit on their business activity, and stress that 'the opportunities are there, but women need more courage and encouragement'.

Sources of support

Aside from strategies to help themselves by engaging in casual labour, buying and selling, self-employment or home-based activities, women are also noted for their manipulation of complex sources of support either external to their own efforts or complementary to it. Support from male partners, manipulation and switching of partners, the family home, kinship and friendship networks, remittances from dispersed relatives and adult working children, gifts from friends, neighbours and employers and hand-outs from state institutions are some of the sources women tap for support. They might also resort to 'Anancyism' or 'working brain', i.e. cunning, in working out their strategies. Women tap these varied sources for goods, services, knowledge and money, either singly or in different combinations to meet daily commitments, becoming, in the process, 'domestic brokers' (Anderson WICP 1986). 'Sources of livelihood', in short, represent a complex of activities which might change from day to day or over the life of an individual, depending on changing circumstances.

In the process women might swing between dependence and independence, according to their circumstances. Regardless of how they go about it, the acquisition of sources of livelihood plays a major part in their lives and consciousness: women are preoccupied with ways of 'making do'. A case-study of poor women in Barbados led researcher Christine Barrow to the conclusion that 'The major desire among all informants is to secure economic support for themselves and their dependents, particularly their children,' and that this preoccupies them continually throughout their adult lives (Barrow WICP 1986a, p. 156).

An examination of the survival strategies of women brings into sharp focus their role as 'resourceful and often successful social actors [who have] definite views about strategies applicable to certain problems in their situations and the ends they hope to achieve' (quoted in Barrow WICP 1986a, p. 132). Generally, survival implies 'active economic involvement' on the part of women themselves rather than passive dependence on men (Barrow WICP 1986a).

Nevertheless, women do receive cash support from a wide range of sources. Husband/partner is cited most frequently as a source of additional income, followed by children and other relatives, especially those living overseas. Unemployed women and those engaged in home services are far more dependent on their partners than others.

While the strategies women adopt show creativity and flexibility, they also highlight the fact that poor women, especially, operate in contexts which they have little power to mould or change, and this underscores their vulnerability (Barrow WICP 1986a). This was brought out in the case-study of poor women in Barbados, women who have been largely bypassed by the process of modernization, a situation which they attribute to their lack of education and training. For such women, as Christine Barrow concludes, 'Life is a series of uncertainties and limited insecure options. Their efforts achieve mere survival and marking time with occasional improvements in standards of living; not social mobility and an escape from poverty (Barrow WICP 1986a, p. 170).

Their high level of parenting responsibilities pushes women into both the formal job market and the grey area of the 'informal sector'. To feed their children, women will exploit any option, including — in the case of one 23-year-old informant — their bodies:

I. How did you come to start working in the clubs, how did you get on to that kind of thing?

R. Well, when I was much younger, my aunt used to go out. I use to see her with nuff money so I ask her where she get it from and she tell me that she use to go out and, you know, hustle and thing. So by then my little boy father use to give me so much trouble and hardly want to give me any money or anything. If I ask him for anything he tell me he ain't got nothing so I had to go and look for myself. That's how I get in.

I. How do you feel about doing this?

R. Well I wouldn't feel no way about it because it make me don't have to get up on mornings and find that I don't have no sugar, no tea, no milk or anything to support the children with.

I. How does your family feel about the work you do, your sisters, your mother?

R. Well, my mother, she was the same thing but after she get older she went and sell, and she got she two houses and she got she car now.

I. Are you hoping sometime to get out of this kind of job?

R. Well I am going to tell you, I never do it for a year good, right? Because you find someone you could talk to and they give you anything, right. I never went steady a year yet. Just a few months, about three or four months and then stop.

I. How about your sisters, how did they feel?

R. Well them ain't feel no way, right? Because when my sister boyfriend giving her trouble I have to look after she, right? Help she get something for she to eat when she was pregnant. So them ain't feel no way about it.

Dependence on males

A woman's dependence on male support will hinge on a number of factors, most notably on how independent she can afford to be. In WICP samples over half of the women with live-in mates cited their partners as their most important source of support, compared with women who were single or in visiting unions, who were heavily dependent on self.

Child support Women in all Caribbean territories have some recourse to maintenance for their children and, depending on the legal status of the family unit, for themselves. However, the law offers far more support to the legally wedded wife than to women in other forms of union.

In the territories, the 'in-wedlock' family has a right to legal maintenance, whether or not a man is present. A husband must maintain his wife (according to the station in life set by him) and legitimate minor children up to the age of 16, so long as she lives with him or has good reason (such as illness, work requirements or his desertion) for living apart. Maintenance is also payable on the termination of marriage. Under the old legislation which prevails in most territories, the wife can lose the right to maintenance by her misconduct, e.g. adultery or desertion, though the rights of children are no longer affected by her behaviour, as they once were. Where a husband fails to provide for his family, his wife can institute proceedings for maintenance in a resident magistrate's court or a high court. In virtually all the territories, maintenance is a fixed sum: in the magistrates' courts the amount fixed by statutes is in the range $EC10–40. In Jamaica, the first territory to establish a Family Court to deal with these matters, the judge determines the sum payable by a means test.

In many territories, a woman is legally obliged to provide maintenance for her husband and children in certain circumstances, where the husband is the needy spouse. The law makes no provision for the maintenance of unmarried women. A childless woman living in a common-law union has no claim to financial assistance, should she need it, except, at the time of writing, in Barbados (Forde WICP 1981; see chapter 5).

Where child support is concerned, the law distinguishes between legal and non-legal unions. In legal unions the father's support is called maintenance. In non-legal unions, the mother has to seek an 'affiliation order' from the court and provide corroborative evidence regarding paternity. As Forde comments, 'the procedure is restrictive and even embarrassing to the woman who is forced to follow it' (Forde WICP 1981, p. 58). Consider the case of a woman who took her partner to court to obtain support of two children she had with him:

> 'On court day he said that the first child was not his. As I had registered the child in my name . . . I did not bother to fight him about the one he did not own as the witness who promised to come to court and testify did not do so. He had a lawyer, but I did not, so I leave it alone. (Jackson WICP 1982, p. 49)

Under new Status of Children Acts in Barbados and in Jamaica, the blood test is used as a means of establishing paternity. Once paternity is established and an order for child support made by the court, a man's attempts to evade it make him a 'rogue and a vagabond' and can result in his imprisonment. However, while maintenance orders are enforceable outside the jurisdiction of each territory, affiliation orders are not.

Although there is legal support for women's claims for maintenance and child support, we must question how reliable these are as sources of livelihood. Many women regard resort to the courts as shameful and prefer destitution to the 'humiliation' and 'scandal' that might result from court action. Many are ignorant of their rights, are unable to understand court procedures and requirements, cannot afford lawyers and therefore might be hesitant to seek this means of support. There is also the humiliation for women who are forced to prove paternity of their children in court. In virtually all the territories, the sums mandated by law are extremely small and do not take inflation into account. Because of the smallness of the sum involved and the trouble of securing it, only the poorest and most desperate women will seek such recourse. For, despite the smallness of the sums, there is still male resistance to paying.

One case-study (Massiah WICP 1982) of 38 women in Barbados who applied for welfare assistance demonstrates how unreliable this source of support can be. These women had a total of 169 children for 76 different fathers; thus there was an average of two fathers per household with a range of one to seven. The researcher argues that, if each father contributed to his child(ren) at the prevailing rate of $10 per week for each child, then household income should average at least $40. But, of the 76 men involved, only 50 provide support of any kind, as they are able. Twenty-six provide no support, either because they refuse to do so, or because their whereabouts are unknown, or because they prefer to go to jail rather than honour the court order. Of the others, 14 had migrated, nine were dead and six were ill, five of them mentally.

We do not know the extent to which women in the Caribbean who need support do resort to the courts. But the figures are believed to be universally low. For instance, figures for the year 1975–6 in Barbados show that there were 1,008 orders, of which 873 related to affiliation cases and 135 to married women's cases. Neither figure is regarded as a true reflection of the extent to which women need this source of income. In the case of married women especially, although the divorce courts represent a viable alternative, the legal fees are so prohibitive that women prefer to seek a magistrate's court order for maintenance or not to use the court at all.

Jamaica's Family Court, the first to be established, offers both legal and social services and attempts settlement of cases through family counselling before resort to judicial processes. The problem of non-compliance with court orders has been tackled by implementation of attachment orders, which permit routine deductions from the father's income or pension, collection by specially designated court officials, and the issuance of a warrant of distress if the allowance falls into arrears. There is nevertheless a serious problem of locating errant fathers. In situations where internal mobility is easy, where emigration is prevalent, and where some men simply prefer to go to prison than settle child-support payments, the problem becomes intensified (see Jackson WICP 1982).

Evidence from a variety of sources suggests that there is throughout the Caribbean considerable difficulty in the enforcement and collection of court orders. Even where a court order is made and the man is located, for the woman the experience can be a humiliating process drawn out over many years. A Jamaican 48-year-old described her experiences over a number of years to gain support for one of her children by her former common-law husband, whom she had left because of his ill-treatment. She first took the father to court in 1972 and he was ordered to pay her $J4 weekly: 'He continued to give the money when he feel like it so in 1977 I was forced to come to the Family Court as when I asked him for money he would say, "when you carry me to the court. I will give you what the Judge tell me to give you.'" The judge ordered him to pay $8 per week, but he still didn't want to pay. She said that she knew that he could pay more as he was a contractor. Despite everything, she was prepared to be reasonable:

> Sometimes when I know that he is not working I wait until he gets work, but after he gets work, he still continues to give me what he feels like. So I have to keep suing him but by the time I get that money, he again owes me back money. The last time I sued him he paid $100 and still owed $76. I am really tired of coming here so many times with this man. He himself say that he is tired of the Court House, yet he has seventy-two dollars for me and by now it is a hundred dollars.

She eventually asked the court to allow him to pay the money over to the collecting officer rather than having to 'hassle' with him every month (Jackson WICP 1982). Often it is the children themselves who are sent by their mothers to their fathers to take the 'hassling' about support.

Irresponsible fatherhood is highlighted by the fact that, in 1970, 70 per cent of the problems taken before the Jamaican Family Court were concerned with non-support from fathers. Of 6,210 cases dealt with by the court that year, 4,101 involved child support. A Family Court official offered one explanation for the high paternal resistance to supporting children: 'It is economics . . . if a man earns $50 per week and has three baby mothers with 12 children, it is impossible to support all of them' (Jackson WICP 1982, p. 58).

While high female fertility is often referred to, the high level of fatherhood is often overlooked. Caribbean men frequently boast of the number of children they have. Over 30 is not uncommon. In the WICP study, one male informant had 27 children with five women and another had 14 children with two women. In Jamaica, a man described as a 'colourful character', whose life style was positively reported on the front pages of two daily newspapers (*Daily Gleaner* 14 May 1985; *Star* 13 May 1985, p. 1), when he died, was reputed to have left 48 children or thereabouts. The death announcement said 48 but one son confided to a reporter that his father had told him that it was closer to 60. His legal wife with whom he had fathered seven, said she definitely knew of 28. His relatives and friends jokingly recalled that:

> on many occasions when his children went to him for support he had to ask them to remind him who their mothers were. The conversation, they said, went like this:
> The child: 'Good morning Daddy, Mommy sent me to you for some money.'
> Charlie: 'Who is your mother again?' Then he would burst into laughter.
> (*Star*, 13 May 1985)

However, he was noted for supporting his children.

The fact that many fathers do not have a feeling of closeness to their children possibly contributes to the lack of a sense of responsibility towards them. The way in which male irresponsibility is widely perceived is borne out by special campaigns of the family planning boards in several territories, which aimed at tying male responsibility to reductions in family size. Men also attempt to link child support to sexual and other favours from the women from whom they are estranged. As one woman puts it, it's a question of 'no sex, no support'.

A residential partner can be expected to provide the most support, but even this source might be insecure; conjugal relations are uncertain and sometimes of short duration, and men might ignore family responsibilities in favour of other women. Despite these problems, many women lack the resources to be independent of males, even if such is their desire:

Right now I have somebody that visit me but when I look on my life I don't feel that it is the life I wanted, it's just that I couldn't do better. This one helps me and he gives me $50–70 each month and with that, I also do a little sewing for myself. It's hard nowadays and I really need help with the rent. You know, if I had a work, I won't worry with a man, they are too much trouble . . . If I really get a job, something to do, I would be be happy. (Jackson WICP 1982, p. 50)

A case-study of the Jamaican Family Court showed that women who resort to the court are those who are most in need and unable to cope single-handed. The women presenting the most affiliation problems were in low-paid employment in the factory, domestic and self-employed categories or were unemployed. The latter also formed the largest group for child-care problems. (Jackson WICP 1982).

Women nevertheless do perceive male assistance as a most important means of making ends meet and, in the process of searching for a reliable, dependable mate, might end up with several 'baby fathers'. The need for economic support is frequently cited as the reason for liaisons with different men. But the fact of a woman having children with different 'baby fathers' can in itself affect a man's sense of responsibility and obligation to his own or any of the children, as excerpts from a 25-year-old Jamaican woman's story show:

His father [i.e. Bobby's — the eldest child] gone away from the time that he is three years old. The Sunday before he went away he came by with some sweeties and $10 but since then he don't write . . . You see this last baby here [six-month-old baby] is not the man I live with own. We had left [separated] for a while and I went to live with my mother. I left the house because the children's father told me to leave [the result of a quarrel] so the next day I come out with Bobby and go to where my mother is and left the four other children with him.

But then she got involved with another 'baby father':

While at my mother, I get fall with this child [current baby] as I started to talk to another man who live in the same yard as my children's father. This baby's father had promised to rent a room for us but wherever my mother found a room for us, he would then say that he can't pay the rent, that it is too high . . . I suppose that I got involved through I was not working and you know when they see you they tell you things, like they would help you and things like that.

Finally, she went back to the first 'baby father' primarily, she says, to take care of their children who were living with him:

Now the present baby father told me not to have contact with the children's father so when he found out that I stayed over, he said that he don't business with me again so he don't give the baby anything since him born. Right through the pregnancy he never give me anything only a tin of feed when the baby born: he don't feel good to see me come back here and the one I have the four children for don't feel good either since the two of them live in the same yard . . . Since I have the baby the children's father don't like to give me money again as he feel I would use it on this new baby.   (Jackson WICP 1982, pp. 51–4)

The economic motivation behind childbearing is further highlighted in the words of one woman who had 10 children with six different partners: 'Sometimes I ask [myself] why I had so many. But having them and having no money — the little bit I had myself couldn't keep them — I had to look for somebody. I wanted children from one man but getting something for one [child] I got the others.' However, this woman asserts, 'I don't regret having had my children though, because it's them who pull me out of a hole now.' If she had had these children for 'fun', then she would feel shame. But she felt that she had nothing to be ashamed of. Some of the men, she said, would not have made good fathers: 'You've got to know a man good before you let him raise the children with you so I prefer to raise them myself.' This comment also highlights the perception of the male as a source of support without expecting him to assume parental functions.

Sometimes a woman's strategy involves not just male support but male assistance in achieving major goals. To secure such assistance, she might employ some measure of cunning and manipulation, of 'working brain' or 'Anancyism', i.e. putting something over on somebody. One young woman, who left elementary school at an early age and who engages in a number of income-earning activities — cooking and laundering for others — and gets support from her 'baby father', described (in a roundabout way) a complex process of reliance and dependence in her life, specifically how she manipulated a number of men to acquire a house in a housing scheme, extend it and furnish it:

> I tell J's father [visiting partner] about getting a house. I tell him I have a certain amount of money and I want a house. And one day I tell this other man, 'Hey S, why don't you get [me] one of these houses?' I don't tell him I have money, right. He said, 'Alright, you want the house?' I said 'yes'. I said to myself, well when you getting something you don't refuse it. So then I threw in the claim and I got the house. Another day another man pick me up and he gave me a ride and he said, 'where you living?' And I told him. He said, 'you don't have a house?' I tell him, no I am paying rent at a hundred and fifty dollars a month. He said, 'alright, I am going to write up a cheque for you at Barclay's Bank'. And I went and cash the cheque. Two thousand dollars.

With this money she decided to improve the house she had acquired.

> I decide I am going to buy the tiles and tile off the whole house. I decided I am going to buy that door. I have some money and the same money is going to buy a front door. Then I said, I am going to put up some cupboards and I sit down and I work out myself how much I believe the material would come to and how much to pay the man to build the cupboards for me. When I got to town I go to the different places that sell chipboard, formica, everything and a man work it out for me; if I buy it ready-cash they will take [something] off. I came home and I tell D [visiting partner] and he went right there and bought them. Then his brother came and measure up everything. He tell me it [will] cost me $1225.

So she gave him the money to do it all. During this time, our informant was not working, but she had a savings account in a bank and was also into 'throwing box' or 'sou sou', an informal savings method (described below): 'I wasn't working because seeing that I have J I didn't have anybody to leave him with. D tell me to stay home so what money he give me I try to put something aside, every month I try to save my money, put it aside, put it aside, until I increase the money to how much I want.'

Kinship and friendship networks

This young woman's story highlights an important element in survival strategy, the importance of 'knowing people'. Family and to a lesser extent friends and neighbours play a major role in the survival strategies of Caribbean women and might be an answer to what outsiders discern as 'no visible means of support'. The interaction with kin or friends might not involve a cash exchange but the exchange of services as well as goods and emotional and other forms of support. 'Hand wash hand' is how the reciprocal nature of such exchanges is commonly described. It is by networking that poor people — women especially — assist each other in coping with their multiple roles and in supplementing inadequate incomes. A sense of neighbourliness still persists in many communities despite trends to urbanization and 'modern' individualistic behaviour. This process seems particularly widespread in the areas of childbearing and child-rearing.

In a preliminary study of social networks in Kingston, Jamaica, by Dorian Powell and co-authors, women disclosed a wide range of support services which they utilized in the raising of their children. One woman's network included the following: her cousin stayed home with the little ones while she worked; she used the day-care centres as they got older; her sister abroad sent money and food parcels; her brother sent vegetables and provisions; her mother, when she was alive, helped with clothes, milk and food. Her employers gave her parcels of rice and sugar (Powell *et al.* WICP 1982).

Networks or 'contacts' are utilized in many other ways, ranging from putting food in the family pot at times of acute distress to raising a roof overhead. One WICP informant described the exchanges in her village:

> Sometimes you see children, you don't even know them, but they are going with their clothes tear down and so you call them and fix them up, especially girls. Sometimes if I am feeling sick, neighbours come and wash the children's clothes free. But you know I have a conscience, they leave their work and come [so] I give them something. And like how I can sew sometimes they come, they ain't have money, I would run up anything for the children or even them. That is how we live. There is a lady right now living below me there, well I can close my eyes and if I haven't got any money she would even buy food, let's say that. I can go and tell her things rough with me and she would say, I have this and I wonder if it's any use to you, and I would do the same to her. That's how we live.

A 26-year-old married woman who augmented the family income by raising vegetables and sewing explained the role played by relatives:

> We'll assist each other. If one of us is sick we don't have to worry who is going to do this and who is going to do that, you just let the other one know and that will be that. They will come and whatever they can, they will do for you. And if you have to go anywhere, like to town or anything like that, and can't get back to do my children lunch or to leave lunch for them, you just tell her and, well, we are all poor, you say after going to town take this and help, and leave lunch for the children and your husband and thing. Well, they would do it and that's all. So you know when you come back the kids have lunch and everybody done eat. You don't have to worry about things like that.

While only tentative efforts have been made so far to study the importance of social networks in the lives of Caribbean women, enough information has emerged to show that communal and fraternal relations are key elements in enabling poor people to survive. Women are especially dependent on the creation of network alliances which permit reciprocal arrangements with other females for child care and household duties, food or cash in emergencies or general emotional support.

Sometimes friendship alliances might be as important or more important than kin. Victoria Durant-Gonzalez in her study of Jamaican higglers (1976) found that participation in higglering, a largely female activity, is facilitated by female kin and friendship alliances for child care, knowledge-sharing and moral support. Such a network ensures transmission of the knowledge of the techniques and practices associated with the activity and provides higglers with uninterrupted income during periods of absence from the market. For instance, when a higgler is unable to go to market through sickness or last stages of pregnancy, she sends her weekly produce by another higgler, thus ensuring continuity of earnings.

In her *Study of Yards in the City of Kingston* (1975), Erna Brodber found that non-kin women exploit their communal life to carry out household responsibilities. The women cultivate other women in the yard for assistance in such areas as child care, child-watching, sharing household chores, participating in 'sou sou', and general companionship, among other things.

A group of women who responded to a preliminary pre-test questionnaire administered by the WICP provide further tentative evidence of how these systems work. They usually rely on close kin, particularly those living near by, for assistance with child care. For financial assistance they usually seek the help of their parents, especially mothers, and siblings, but for other kinds of problems they turn to other kin, friends and authority figures such as the parson or the doctor. But women also drew a great deal of support from their partner, their baby's father, or a good friend of either sex: 'Someone you can rely on and they can rely on you. Someone to talk things with which they don't repeat. Someone to trust. I prefer male friends. Women don't keep their mouth shut. Men fight and 'gree again. Not women.' Yet girl-friends are most frequently cited as persons to whom women turn when problems arise:

> I can ask her to do anything for me and she is always ready and willing. She would do for me first and leave herself out.

> She is a good conversationalist. We help each other financially and otherwise — with work and so.

> She is a good woman and she has the time because she don't have her own children. I can call on her for help.

Sometimes there is surprising largesse from non-kin, especially in providing assistance for major purchases such as land or a house. The woman who became a successful businesswoman after many years of hardship described how she and her husband acquired a house: 'A gentleman friend bought it for us and we paid him by the month or the quarter. This man had this home and he fix it up and sell it to my husband, so he paid him a certain amount of money and then paid him by how he fix it up.' This 'friend' provided other forms of assistance:

> Because the children I raise for my husband, those children mother died, they came to me and I took them and I had to find means to support them. And a kindly gentleman gave me about a half acre of land just below the road there — it was a pasture — so we work this land, and he say don't plant no cane, just plant something valuable to the children. Because he said my husband was nice to him and he had that land just lying down.

She used the land to plant vegetables to help feed her large family and sold the surplus.

In some cases employers will reward employees of long service in tangible ways. One domestic servant reported:

> The galvanise was very cheap in those days and lumber was four cents a foot. Well every month I'll put something aside and then I would trust [credit] and pay until they put on the body of the house. Then when he [her employer] was going to die he told his executor to give me some money and I took it and put on this place here.

As one young woman implied, how people perceive you and your businesslike or ambitious nature are important factors in their aiding you:

I. Do you think you will ever start your own business?

R. For me to start my business I have to work and show interest in the work. People will help you and the people you work with they will see you have an interest of doing something and then you propose yourself to them and say, well, I like to do so and so but just don't have all the money. Then they say, alright, how much money you have? I'll say I have, maybe, three thousand dollars. And they say, how much more you want? I want three more thousand and I am going to get that and I am going to work and pay you back until I finish, so that's the way you have to do it.

Survival strategies can sometimes involve a combination of all the factors mentioned so far, plus scheming, ingenuity and faith. A single mother who raised eight children almost single-handed — 'I was both mother and father' — explains how she acquired a house:

I. Eight children. Six through secondary school. How did you manage that?

R. When I needed somewhere to live, I put it to the gentleman I was working with. He say, 'how much money you have?' I said I don't have a cent. He said, 'how you expect to get house without money?' I said I just know that God will help me. I want somewhere and I must get something. During the time that I was working I was throwing a little sou sou and when I get that money I put it aside and from time to time I would put it in the bank and give it to the same gentleman and let him hold it.

She found a piece of land to buy and needed $144: 'So I wrote and asked some of my relatives and most of them said they wouldn't be able to help because they have so much bills to pay and what-not. They're in America. I said okay, no problem.' Next she wrote to the father of one of her children, who was living in England:

I send and tell him the whole situation. He send me some money and I put that along with what I had and after finish paying off for the land, I get it clean up. I start buying cement and I get a few fellas and they start putting down the thing for me. I used to just feed them and they put down the foundation.

Then her money ran out:

So I come and look for the gentleman. I said I want to go in and ask if the Government Central Housing [Authority] will be able to take it over for me. So they told me yes but I will have to pay down a thousand dollars before they could even give me help. I said, Lord, where this coming from now? I said, I got to believe you, because I believe in you. So a couple days left, the gentleman who I work with he bring back a thousand dollars for me from the bank. I went in and I sign and two weeks after they [Housing Authority] took over the building.

When the house was completed she agreed to pay back $20 monthly. Her daughter started working and she also contributed until the debt was paid off: 'The first night when I go in and I lie down and I look up I said, 'Father, I thank you' seeing how my mother come from Barbados she dead she left not even a little chicken and to see we had to go all out and to start life all over again. You know, I felt very good!'

Family home (pooling resources)

In the Caribbean, the family home often remains a source of support long after children have taken the first step into adulthood. Part of the reason is economic.

School-leavers often have a hard time finding employment and will usually stay in the family home until they do. This is especially so of female members. But it is also a traditional practice. A common pattern is for young girls to be supported in the family home as they start adult life and until they have borne at least the first child. Many remain even after bearing a number of children, to extend the generation structure of the household. Depending on circumstances, the young mother might engage in income-earning activities while her own mother stays at home to mind the children; or the reverse occurs, the mother who is already in a job contributes to the financial upkeep of the home while her daughter looks after domestic needs and the children. In many cases near and distant relatives will be tapped for assistance in the raising of children and for specific needs such as school fees, exam fees, books and the like.

The older woman in low-paid employment who took over responsibility for her grandchildren described a family network of assistance:

I would send to all my relatives, some know them and some don't know them, but they know I have these children and I would send to tell them when I want to send them to school and they know I haven't got it and if they can help they does help. My sister have some children, that same girl in the States, she always would send a little something for me just to keep those children you see. That's the way I live. It's not that I am getting anything from the government or from any organization, but I will write and I will plea my distress. Not for me, for them. Because I say, well, if they move to something I may get bread in my older days. I don't depend on the mother alone to find books for them, I will drop a few lines. This is a cousin I just writing here telling him the children pass [exam]. And if it's a five pound, he will send it to help them to get books.

In many cases women ensure survival by pooling the resources of the different members of the household who are earning, with assistance from outside. A mother of eight children recalled:

R. My husband was a tailor and he used to get nuff work, that is the thing, and then my mother [who lived with them] had children, my brothers and sisters so that we could get a little something if I didn't have.
I. When you say she had children, you mean overseas?
R. Yes. Had a brother in America. A sister in Trinidad used to send money for her every month. Then she had a son in Curaçao and my other brother was in Trinidad, he was sending money every month.

For the young person, the support which can be provided within the family home is, however, limited, usually to the provision of 'shelter, utilities and food from a common pot', as Barrow found in the Barbados case-study (Barrow WICP 1986a). While there is sharing, adult working members are expected to make a contribution, according to their earnings and the overall income of the household. 'Thus, while the family home may be a . . . secure base, the support received within often ensures little more than basic survival and it may constitute a drain on the finances of the more economically active members' (Barrow WICP 1986a, p. 157).

Often, too, conflict over values will ensure that this means of support will not be sustained by parents/older relatives indefinitely. While the young female with her first child will be tolerated according to the norms of the community, repeated childbearing might lead to her being thrown out of the nest, and, if there is no steady partner to support her, she herself must begin the precarious search for a livelihood of her own, a search which often leads to a succession of partners — and children.

However, one does not have to live in the family home to benefit from what is owned by the family. In some territories, traditional patterns reinforce the notion that descendants should benefit from joint ownership of 'family land'. In Jamaica, as Edith Clarke noted in the 1950s, it is expected that direct descendants not only have an inalienable right to occupy family land but that those who live on it have an obligation to supply the rest of the family with some of the yield from the land. As Clarke explained, 'When the crops are reaped, baskets of foodstuffs are sent from the home cultivation to . . . relatives working in Kingston [the capital city] or elsewhere, and in return, those who can, reciprocate with small sums of money or gifts of clothing' (Clarke 1957, p. 63). In situations of poverty, even occasional gifts are meaningful in the strategy for survival.

The increasing fragmentation of West Indian family life under pressures of migration, urbanization and modernization is probably undermining the concept of tangible family assistance from one's rural roots, though they still remain a cushion in times of acute distress. While the concept of inalienability of 'family land' serves as a means of keeping kin relations close to and supportive of each other, it is only one of a whole series of networks of kin/friendship relations which are a significant element in the survival strategy of Afro-Caribbean women especially, and which need to be more fully explored.

Adult children

The data suggest that, in the Caribbean, dependence on children for economic support is not widespread, owing to the great value attached to schooling, though in places such as Kingston, Jamaica, where economic pressures are most acute, child labour is found to be growing. Except in extreme cases, households usually derive cash benefit only when children leave school. Because there is high unemployment among school-leavers, or most find jobs which are low-paying, income from this source is marginal or uncertain. Indeed, adult children can continue to be dependent on the family home for a long time due to economic circumstances, and, with the rising incidence of teenage pregnancy, might put extra strains on the already fragile resources of the household. Nevertheless, working adult children do provide a significant source of livelihood for many mothers:

> He [her husband] didn't do tailor work for long, he does do little painting out sometimes when he get a job. But I have some children that really don't let me down, they does help me every month. Four of them working. One's a fireman and he ain't married yet, so when the month come, he would bring in. Another one he would bring in by the week and another one, he's on a course so he still leaves his salary, you know. A boy in England and a girl in Canada, they help out, help the family.

In the WICP survey, adult children were ranked second to males as a source of cash support, but were far more of a support to single mothers than to those in unions. Support from children is usually voluntary and is based on the mother–child bond. It is usually expected by both parties that such support will diminish or cease altogether as the children enter into unions themselves and establish their own households.

In many cases, as we have seen, substantial family assets can be acquired through the joint effort of parents and adult working children. Indeed, the very struggle for survival itself ensures the continual forging and reinforcement of family bonds as a coping strategy.

Institutional benefits

While forms of 'welfare' assistance are available to women in developed countries, it is not a source of support that can be tapped by the region's women. There are, however, a number of institutional benefits including maintenance payments for children, widows' benefits and other forms of national insurance benefits. However, social support schemes, where they do exist, are in their infancy and the level of support which can be provided by these means is often minimal. They should be considered as options available to and usually utilized only by the poorest of the poor.

Supplementary benefits may take the form of national insurance benefits, allowances permitted on income tax and public assistance. In addition, a range of benefits are provided under the various health and education services. No specific schemes are available for women who head households. Those who support themselves by regular employment can derive benefit from tax allowances and national insurance benefits. Those who cannot support themselves are forced to rely on public assistance. There are no data to indicate the relative importance of these various sources of supplementary income to women who head households. Available data for one developed country indicate that at least half of the fatherless families there rely on supplementary benefits provided by national assistance (Massiah WICP 1982).

Ownership and management of resources

Although Caribbean women place a high value on personal independence and recognize ownership of property as a means of realizing this (see Brodber WICP 1986; Odie-Ali WICP 1986), the large majority of women surveyed by the WICP owned no substantial assets. An exception are the women engaged in farming in the Guyanese case-study, who are mainly East Indians. Thirty per cent of that sample owned land, 8 per cent owned housing and 24.2 per cent owned land and house. The Guyanese women also owned furniture, appliances, jewellery and livestock (Odie-Ali WICP 1986).

This contrasts with the Caribbean islands where 48 per cent of women surveyed in St Vincent and 17.4 per cent in Barbados owned nothing (WICP country reports 1982). Furniture was the major item owned by women (58.1 per cent of respondents in Barbados and 27.4 per cent in St Vincent), followed by jewellery (Barbados 36.4 per cent) and life insurance (19.1 per cent in Barbados). Only 2.5 per cent owned land, 15.8 per cent house and 6.8 per cent land and house. Nearly two-thirds of the women (62.8 per cent in Barbados) did not own anything jointly with a male partner. Joint possessions were mostly furniture (19.3 per cent), houses (12.5 per cent), land (3.3 per cent) and land/house (9 per cent in Barbados; 19 per cent in St Vincent). An interesting feature was the difference in the pattern of ownership between males and females, which reflected traditional gender roles and values, the females owning mostly items of domestic utility, the males owning less of items such as furniture but more of items such as motor vehicles.

Of course ownership of resources is linked to the capacity to accumulate funds to make purchases. Given that making a living is a precarious endeavour for the majority of Caribbean women, who are locked into low-paying, dead-end jobs or *ad hoc* methods of 'making do', the low level of ownership is not surprising.

Another way of establishing possession of resources is to look at savings, and this was also done in the WICP survey. Again, Guyanese women farmers were best off: 80.7 per cent of the sample were able to save (Odie-Ali WICP 1986). But, for the majority of Caribbean women, planning for the future is virtually impossible since it is difficult to save and, where savings are accumulated, these frequently have to be diverted into family welfare.

In St Vincent, for example, a little over 1 per cent of the women surveyed were able to accumulate savings for long-term benefits such as land purchase (0.4 per cent) or studying (1.2 per cent). In all, over one-third (36.7 per cent) of the women surveyed in that country had no savings at all.

In the case-studies, it was found that the only women capable of saving were those who were regularly employed, and not all of them had cash left over for saving since family responsibilities were a constant drain on these resources. Of the women interviewed by the WICP, only 12.6 per cent with savings were able to retain them in St Vincent. Guyanese farmers were able to plough back only 32.2 per cent of savings into their farms since the rest was normally consumed by family sickness or emergencies. Barrow concluded that, among her Barbadian informants, only those gainfully employed had cash left over after covering basic expenses, and, while most of this was spent on clothes or additional household items, only they, and only while employed, have managed to accumulate long-term savings as security in the unpredictable circumstances of their lives (Barrow WICP 1986a).

Methods of saving were found to be mainly informal. Guyanese women farmers claimed that they saved weekly sums at home and then deposited these in the bank. The East Indian farm women saw owning jewellery as a form of investment: 'You could sell your jewels or pawn them in times of emergency. Owning jewels is like owning money' (Odie-Ali WICP 1986). In St Vincent one-third of the savers used banks. A small number saved in building societies and credit unions, but most women surveyed preferred informal methods of saving such as 'sou sou' (70 per cent in St Vincent). In Barbados, Barrow found that credit union participation was generally restricted to the better-off working for a regular wage but that credit unions were preferred over commercial banks because they provided loans for those members in good standing without the tight restrictions of the commercial banks. Commercial banks, for years the exclusive preserve of the wealthy, are still viewed by poor people, particularly the older generation, as alien institutions not catering to their needs and not to be trusted. (Barrow WICP 1986a). One informant told her, 'I would feel funny going in with my two little dollars when the rest of the people carrying their thousands.'

The savings method which many women still prefer is an informal credit association known variously as 'meeting turn', 'credit turn', 'partner', 'throwing box' and 'sou sou'. Yoruba-derived, it is widely used by people of Afro-American origins to save and to meet financial obligations. It functions according to networks of kin, friends or co-workers. What is most important to the functioning of the 'sou sou' is that participants trust each other. Particularly important is the position of the 'banker'. Each set time period — week, month or fortnight as agreed — a network of people contribute a 'hand' or set sum of money to the banker. Each set period, the total take is paid out to one person in turn — the 'meeting turn' or 'credit turn'. By this means poor people can count on getting their 'hand' or 'turn' to meet heavy obligations such as a down payment on an appliance, children's clothes or school fees, or payment of debts. Women in the WICP discussed the importance of the 'sou sou' in helping them to meet their responsibilities:

R. If you need something you would say 'when I get my sou sou hand I will buy so-and-so'. Because the other money is to run the house and so on. Let's say something happen to you: an emergency. Even though you had your own hand already you could always run to that person and say, you know what, I get in trouble. I would like that set of money to do something. According to the co-operation they have, they will quickly hand it out and say go and fix up yourself. Wherein if you had the money in the bank you just can't go and do that, you just have to take what you pay so I think that's the advantage of it.

I. So it's possible to get two hands at the same time and then you miss a turn next time around?

R. Yes. It's just according to how much you pay up you know and how long you there. You could be trusted then.

One woman described how her 'sou sou' helped with a major purchase:

It was a lot of us in the sou sou and we heard about the Singer machine came in. You pay twenty-five dollars down and eight dollars per month. I told them that I wanted to purchase this machine and I would like to get a hand, you know. Well it was years I was in the sou sou, even sometimes the lady go away she use to ask me to carry on for her, so I had no problem getting it.

A young woman who is in a 'sou sou' with family members was asked:

I. How do you decide who is going to hold the box?

R. Well we sat down and talk about this.

I. How much do you throw a week?

R. Then we throw twenty. You can throw forty, you can throw two hand like a half and then a whole hand.

I. Explain that to me. A half-hand, how does that work?

R. That's ten dollars. And you throw another half-hand, that's twenty, cause me and you is pal, right. So we just throw two half-hand plus the whole hand that we throw, twenty for you and twenty for me. So then when the money comes out now we share it up.

Edna Manley, *He Cometh Forth*, 1962 (Purple heart wood, 79½ × 113″)
Edna Manley Memorial Collection, National Gallery of Jamaica, used with
  permission of the family of Edna Manley
Photographer: Maria La Yacona

8 Women in the Public & Political Domain

'Rebel' women

Caribbean women have never been passive actors in the public and political arena. Afro-Caribbean women have long been involved in the economic realm, and the social services of the region have been pioneered by women. A strong thread of women's active involvement in the struggle for justice runs throughout our history.

Lucille Mathurin Mair and others have begun to document this struggle in the period of slavery, when men and women shared equally in work and punishment. Mair also records their equality in their reaction to enslavement. Women, like men, plotted, conspired, murdered and became runaways and guerrilla leaders. They were arrested, tortured, hanged, transported and imprisoned; in short, they were subjected to the range of punishments laid down under West Indian slave laws. The only difference between men and women was that pregnant women sentenced to death had their sentences stayed until the birth of the child, who would count as one more plantation hand. Women also developed and used particularly 'feminine' strategies (see Mathurin 1975). The position of women as antagonists to the system is exemplified by Nanny of the Maroons, who was not only her people's leader but their military tactician and priestess, occupying a role similar to that of the Queen Mother in Asante culture (Brathwaite 1977).

Freedwomen were also active in the struggles leading up to emancipation in 1838. When missionary activities were suppressed as being inimical to the interests of the ruling class, it was often the women who at great risk to themselves kept congregations alive, even though their own roles in organized religion were circumscribed.

Although women's history is unwritten and therefore 'invisible', the glimpses that we get from the work of scholars such as Rodney (1981) and Reddock (1988), and from the official reports of disorders and civil disturbances throughout the century after emancipation show that women individually and collectively continued to be in the forefront of the struggles associated with the developing labour movement. Often they acted in support of male leaders, but many acted on their own. For instance, Rodney shows how official accounts of the Georgetown riots of 1905 paid considerable attention to the role of women. Governor Hodgson, who had formerly held office in West Africa, saw similarities between resistance of the women there to colonial rule and what was happening in Guyana, and 'tried to persuade the men of Guyana that the women were the ones causing the trouble and that they should be kept quiet' (Rodney 1981, p. 208). Swithin Wilmot shows in his work on labour relationships in Jamaica in the immediate post-emancipation period that women labourers could often be far less conciliatory and more militant than the men (Wilmot 1984, 1986). Caribbean history abounds with 'petticoat rebellions'. Maroon Nanny's act of defiance in lifting her skirt and showing her backside to the British soldiers sent against her people was symbolically replicated in many ways by women in their struggles against colonial domination.

Until the last few decades, women who acted in the public arena were *de facto* rebels, for they were effectively excluded from the corridors of power, which were the preserve of males of a certain class, and were acting outside their own domain, which was viewed as strictly domestic. In the pre- and post-emancipation period, 'respectable' black and brown freedwomen, like white women, were expected to conform to patriarchic structures. In Barbados, Handler (1974) tells us: 'There were freedwomen whose standard of living and property holdings were comparable to those of many males, but males provided the leadership in community affairs, and women were neither expected nor allowed to participate in activities that could be defined as political . . . Freedmen charitable, religious and social organizations were primarily male organizations.'

The 'rebel' woman was usually the lowest in the society, black or coloured slaves or freedwomen, later wage-labourers or self-employed women, who valued independence or justice more than 'respectability'. In creole society, it was only outside the formal power structure that women could hope to assume positions of leadership, power and prominence in their local communities. In African magico-religious practices they were healers, priestesses and leaders or otherwise had important roles to play in rituals and ceremonies and, indeed, even founded their own churches. Later, Afro-Caribbean women also played leadership roles in the indigenous clubs, friendly societies and credit associations which began to proliferate from the late nineteenth century.

Upper- and middle-class women, who were socialized into Western values, continued to function outside the home only as appendages of males — in subordinate, supportive roles — except in charitable activities, where a 'public role' was permissible. Thus upper-class women were instrumental in pioneering much of the social welfare activities throughout the region. The roles of other women were never so circumscribed because, at the lowest levels of society, women, like men, were exposed to the harshest realities of everyday economic life. Women of the working class in Guyana — and no doubt in other countries — who were active in civil disturbances were not only backing their menfolk, 'they were fighting for themselves and for the reproduction of their families' (Rodney 1981, p. 207). Poor women also participated in large numbers in the most significant social and economic process of the post-emancipation era — that of large-scale emigration in search of wage labour overseas. Some went to join their men but equally large numbers went on their own to seek jobs in Latin America, Cuba and the United States and later, in this century, to the United States, Britain and Canada.

The early emigration experience, coupled with international events such as the suffragette movement, contributed in the 1920s and 1930s to a growing consciousness of the need for the emancipation of women, as opposed to the emancipation of subjected peoples to which the women's battles had been largely directed. Women were beginning to benefit from opportunities for better education provided through secondary schools and teacher training institutions, to which they now had greater access; women who were now beginning to have professions as nurses, pharmacists, teachers, social workers, secretaries and clerks were in the forefront of fledgeling efforts to gain 'women's rights' (see, for example, Brodber 1986). It was also from their group that many of the earliest nationalist writers came (for example, Smilowitz 1983).

In the period from the 1930s, working-class women and some progressive middle-class women were also beginning to participate in the embryonic labour/political movements in the Caribbean, rallying around the strong nationalist male leadership that was emerging and, with the advent of universal adult suffrage beginning in 1944, exercising in large numbers their right to vote. Dominican Prime Minister Eugenia Charles has stated of her own country:

> Sixty years ago, our mothers, and some of our grandmothers took an active part in determining the policies of our region. I remember clearly seeing the women in the community, standing behind the men, but pushing the men the way they wanted to go. They didn't take part in the front position, but don't underestimate the work they did in laying the foundation. From the 40's women have been active and visibly in the front line of power.
> (Gregory 1985, p. 6)

While women have a record (still to be properly investigated) of active participation in rebel action, labour movements and social developments over a period of several centuries, women's participation in political life over the last few decades is viewed by many observers as disappointing (see Clarke WICP 1986; Massiah WICP 1982; Drayton 1983; Duncan and O'Brien WICP 1983; Anderson 1985), especially since this period has coincided with women's widespread access to education. And yet, to evaluate how far women have come in public and political life, we need to look at where they are coming from.

The West India Royal Commission of 1938 is a good place to start, for the Commissioners took special note of the status of women. They found that women were effectively debarred from participation in public life with respect to voting rights, elected office, administrative posts, equal access to civil service jobs and the field of justice — women magistrates were unknown and women did not serve on juries. Although women in Jamaica had achieved the right to vote as early as 1917, women did not have the vote in several of the other territories, including Barbados. Even where they could vote and stand for elections, women for the most part were unable to exercise these rights because they could not meet the stringent property and income qualifications. In three of the colonies, the age at which women could vote was higher than for men. Also in three colonies, women were debarred from seeking elected office (in the Legislative Council) and, even when they were allowed, none had yet sat on that body. The Report also noted the absence of women on all boards and local and municipal authorities. In short, Caribbean women up to fifty years ago had virtually no opportunity to participate formally in the shaping of their societies.

Women's public status

In seeking to define women's status, the WICP identified access to 'power and authority' as one of the components by which their total well-being should be judged (the others being 'sources of livelihood' and 'emotional support') (see Massiah WICP 1986b). The WICP sought to identify the extent of women's power and authority in several areas: in the familial, the economic, the social and the political spheres. We have already looked at the exercise of women's power and authority in the home (chapters 1, 2 and 5) and in the economic sphere (chapters 6 and 7); in this chapter we will look at how women exercise power and authority in the public domain, i.e. in the social and political arena.

WICP researcher Roberta Clarke (WICP 1986) argued that women's participation at policy-making level is a key indicator of their status in their societies and of the importance attached to their contribution to national development. If this is so, then women's status in the Caribbean might be judged to be very low indeed. Granted that there is a lack of data that will enable us to make any definitive statements on women's actual status in the various territories, but the information that does exist supports this view.

While women today constitute a substantial number of registered voters (indeed, a majority in Barbados) and turn out to vote at elections, while they are active as party workers, especially in 'women's arms' or auxiliaries of national parties, and although women do serve if nominated to senates or upper houses of parliament, official boards and commissions (but only a token few are), they are hardly represented at all in the highest reaches of political power — as elected representatives in national parliaments. They do not generally play a major role in the inner circles of their parties and have never introduced specific women's issues into Caribbean national electoral politics. Although they campaign for the rights of workers and are active in trade union movements, they play a minor role in trade union leadership (25 per cent regionally). In other areas of public life — the church, media, civic and business organizations — women for the most part continue to play secondary and subordinate roles, except in specifically 'women's organizations'. But, although such organizations proliferate, their national impact tends to be limited.

The WICP survey showed that few women are really joiners (though many approve of organizations) and leadership roles are usually the preserve of upper- and middle-class elite women. Despite the high visibility of a few individual women in public life in each territory, they are not necessarily furthering women's interests. In the public domain, the majority of women might truly be said to be standing where Eugenia Charles placed them at the birth of party politics in the region — 'behind the men'.

The WICP investigation of the status and performance of women in the public domain included material from the survey of three eastern Caribbean countries, supplemented with interviews with key figures in organizations there; in-depth interviews with women in public life in the eastern Caribbean; and a study of women in politics in Barbados. This material permits tentative examination of the subject in two areas, women in organizations and women in politics.

Women in organizations

Participation by individuals in organizations is recognized as important to personal growth and national development, for a number of reasons. Collective activity can provide access to political power, especially for those far removed from decision-making; it can serve as a kind of lobby and stimulate political action; it can provide the vehicle for the dissemination of information and services and furthering of contacts for the benefit of members; it can give participants experience in leadership, management and other skills which can be transferred to other spheres. Involvement in organizations is also an important channel for recruitment to participation at higher national levels (see Clarke WICP 1986).

The need for collective action by women is perceived as one factor which will contribute to their greater integration in the development process and their participation in organizations a means of furthering this. But this assumes that organizations are dealing with issues that are of direct concern to women; that women perceive that they have 'common cause', that there are 'women's interests' and 'women's issues' that are separate from those of men (Clarke WICP 1986).

Roberta Clarke, from her analysis of the data available, has concluded that, generally speaking, there is no evidence that Caribbean women have recognized collective interests or that there is a feminist political consciousness or feminist activism in the region. The evidence comes from the nature and types of organizations to which women belong, the interests served by women's participation in politics, and how women conceptualize gender issues.

The WICP survey revealed that most women are not members of any organization. Highest participation rate was in Antigua (36.7 per cent) and lowest in St Vincent (26.8 per cent). Yet over 90 per cent of the sample said that they felt membership in organizations to be important. Organization members ranked social incentives very highly, i.e. they joined for personal improvement or self-development, to make friends and meet people and get away from home, and for access to new ideas and skills. 'It adds something to life,' one woman said of organizations, 'life becomes monotonous if you just go home, then up and back to work. You need something extra.' Another averred that a woman 'should be out and stop behaving like she sign a contract to the house'. A third commented that such activities help her become a person outside the home.

Clarke's analysis of the survey data revealed that economic incentives also ranked high: membership in informal credit associations, i.e. friendly societies, 'sou sous' and burial societies, was found to be important. Spiritual enrichment and fellowship were also cited and borne out by the fact that most women who belong to organizations belong to church-related groups.

Church groups

These groups are affiliated to Christian churches and are widespread throughout the territories; for example, the Anglican Mothers' Union, the Methodist Women's League and the Moravian Christian Fellowship were prominent in the three islands. Clarke found the aims of all the church groups to be similar: concern for the quality of Christian family life, the promotion of unity of women in the church, and more generally to help women develop spiritually (Clarke WICP 1986). Enrolled membership in these organizations tends to be relatively large (for example, over 2,000 in the Barbados Mothers' Union) and participants tend to have a low income and to be in the age range 45–60. But leadership at community and national level was found to be concentrated among middle-class and elite women. The main activities of the groups are supportive in nature — fund-raising for the church, charity-oriented activities and spiritual uplift. Though training in leadership is encouraged, this is confined to leadership within the organizations and not within the church itself; the respondents felt comfortable with male domination in the church (Clarke WICP 1986) — which might explain the absence of a vocal movement by Caribbean women advocating the ordination of women. In short, women's roles in these groups reflect the traditional female one — that of supporter and nurturer.

Other organizations investigated by the WICP included government machinery, umbrella organizations for women's groups and non-governmental organizations.

Government machinery

In the euphoria of the decade for women, virtually all Caribbean governments established women's desks or women's bureaux or other machinery specifically to address the needs of women.[1] Most of these bureaux are concerned, for example, with co-ordinating activities of other agencies, developing income-generating projects and skills training. Clarke found that, of the three countries examined, one had no women's bureau and the bureaux in the other two suffered from constraints in staffing and funding which severely limited their activities and impact. She attributes this to the fact that the concerns of women are perceived by governments as 'secondary' and that the lack of commitment to these mechanisms might be partially attributed to the manner in which they are constituted, especially if they were set up in the absence of any consistent pressure applied by a majority of women. It is unlikely that any government would commit extensive resources to significantly aid unrepresented sections of the population unless groups develop a sense of their own interests and are able to forcefully articulate demands on policy-making centres (Clarke WICP 1986, p. 121).

Umbrella organizations

In recent years, voluntary umbrella organizations embracing all existing women's groups have developed in the three project territories (and also exist in some other territories). The main aims of these organizations are to (i) provide a communications channel through which women's organizations can liaise and co-ordinate activities; (ii) stimulate income-generating and skills training projects; (iii) sensitize women to their roles in national development efforts and the options available to them in personal development goals, for example, employment and educational opportunities.

Councils were found to be engaged in such activities in all three countries and some were quite effective. But their potential for providing a base for increasing women's participation in national development goals was undermined by the fact that the various groups had differing perspectives on the role of women and the functions of women's organizations. For instance, the church organizations had pulled out of the National Organization of Women in Barbados because they felt it was 'too politicized'. Women in these groups had not yet managed to elaborate some form of consensus or ideology to provide a base for unified action. Clarke, in interviewing people in the various organizations, also felt that their explanations for limited membership displayed many of the stereotypes held about women and women's organizational performance, for instance that a collectivity of women would only engage in gossip; hence women seemed to regard these organizations as irrelevant or a waste of time.

Non-government organizations are also active in the various territories and are broadly concerned with improving the status and conditions of women, especially the poorest in these societies, with varying degrees of success. These

---

1 The Jamaican Women's Bureau was established in 1973, one of the first in the world, on the initiative of women activists in the ruling People's National Party. In June 1977 a regional plan of action emerged from a meeting in Jamaica of representatives of twelve Caribbean governments, the UWI, CARIWA (Caribbean Women's Organization based in Guyana), international development agencies and other organizations to develop a regional position in relation to the then existing United Nations Decade for Women. A number of regional initiatives followed, including the establishment of: national women's machinery (desks, bureaux, etc.); a women's desk within the Caribbean Community (Caricom) Secretariat, based in Guyana; the Women and Development Unit (WAND) of the UWI Extra-Mural Department based in Barbados; the Women and Development Programme of the United Nations Economic Commission for Latin America and the Caribbean (UN/ECLAC) based in Trinidad (see Reddock 1989).

organizations — some funded externally — offered among other things skill training and income-generating projects. Most were engaged in helping low-income or
unemployed women and had developed guidelines and provided funds, resource
persons and materials. But such activities were seen by WICP researchers as likely
to encourage dependence and stifle local initiative, since few of the groups actually
involved local women in the planning and implementation of development strategies. Many of the projects implemented domestic activities such as needlecraft and
housecraft, which merely served to reinforce women's domestic roles. These
organizations were also not engaged in helping women to get involved in the broader
political process as a means of changing their conditions.

Characteristics of organizations

Generally, the WICP study revealed that women do not actively participate in the
political or policy-making arenas of their societies; nor have women's organizations
been pushing for the realization of this ideal. Activities of many of the organizations
are supportive of male-dominated institutions and are welfare-oriented. Thus they
appear to reinforce and perpetuate women's identification with their domestic
labour functions (Clarke WICP 1986) This follows the pattern described by Patricia
Mohammed for Trinidad and Tobago: that women's organizations, no matter how
powerful, have been reformist in nature and have not challenged or questioned to
any significant extent the existing sexual division of labour. Only since the 1980s
have new movements been springing up in the larger territories which are question-
ing gender assumptions and addressing 'women's issues' such as sexual violence,
equality of rights, equal pay and so on (Mohammed 1985; see also Reddock 1989).

Another characteristic of existing organizations is that middle-and upper-income
elite women are found to dominate key decision-making. How this affects the constitution of 'women's issues' as reflected in organizational activity remains to be
explored. No doubt, though, ideological outlooks are determined to some extent by
material conditions. Thus the differing material realities among women may influence what issues they consider as women's issues (Clarke WICP 1986, p. 49).

At the same time, elite women because of their connections do have access to
decision-making centres of the political process and might be good channels for gaining support. (Clarke WICP 1986). In the Caribbean, in fact, it is largely the elite
women who have so far been able to mobilize support for whatever changes have
taken place in the status of women.

Women in politics

The situation of women in politics mirrors that of women in organizations and in
society as a whole. Although women have been actively participating in politics for
some decades, their role has been largely supportive. They have been active as cam-
paigners and party workers; they have exercised their right to vote. But few have
offered themselves as candidates for elected office; fewer still have won.

However, hard data are lacking as the gender aspects of politics have been little
investigated, and efforts by WICP researchers to do so demonstrated how difficult
such information is to come by. There are no general surveys on the subject and
reports which are officially issued after each general election in each territory give
no breakdown as to registration of female voters or female voter turnout. Post-
election surveys which might yield this type of information are still relatively rare

in the region. Duncan and O'Brien who researched women and politics in Barbados for the WICP, noted the herculean task involved in piecing together information from varied sources to establish some sort of pattern.

Our observations about women in politics are therefore of a general nature. But even this is instructive. Patrick Emmanuel (1979) analysed general elections in the eastern Caribbean and Barbados from the period covered by the full attainment of universal adult suffrage to 1980. His analysis showed that, of 821 candidates contesting elections, 28, or 3 per cent, were women; the 28 faced the polls for a total of 50 times, lost on 28 occasions and won on 22. But 11 of the wins are accounted for by the fact that in two of the territories the wives of leaders of winning parties won their seat on every occasion they faced the poll.

The *Caribbean Yearbook 1977*-8, the source used by Massiah (WICP 1984), yielded a broader picture. Houses of Representatives in nine of the territories had a total of 237 members, of whom 214 (roughly 90 per cent) were men and 23 were women. In the Senates or Upper Houses, to which both government and opposition nominate members, of 94 senators in ten territories, 11 were women. There were 111 cabinet ministers, of whom 5 were women.

At the level of individual countries, we have information for three. Duncan and O'Brien (WICP 1983) show that, in Barbados for the period 1948–81, three women served in the Legislative Council (which preceded the establishment of the House of Assembly) and seven served as senators (including one who had previously served in the Legislative Council). Of 186 candidates in elections from 1951 to 1981, 10 were women and 3 of them won seats. Two have held positions at ministerial level, and one as a cabinet minister. Women's record as serving members on statutory boards, commissions and public corporations is marginally better. Of a total board membership of 462 for the period, there have been 81 women, representing 17.5 per cent.

The situation in two of the smaller eastern Caribbean islands — St Vincent and Antigua — was also examined in the WICP survey. St Vincent at the time (1982) had six senators, of whom two were women, and no woman in the House of Representatives. The first female elected member had served in the previous government. In Antigua there was one female senator (the first) and no elected member. There had only been one elected member in each country; both happened to be the wives of the then premiers.

Although at the time of the WICP research the Caribbean boasted its first female prime minister in the person of Eugenia Charles and at the time of writing Jamaica had a female president of the Senate, these cannot be taken as indicative of the real status of women in politics in Dominica, Jamaica or elsewhere in the Caribbean. Although the situation in the larger territories such as Jamaica might reveal a better record of women politicians than the situation described for the smaller islands (see Table 8.1), women's performance in politics *vis-à-vis* men, though improving, is still abysmally low.

In Caribbean politics it is widely acknowledged that women play a strong role in campaigning and are active in women's arms or auxiliaries of political parties. Clarke (WICP 1986) examined auxiliaries in Barbados, Antigua and St Vincent and noted that 'All of the groups examined included in their objectives, the promotion of the full participation of women in all aspects of national life.' To join the group, women had to be party members. The autonomy of the auxiliaries is limited and they are constrained in activities 'by party structure and politics and have so far always been available for fund-raising, campaigning, or the mobilisation of other women in membership drives' (Clarke WICP 1986, p. 123). Clarke also noted that,

Table 8.1 Female Participation in Electoral Politics, Jamaica, 1962–83

Year	Total cand.	Total female	% female	Total females elected
General elections 1962–83				
1962	114	3	2.6	1
1967	114	5	4.3	2
1972	113	5	4.42	2
1976	120	5	4.16	4
1980	126	13	10.3	6
1983[a]	66	7	10.6	7
Local government elections 1969–81				
1969	520	31	5.9	16
1974	558	51	9.14	25
1977	558	65	11.65	31
1981	552	70	12.68	38

[a] Not contested by main opposition party–PNP.
Source: Maxine Henry, 'Women in Politics in Jamaica' (unpublished m.s.)

as is the case in other organizations, while membership is made up of mostly low-income middle-aged women, leadership is dominated by middle-class women. Younger women are also found to be poorly represented.

Apart from fund-raising and campaigning, the auxiliaries are also involved in social welfare functions which relate to women's nurturant roles (Clarke WICP 1986) such as involvement with child care, orphanages, mutual aid, and sick visiting. Vocational education offered is limited to 'female' areas such as typing, nutrition and food preservation. While some of the auxiliaries have moved towards income-generating projects, in one case the project employed men rather than women and profits were ploughed back to the party.

Yet the women involved in these auxiliaries who were interviewed were proud of the instrumental roles they played in the successful campaigning for their parties. 'Women have more stamina than men and they tend to be more enthusiastic,' one said. Another commented: 'Women did the major part of the campaign.' One highly placed woman politician (WICP, Interviews with women in public life) claims that women in politics are more reliable and more loyal, work harder and 'know what they are doing'. Another prominent woman noted of her country: 'If you call a meeting tonight . . . it will be a woman sitting down there first, it's always the woman leading and if you see with those women on the streets you have to wonder if the party belongs to women and no men in the party.'

Women are absent, though, from the highest levels of their own parties; the women's auxiliaries are allowed at least one representative on their party's executive council, the central decision-making body; this, however, bears no proportional relationship to female membership or activity. In the two Barbados parties examined, one had 4 women out of 23 members of the executive council and the other 7 out of 41 — at a time when female registered voters exceeded male.

Women are not entirely happy with the status quo. Several female politicians interviewed would like to see a more prominent role for women in their parties:

> I feel it's because of the men, they're not ready for women to participate fully in decision-making, they are scared of women, they say women are contentious and that it isn't easy to get them to make a decision, they talk a lot. I think you

must criticise, I don't think people can just make decisions by sitting down. People have different views and these views must be put forward and why not . . . women? It is said that most decisions are made in bed by husbands and wives and so the man goes forward the next morning to Cabinet or whatever, and he puts the thing forward, but maybe it was because of his wife . . . What I am saying is, if they can do it there, why not go out in Cabinet and help to make the decisions.   (WICP, Interviews with women in public life)

But, despite such private feelings, women have not openly challenged male-dominated political structures. Some possible reasons will be discussed below.

Why not more women in politics?

Certain key factors can be identified among the reasons for the lack of female politicians. These relate to women's socialization, attitudes to politics, role conflicts, lack of male support and lack of female support.

Socialization   How women conceptualize themselves and their roles depends a great deal on their socialization. Politics represents the exercise of power but women are socialized to be non-challenging, to see power as 'masculine'. The suggestion is that, in seeking power, women must abandon their femininity and are forced to 'become men'. Those who do acquire power often feel that they must be 'more men than men' (Anderson 1985).

Politics is definitely associated with loss of femininity in the minds of women who are active politicians. One woman who is prominent in her party in a non-elected position said, 'women are scared away from being politicians . . . because people will see them not as feminine as they feel they should be' (WICP, Interviews with women in public life). And a female member of parliament asserted: 'There is always the perception that women who become involved in politics must possess extraordinary qualities, which rob them of their femininity, charm, grace, and other lady-like characteristics.' She further noted: 'The husbands of women politicians are always seen as female dominated. Women in politics are expected to be either easy pushovers by their male counterparts or they are said to be hard — MORE THAN ANY MAN' (Gregory 1985, p. 21).

Politics is perceived by women as not only unfeminine but also 'dangerous' and 'dirty': 'Politics is still seen as a man's world. What is more detrimental to our cause is that it is perceived as a dirty game' (Gregory 1985, p. 21). A highly placed female politician said: 'Politics can be highly dangerous you know; women don't like it, they can't stand the abuse, they can't stand stories being told about their mothers and their grandmother in their earlier lives and so on. You have to have a high strong stomach to do this.' As for herself, the Opposition 'made their abuse even more bitter and deep, you see, because I'm a woman . . . I don't think they believed it themselves but they were using it, you know' (WICP, Interviews with women in public life). Women are reluctant to run for office 'because of fear, fear of those men politicians that ridicule them and say all sorts of things about them' (WICP, Interviews with women in public life).

There is the suggestion that the 'dirty' element in politics was introduced by men to keep women off the platform in the first place. According to Eugenia Charles: 'From the 40's women have been active and visibly on the front line of power. It is only in the 70's that some unenlightened males, fearful of the power of women, attempted to frighten women away by the use of abusing and denigrating behaviour.' Miss Charles asserted, 'they failed. They failed miserably' (Gregory

1985, p. 6), but this might be more rhetoric than fact since there is so much evidence that women's fear of the 'dirtiness' of politics and the impact this will have on their reputations and their families is what has kept many out of the political arena. This came out in many of the interviews with women in public life:

I. Were you ever interested in contesting elections?

R. Never, never, no, no.

I. Why?

R. I don't like the type of politics that obtains in these small Caribbean islands . . . for instance, the canvassing for seats. You don't have anything good to say about the person, you look for the worst and you continue, even if you say that it is only an election gimmick.

A leader of the women's arm of her party asserted: 'women are scared away from being politicians by men, they are scared away by the way that men seem to dishonour women on a political platform.' Another prominent woman in another country said: 'If I had to become a politician I would hesitate because I know how dirty it can get here. If it change tomorrow and they didn't get on platforms and abuse one another I would be right in there asking the men and even the women for their vote.' One who was an unsuccessful candidate for election said: 'Many women will tell you they are afraid of going out there and men abusing them.' Thus it appears that women in public life — including those who are active politicians — endorse the view that politics is 'dirty', 'dangerous' and 'unfeminine'.

Part of the process of socialization is expressed through role modelling. There is evidence that those women who have so far been successful in politics or public life in general were in their early years exposed to political discussions at home and had relatives — male and female — who were actively involved in early nationalist politics. This comes out clearly in the WICP interviews with women in public life. An examination of these interviews also suggests that most of these women grew up in strong family situations; that they had a sense of 'belonging' and of being 'rooted' in their societies, and were encouraged from an early age to get an education; independent thinking was also encouraged. Additionally, they had strong female role models in their school principals and teachers as well as their mothers and other female relations.

A successful politician, the Hon. Billie Miller, who was the first female government minister in Barbados, seems to endorse the importance of early conditioning:

> exposure to the political system and its proponents, whether early or late in life, and/or active involvement in civic or professional or trade union or social work, predisposes women to entry into politics in much the same way that men were predisposed in the early years of their active involvement. Men enter political life nowadays motivated by a wider range of influences.
>
> (Duncan and O'Brien WICP 1983, p. viii)

The importance of early conditioning, role models and other factors in shaping future 'public' activities needs to be properly researched. At this stage we can assert that, on the whole, Caribbean women have few role models in politics; even those women who have made it to the top are subjected to scorn and ridicule and generally negative images are projected about them.

Role conflict A woman experiences severe role conflict in deciding whether or not to run for public office. The manner in which her family and family life might be affected by her decision acts as a powerful constraint. Male politicians presumably expect their wives to keep their family life going. Female politicians need to be able to count on the same sort of support: 'There would have to be a very understanding man who would say, well look, if you have to go out tonight, I would stay with the children. He would have to understand. It cannot be a one-sided affair' (WICP, Interviews with women in public life). A woman politician explained:

> To enter into politics, you should first have the support of the family . . . the pros and cons must be taken into account as to what it will mean to the family and how it will affect the family. Some husbands are reluctant for their wives to enter politics. There are many reasons for this. They feel the love and affection will be taken away because politics takes a lot of time and jealousy comes in at times. Sometimes, husbands . . . feel that [the] wife is to be [in] the forefront and she is getting all the attention; in some cases husbands or boyfriends become so bitter that they are non-supportive.   (Gregory 1985, p. 19)

One politician said that she got involved in politics only after she separated from her husband 'because, with due respect, men are jealous and I had that to live with [with] my husband. So I kept to myself. And after that, I just got out and got involved' (WICP, Interviews with women in public life).

The old fears of abuse, slander and ridicule are compounded by their possible effects on family life:

> Because the minute they're going to start abusing my family that's a different story, they're going to abuse me and call me names, wash all my dirty linen in public, that's okay, but if my children and grandchildren and husband have to suffer . . . If I had to become a politician I would hesitate because I know how dirty it can get.   (WICP, Interviews with women in public life)

The same woman underscored the double jeopardy when she asserted, 'I would be a politician if I didn't have a family. I would be a politician in spite of having a family if politics was not so dirty.' One highly successful politician admitted that it had been easier for her to devote herself to politics because she is unmarried.

Economic factors   Another gender-related problem is the economic aspect. Running for office is an expensive business. Women must have independent means or access to funding or, as one politician claims to have done, be able to generate income-earning activities in the constituency (Gregory 1985). Problems will arise if she is wholly dependent on a mate: 'It just can't work if you have to depend on a man for financial support as he is going to object to how you spend in the political avenue, buying gas to go to meetings and campaigning etc.' (Gregory 1985, p. 20).

Because of their lower occupational statuses, women as a group have fewer economic resources available to them than men; this might be another constraint against women running for public office. Because of negative male perceptions of women in public life, and the lack of the equivalent of the 'old boy network', they might also find it more difficult to tap corporate and other traditional sources of campaign funds.

Lack of male support   Lack of male support emerged as a definite reason for more women not playing a bigger role in politics. The perception about politics reflects perceptions about the larger society. Politics is definitely perceived as a 'man's world' by both men and women and their behaviour and attitudes reinforce this.

Even where women believe in their own capabilities sufficiently to want to run for office, too often they encounter a lack of male support if not opposition even within their own parties. An MP noted that, although women were beginning to play a leading role in her country, 'there is still the feeling held by some men that women should not be there . . . Sometimes the men voice it that when it comes to the decision-making positions, men should be in charge. Personally, I have experienced a lot of prejudice.' She asserted that 'the prejudice against women, the abuse, the feeling that the political career belongs to a man, have resulted in few women entering the arena' (Gregory 1985).

Several of the women interviewed attributed lack of male support within their political parties or trade unions as definitely a factor working against women moving up in the hierarchies of their organizations. One woman who stayed for a long time in the highest reaches but never quite managed to make it to the top of her trade union organization did not ascribe this to any inadequacy on her part but to the 'fear' of her male colleagues who did not feel that a woman should hold the top position: 'It was the people themselves who did not know how far they could put me, you know, men were always at the head' (WICP, Interviews with women in public life).

A politician who was prominent in her own country noted that, although she had been active in party politics for a very long time and had even helped to form her own party, she had never been asked to run for a seat. She ascribes this to the fact that 'maybe at that time they weren't ready to accept women'.

In another context, Beverley Anderson Manley, who was active as leader of the PNP's women's movement in the 1970s when her husband was Prime Minister of Jamaica, recently noted that in her party, 'While the women played the role of auxiliaries to the men, there was little tension or conflict . . . Later, however, when the women became interested in genuine power sharing at different levels of the party, the men felt threatened' — and this was within a regime that had carried out many programmes for the benefit and advancement of women (Anderson 1985).

The fact that women's political aspirations might not be supported by their party leadership has many implications for the success of women in politics. For one thing, prejudice against women could exclude them from the sharing out of rewards for political support and service, which is a recognized aspect of political life. One way of rewarding outstanding party workers is to groom them for electoral office. This does not seem to apply to women to any great extent, considering that much of the donkey-work in all the territories is done by women. Political activity at constituency level also serves as a means of building up grass-roots support, and the dispensation of patronage at that level helps to pave the way for political aspirants. In other words, the party machinery usually functions for the benefit of political aspirants. We would need to know the actual level of responsibility that women have within their own parties to evaluate how far their own political aspirations are being retarded or enhanced by the machinery. It seems clear, however, that, if women are not near the centres of power and decision-making, then they do not have the same opportunities for political education and for political 'grooming' as men. Women on the whole seem to have fewer opportunities than men within their parties to gain political awareness, leadership training, self-confidence and grass-roots support that are some of the stepping-stones to nomination for political office. Precisely what the status of women is within the parties they support and how they are helped and hindered by the political machinery are questions that need to be further explored.

Lack of female support   If women are not high in the ranks of their parties, part of the reason can be found within themselves, their own lack of self-confidence and lack of support from other women. A prominent female political leader of an earlier era identified the importance of female self-concept when she noted that despite the high level of female involvement in party politics in her country:

> women never had a chance of getting to the top, we're always left at three-quarters level. They felt that men were the ones that's supposed to lead, that is how the women feel; it's only the younger folks like my children are coming up to say, well, we're all flesh and bone, men and women the same thing, but women of my age group they always feel that the men should be at the head.
>
> (WICP, Interviews with women in public life)

If women feel that 'men should be at the head' then there is little likelihood of their challenging males in the race to get there.

There is also evidence that female aspirants for political office cannot at this stage automatically count on female support. The evidence is very tentative and comes from only one country, Barbados. There is a high level of female voters registered in that country but their voting behaviour does not demonstrate any particular support for women candidates. Duncan and O'Brien (WICP 1983) noted that while one seat in the 1981 campaign in that country was won by a woman, Billie Miller, there is the suggestion that her victory did not depend on female voters, as the female turn-out in her constituency was 64 per cent, significantly below the national average of 71.6 per cent. On the other hand, although the female turn-out in two other constituencies where women ran exceeded the national average, both candidates lost, suggesting to the researchers that they did not appear to have received special support from female voters.

Women's issues One final reason for the low level of female participation in politics and public life generally might be that female consciousness in the Caribbean has not yet crystallized around specifically women's issues, that is, issues which indicate that women have some interests that are different from those of men and which need to be articulated in a particular way. Nor do women seem to perceive the need for collective or group action to address those issues, either in politics or in other types of organizations.

Clarke's analysis (1986) of the three project territories showed that there are not and have never been women's issues in the politics of these countries. There is evidence that the situation is similar elsewhere. One woman who has been active in the politics of her eastern Caribbean country for over 40 years noted that she was not aware of any women's issues having arisen during that time (WICP, Interviews with women in public life). None showed up in the Barbados case-study or in Carl Stone's study of the Jamaican election of 1972 (Stone 1974).

However, some recent experiences suggest that the perceptions are changing and that genuine women's activism is developing, albeit in a small and fragmented way. Reddock (1989) cites, among successful recent campaigns by women, one which ensured swift passage of a maternity leave law in Jamaica in 1978-9, a campaign against violence to women on St Vincent and the Grenadines in 1985-6 (after the WICP study), and a campaign against offensive clauses in a Sexual Offences Bill in Trinidad in the same period (see Johnson 1988 for more on this bill and the controversial 'clause four'). Reddock has suggested that the issue of sexual violence has become a key factor in mobilizing women throughout the region, transcending class, race and ethnic groups; further, that these new developments 'have served to radicalise the established women's organisations and force them to refocus away from charitable works to their original concerns, the emancipation of women' (Reddock 1989, p. 10-11).

The lack or otherwise of women's issues is as much a reflection of how women perceive themselves as of societal factors. Caribbean women operate in political systems that are highly polarized in terms of party politics — in some countries even 'tribalized' — and this at present is the dominant factor which determines their political behaviour (Anderson 1985). Thus women's political involvement and support are of a partisan nature. In conditions of poverty, politics is seen as the means for distributing scarce resources and women — like men — hope to gain tangible rewards for their party support. Thus bread-and-butter issues will have greater salience than gender issues. At the same time, the intensely antagonistic nature of Caribbean party politics might turn away many women (and men) who would prefer to conceptualize political issues in non-party terms but who do not have the channels for doing so. But there is another dimension and that is related to how women view gender issues.

Clarke's analysis of the WICP survey revealed that the majority of women questioned the idea that gender had retarded their development. The proportions who did not believe it had were: Antigua 82.5 per cent, Barbados 91.6 per cent and St Vincent 86.4 per cent. Yet direct quotations from some of these women revealed that generally they had a fatalistic attitude to the subject, which revealed either acceptance or adaptation. Comments indicating acceptance included the following:

God made me a woman so it couldn't keep me back. Anything I want to do, I do — I very masculine.

I accept being a woman and never try to do anything like a man.

As long as you have the spirit, no man can turn you back. God made us all equal and once you have that understanding you can do anything without feeling embarrassed.

I have always learnt to be a woman and make my decisions. Being with a man has held me back but being a woman is nothing.

One who felt restrained commented: 'If I was a man, I would not have any children to keep me back.' Another noted: 'In jobs they favour men. We are equally qualified but we seem to take longer to progress than men.' Clarke concluded that the women's comments reveal that women seem not to consider their interpersonal relationships (especially as mother or partner) or the nature of how other people relate to them as reflective of the constraints placed on them by the fact that they are women (Clarke 1986, p. 144).

Indeed, notions of social inequality appear to have greater impact on women's perceptions than gender inequality. Thus women's concerns so far have not been with 'gender issues' so much as with socio-economic ones, with improving the status of themselves and their children, i.e. they are more concerned with individual status than with women's status. This would tend too to reinforce their support of party politics in the Caribbean, where identification with party can be seen as a means of garnering scarce resources for individual enhancement.

Generally speaking, there has so far been little pressure from the majority of women to change their status in the public sphere. The status and moribund character of some of the women's bureaux and women's desks, established by governments with such a fanfare in the 1970s, are a telling indication of both how women's interests are viewed and how women themselves view their interests.

Women's acceptance of supportive or subordinate roles in politics and other institutions such as the church mirrors their subordinate role in the home. The activities of many women's organizations appear to reinforce and perpetuate women's identification with domestic labour functions (Clarke WICP 1986).

But women are involved not only with child care and housekeeping (i.e. with reproduction) but with production as well. Even those women who do not work out are involved in the economic management of their households and are major consumers. Thus economics and politics, 'public' issues, do impinge on their day-to-day activities and are of direct concern to them. It is this interplay between women's private and public roles that is often not recognized, by society at large and by women themselves (Clarke WICP 1986).

Clarke has concluded that the relative exclusion of women from centres of power and authority in public life may be attributed to a complex mix of determinants related to race and class as well as to gender. Part of this has to do with women's assumptions of heavy economic burdens with little support from institutions or irresponsible fathers, which for them make 'bread-and-butter' issues, issues of survival, of far more importance than gender ideology. At the same time, these women 'have so far managed resourcefully their life situations, against all odds' (Clarke WICP 1986), which might give them confidence in their own individual capability, in their ability to 'make do', and prevent them from seeing how organizational activity can help them.

Most importantly, women's responsibilities in the home leave them little time for participation in public life, while precisely this freedom from domestic labour and child-care duties is what 'frees up' men to engage in activities outside the home.

A proper interpretation of women's seeming lack of concern with public roles, public issues and gender ideology can only come about through further study. The roots of women's lack of self-confidence and their distrust of other women and of women's ability to lead and perform successfully in organizations also need to be pin-pointed with some exactitude.

We also need to explore other factors present in Caribbean culture which might reduce women's need to join organizations — such as the services and support they derive from informal networks — and whether or not they have the means of achieving power and status at community level outside the conventional route of formal organizations.

9 Women & Men

General views of male/female behaviour

It has been argued that it is in childbearing and child-rearing that Caribbean women 'find the greatest opportunities to exercise independence, responsibility, decision-making autonomy and control over self and others'. In these domains, women are said to surpass men in status. It has also been argued that the converse is equally true, that it is in the domains of sexual and emotional involvements with men that women appear to be weakest (McKenzie WICP 1982, p. viii).

The ambiguities of male–female relationships throughout the Caribbean are perhaps best highlighted by the fact that, while the women surveyed by the WICP on the whole expressed themselves as satisfied with their unions, analysis of the in-depth interviews with some of these women reveal quite different stories. We find women citing certain negative behaviours on the part of men which our informants almost seem to take for granted as part of the male repertoire. These include unreliability, infidelities, and a wide range of oppressions including physical violence, humiliation, mental cruelty, drunkenness, desertion, financial irresponsibility, etc. We find women asserting their desire for independence while yoking themselves to unsatisfactory partners. We find women rejecting males they consider unsuitable but exercising options that yield results which are just as oppressive. We find, more than anything else, cynicism and resignation about the man's behaviour. We rarely find women rejecting men. Even women with life-histories filled with tales of male rejection, ill-treatment and ultimate abandonment continue to affirm the power of male–female relationships in their lives. An Antiguan in her forties asserted:

> I don't think a woman can live without love. I don't think we women were made to live without love. Women need to be loved. I don't think the world can exist without love, nobody can exist without love I mean when you're loved you feel wanted, you feel appreciated, somebody loves you, you have somebody that you can talk to, you can exchange ideas with, you need a companion you know.

There is no doubt, however, that Caribbean men and women hold negative views about each other's behaviour. Barrow concluded from studying male images of women in Barbados that 'the Barbadian male image of today's women . . . is almost totally negative' (Barrow WICP 1986b, p. 61). Henry and Wilson after a survey of the literature which chronicled such relationships in the Caribbean concluded that 'Role relationships between men and women are ambiguous, unclear and consumed by strategies or "games playing"' (Henry and Wilson 1975, p. 165). Trinidadian novelist and critic Merle Hodge has commented that 'the whole range of mental cruelty [from men] . . . is part and parcel of women's experience in the Caribbean' (Hodge 1974, p. 113).

While the topic has been subjected to little serious analysis, there seems to be such consensus on certain aspects of male–female relationships that such beliefs appear almost stereotyped. Male–female behaviour has been the subject of commentary mainly in the idiom of popular folk culture, including folk-songs and sayings and calypsos, and of literary work. But up to recently most of these commentaries have been expressing a male viewpoint. It is only in recent decades that Caribbean women have begun to find a public voice and are beginning to name their experiences and voice their consciousness.

Female images in calypso

Of all the images portrayed of Caribbean women, those most frequently cited have been in the idiom of the calypso. Although the calypso originated in Trinidad and is identified mainly with the southern Caribbean, it is an art form which is well received by both men and women throughout the region. Elder, writing in 1968, tells us that 'the calypso is predominantly a man's song about his own emotional confrontation of the world of rivals, his conquests and his defeat, his hopes and his fears' (Elder 1968, p. 29). The male singer's portrayal of women has constituted the core of calypso music for the last several decades, a fact which has been noted by many observers (see, for example, Elder 1968; Rohlehr 1970; Warner 1982). Gordon Rohlehr notes that 'The calypso . . . is of prime sociological importance to anyone who seeks to study some of the attitudes of the West Indian male towards women' (Rohlehr 1970, p. 89).

What are these attitudes as revealed by calypso? Elder, using statistical methods to analyse Trinidadian popular music by leading singers over a 50-year period, concluded that 'the female figure as theme predominates over the whole calypso tradition . . . aggressiveness in calypso towards the female figure has increased steadily throughout the calypso tradition' (Elder 1968, p. 33).

Male/female themes might be roughly collected under four categories. First are those which centre around the uneasy relationships between the sexes. The male–female relationship is portrayed as based on mutual suspicion, mutual exploitation. For the male it is often 'pursuit, conquest, desertion' (Rohlehr 1970), although he frequently refers to the 'smartness' of women. 'Man smart, woman smarter' is the challenge to warlike and mutually antagonistic behaviour to prove otherwise.

Secondly, there are the calypsos based on male 'ego-inflation' (Warner 1982, p. 99). As Warner explains it in his book on calypso, 'by far the most overworked theme is that of the calypsonian's alleged insatiable sexual appetite, which causes innumerable females either to cry in ecstasy, beg for more or groan in agony if they cannot cope with their too-ardent lovers'. Calypsonian Sparrow, says Rohlehr, 'has done more than anyone else to project the idea of the West Indian male as a walking phallic symbol'. As Sparrow's 'Village Ram' boasts:

> . . . if a woman ever tell you that I
> Ever leave her dissatisfy
> She lie, she lie, I say she lie.

And Mr Rake-and-Scrape avers that, for him, any woman will do for his sexual gratification:

I'm a busy man with no time to lose
Ah don't pass my hand, ah don't pick and choose
So any kind o'woman, one foot or one hand
Dey cannot escape from me Mr Rake-and-Scrape.

Thirdly, there is a large body of calypsos which deal with 'denigration and degradation' of the female (Warner 1982, p. 99). In the crudest possible terms, women are castigated as being ugly, dirty, stupid, vile, predatory, smelly, evil, etc. (see examples given in Warner 1982; see also Rohlehr 1970; Hodge 1974). Part of this includes the categorization of women by stereotypes which convey 'semantically offensive overtones' (Elder 1968, p. 25) such as 'Hog-mouth Mary' and 'Gate-way Janie'.

Finally, there are those calypsos which deal with 'pejorative accounts of female acts', in which the male is frequently victim (Warner 1982). The woman is cast in various negative postures: demanding money for sex, attempting to saddle the male with false paternity, cuckolding him, trying to ensnare him with witchcraft, etc.

Throughout, the woman as the victim of male condemnation is also subjected to threats of violence and verbal abuse as a means of keeping her in line. 'Girl you looking for blows,' Sparrow warns his sweetheart Rose. He tells the world:

Every now and then cuff them down
They'll love you long and they'll love you strong
Black up dey eye, bruise up dey knee
And they will love you eternally.

However, the female is also seen as quite capable of defending herself physically. Shadow's Jane in 1976 was threatening that

I might pelt a big stone and mash up your jawbone
You better leave me alone.

The calypso is recognized as double-edged. Matched against the calypsonian's bravado and contempt is his fear of the female, whom he perceives as scheming and untrustworthy, and who, when all else fails, will resort to trickery including obeah and black magic to bind him. Views of the female as scheming were also held by the men in the Barbados study, who described women as 'avaricious, materialistic and calculating'. These men, like the calypsonians, viewed their relationships with women as 'uneasy' and 'dangerous' (Barrow WICP 1986b).

It is of interest that the more recent development of popular music in Jamaica — the ska to reggae to dee-jay tradition — has followed the same pattern as calypsos where themes are concerned. The earliest themes dealt mainly with issues of social protest and were against male authority figures such as the police, judges, soldiers, the rich elements of society castigated as 'Babylon', etc., just as Elder found for the earlier period in Trinidadian calypso. Analysis of contemporary Jamaican popular music would show that an inordinate amount of song themes, especially in the newest dee-jay style, are similar to the calypsos in so far as they deal in female denigration and degradation versus male elevation.

Male perceptions of women: mother vs. 'other'

We noted (chapter 2) that males at an early age distinguished between the tender treatment to be accorded mothers and the treatment of other women who are likely to become their sexual partners. Various scholars suggest that this distinction arises from (i) the powerful role played by the mother/weak role of the father in the young boy's life and his subsequent close attachment to his mother; (ii) lack of socialization of boys and girls in how to relate in a normal and healthy way to each other as individuals; (iii) lack of socialization of young men into their future responsibilities as fathers and towards women as partners. Of course historical factors should not be overlooked, such as the highly esteemed place of the mother in many cultures, especially African culture, and the strength of the mother–child bond which developed during slavery and which has continued to this day as the most lasting of family bonds.

While we do not have information that would enable us to make a direct link between these factors and subsequent behaviours, it can be observed that in the Caribbean the adulation of the mother might be tinged with hostility, and is off-set by cynical treatment and behaviour towards other women. Several observers have noted this in calypsos; favourable portrayal of women, except for mothers, is rare in this art form. Kitchener observed:

> Well for me I'm holding on to my mother
> And my wife she'll have to excuse Kitchener
> For I can always get another wife
> But I can never get another mother in my life.

While Mighty Destroyer avers:

> You can have diamonds, rubies and pearls
> But a mother is the greatest thing in the world.

However, a discordant note is struck by Striker in his Mother's Day song:

> M is for the million things she gave me
> O means that she is only getting old
> But all my mother used to give me heaven knows
> Is to kneel down on grater with plenty blows

and alerts us to the fact that the adulation of the mother cannot hide the paradox 'whereby the calypsonian can simultaneously applaud the courage of the mother who fathers her bastard son, and the cynical cunning of the male who has deserted her' (Rohlehr 1970, p. 91).

While the content of calypso and other forms of folk and popular music can be seen as expressions of the singer's response to his social environment (Elder 1968, p. 25), another dimension has also been suggested, that utterances of this kind also serve as a tension-releasing mechanism which helps to satisfy some of man's emotional needs and drives (Elder 1968). Thus calypsos and dee-jay songs might be seen as part of an adaptive strategy whereby males and females work out their conflicts with each other. In some African societies ritual songs of ridicule are one of the 'institutionalised mechanisms for releasing tensions', including tension between the sexes (Steady 1981b, p. 33).

Calypso (and to a lesser extent reggae music) has been largely a male tradition and only in recent years have females been emerging in some numbers and prominence. Where they have dealt with male–female relationships, the women not unexpectedly have been defending the female against male ill-behaviour, giving such explicit advice as Singing Francine in 'Run Away' (1979):

> Cat does run away, dog does run away
> Fowl does run away when you treating them bad
> What happen to you?
> Woman, you can run away too.

Attitudes and expectations

It can be argued that throughout the Caribbean there is little remaining institutionalized discrimination against women. Nevertheless, sexual inequality widely exists
and takes subtle forms, some of which we have mentioned throughout this work,
e.g. the role played by institutions such as media, schools, churches, etc. in projecting and reinforcing gender-role stereotyping; inequality of access to resources;
oppressions in the social and economic spheres. To these we might add inequalities
in male–female relationships.

To the outsider, the Caribbean woman for all her vaunted 'strength' and 'independence' seems to 'put up with a lot' from her man. 'A lot' frequently includes
unfaithfulness, physical and mental abuse and cruelty and a shouldering of unequal
family responsibilities.

There is ample evidence to suggest that, in general, females as well as males seem
to accept sexually defined roles and male dominance. As Elsie LeFranc observes,
'Male and female perceptions about each other display not only mutual distrust and
suspicion, but also the continuing subscription to the traditional expectations about
behaviour. For example, man should be the dominant hunter and woman the submissive and respectful home-maker and child-rearer. It is of some interest that both
sexes hold similar views' (LeFranc WICP 1983, p. 92).

Barrow's survey (1982b) showed that the men in her study accept it as natural
for males to be dominant, a view certainly articulated by the most vocal elements
such as calypsonians. Men in Barrow's survey also expressed the view that women
have no identity outside their partners, and that the marriage certificate gives a man
the right to correct his wife, including physical punishment.

The cultural expectations of men (as expressed in Barrow's survey (Barrow
WICP 1986b) and various other sources (e.g. Sutton and Makiesky-Barrow 1981)
might be summarized as follows: a wife's role in marriage (legal or common law)
should be to (i) assume responsibility for domestic duties, housekeeping and child-
rearing; (ii) be a good manager of household finances and economic resources
generally; nowadays women are also expected to contribute to household expenses;
whether wives work or not, domestic responsibilities are theirs exclusively; (iii) look
after the man, i.e. take care of his clothes, prepare his favourite dishes, see that his
meals are on time and cater to him generally; (iv) treat his friends well; (v) not
'shame' him, and this includes not being unfaithful or playing around with other
men.

These expectations also seem to be shared by women: interviews with women in
the WICP revealed this. The self-image of the 'good wife' was frequently bolstered
by biblical precept. A Pentecostal minister's wife in her thirties stated:

> I never believed that women should be above the man because the Bible tells
> us that God make man first and he take a rib from the man and he make the
> woman and that is telling us that the woman was made for the man but the man
> was made for God and the woman is the glory of the man and the man is the
> glory of God. And woman should not try to make themselves to say I am the
> boss, I am the boss. Woman should know that we are the weaker vessel and we
> must be in subjection to the men, that's how I think it.

This woman sees the economic role performed by Caribbean women as resulting
exclusively from the failure of the male, and the nurturing role as the only proper
one for women:

> We know that a man is the head of the home, a man is suppose to be the breadwin-
> ner, he suppose to go and bring in the money. In the first place we women should

not have been working we should have been home taking care of our home, taking care of our children because the Bible say young women must have children, train them in the fear of God. That is what a woman is there for. But men fail and because men fail that's how women have to go out.

Pleasing a husband is seen as an important part of the wife's role:

If your husband coming in now and you know he's a fretful person then you will study well, my God, let me see if everything is in order. And you will try to make sure that everything is in order because you don't want him to fret when he get in, you see. You will try to do your best to please him. Well my husband, he want to see the house clean and his clothes ready, nothing else. If he come in now and they ain't no food, he don't mind. But let him meet those clothes on the hanger and let him see everything clean.

The old folk song which complains about the useless wife:

Hand full a ring and she can't do a ting
Send she back to she mumma-o

would still find currency today.

Another woman in the WICP survey viewed acquisition of homemaking skills as a prerequisite for the good wife. She herself acquired these when she started working as a domestic at an early age:

I. And you can do this before you marry?
R. Yes, yes, and when you marry now your husband wouldn't say 'oh you can't do this, oh and you so worthless, you can't enjoy nothing you can't even fix yourself a good meal, you can't do nothing'.
I. So this gives you knowledge for marriage?
R. Yes. You watch how other people live so if you marry it wouldn't be no hardship because you know how to set your home for yourself.

The Caribbean woman also has certain cultural expectations of the male. These may be summarized as follows: (i) he is expected to contribute to household finances and child-rearing expenses and treat the children of the household well, including hers by another man; (ii) he should not divert his income elsewhere, i.e. to other women, gambling, etc.; (iii) he should be considerate, affectionate, not indulge in physical abuse, etc.; (iv) he should protect his wife from dangers and physical assault, though the woman is expected to be able to 'speak up for herself'.

Problems arise when both males and females stray from these prescriptions of behaviour — as they invariably do.

Behaviour and experience

Fidelity

The double standard of sexual morality which is applied to the socialization of adolescents is absorbed and becomes part of the pattern of behaviour of both sexes as they mature: the stereotyped belief is of the straying male, faithful female. This does not mean that both males and females might not be unfaithful, but where male infidelity is recognized, where 'playing around' is seen as natural for men, whether married or not, the same sort of behaviour by women is roundly condemned and for women in unions might lead to beatings, denunciation and abandonment. A palindrome given by a Trinidadian summarizes the attitude which pervades all classes: 'When women are wild you call them rats; when a man is wild you call him a star!' (cited in Rodman 1971, p. 71).

Males in the Barrow study argued that:

> Caribbean man perceives women as existing for his sexual pleasure. The tendency to be simultaneously involved with more than one partner is perceived as natural to a man — 'to keep you knowing you is a man' — but not to a woman. For their sexual performance men are complimented as 'hard-seeds', while women become 'whores' and are 'dragged in the gutter'.
>
> (Barrow WICP 1986b, p. 58)

The double standard in male–female relationships is a particular source of conflict and sexual inequality (Sutton and Makiesky-Barrow 1981). Thus men will accept as 'normal' and women will tolerate the man's outside affairs, accepting it as part of man's 'nature', no matter how painful and humiliating to her the whole affair might be. As one woman describes her marriage:

R. The first two years were good. Well, after that you know men going to be men. So he had his little flings and we broke up once through that. We were separated for a year and we got back together. I suppose he still does his thing and it doesn't worry me in the least.

I. You said 'men will be men'. Does that mean this is something that's natural for men to do?

R. It would look like that.

I. Why does it look like that?

R. Because they always do it. If they don't do it early in life they do it later. My husband had his flings but I never could say that I actually saw him. He would always be discreet. But I have some friends who meet openly with other women. They don't care.

She was asked:

I. When you hear [about your husband's behaviour] how do you feel and who do you hear from?

R. Sometimes friends mention it, sometimes you just talk and it might come up. But I will ask him if I hear.

I. What does he say?

R. Sometimes he does laugh and he would say nothing but I know him so well according to his reaction I know whether it's true or not.

I. Let's say if the situation was reversed, if it was you having an outside relationship, what would be your husband's reaction?

R. That would be the end.

I. Would he get explosive about the whole thing?

R. Yes.

I. Then why is that?

R. That is just how he is.

I. Do you think that most men would take this position?

R. No. Not all the time, because I have a lot of men friends and we chat and sometimes one would say well if I were to catch my wife with a man I would forgive her because I realize sometimes just like how a man could look at another woman and feel that he wants to have a fling I feel the woman could be the same way too. But he's [her husband] never in sympathy with that, you know. Once a woman does that she's bad, that's how he thinks of it.

Women of widely varying ages and backgrounds seem to share this view of male infidelity as 'natural'. A 23-year-old Antiguan high school graduate said: 'It's Caribbean ways, the married men are there for the single woman comfort. You find the young girls say that married men treat them better than the single ones.' An older Antiguan takes a more cynical view of male philandering:

    I. You said the problem with some men is that they want more than one woman?
    R. Yes, all the time, and they can't manage one you know.
    I. Why are men like that?
    R. I couldn't tell you me dear love, it's just their minds.
    I. Now what kind of problem does that create, when a man has more than one woman?
    R. When he have more than one, some outside does get and you inside get nothing and that cause contention all the while.

Family responsibilities

Although men in the Barbados study generally admitted that 'leaving out' wives and children in favour of other women was wrong, especially with regard to the children, they felt that such behaviour was justifiable in certain circumstances: for example, '(i) if a woman's behaviour does not conform to her partner's requirements, (ii) most certainly when she has or is suspected of a relationship with another man, and (iii) if she is suspected of wrongful paternity claims or if she turns children against their fathers' (Barrow WICP 1986b, p. 59).

Men are especially afraid of being given a 'jacket', that is, taking on unknowingly the responsibility of minding a child conceived by another man. Frequently, a man in a visiting or common-law union will wait until the child is born to see if there is a resemblance to him before assuming paternity. The concern with being saddled with false paternity is a constant theme in calypso.

The fact that the child does not resemble him is frequently used as a dodge by the man to get out of paying child support, even leading to the absurd situation cited elsewhere in this book where a father of twins accepts one child who resembles him and rejects the other who doesn't.

An examination of the 38 in-depth interviews in the WICP study yields some insights into female attitudes on the subject. The general feeling among the women seems to be that a father should provide for his child. Thus tolerance will extend to the children of extramarital affairs, though not usually to the 'baby mother'. A 30-year-old St Vincent woman, a professional, was asked:

    I. If your husband had an outside child how would you feel about it?
    R. If I know that he is not taking care of that child, I would see to it that the child is being fed and things like that.
    I. Would you feel anyway towards the child?
    R. No.
    I. What about the child's mother?
    R. Well now, I don't know what to say.

A woman who is already sharing her common-law husband with another steady woman was asked:

    I. If he's having sex outside, what would happen if one of those ladies got pregnant?
    R. Well he would have to just see to his child.

    I. How would you feel about that?

    R. Nothing, I wouldn't feel nothing. While I watch the child and the child looks like him and the woman say it's his, he will just have to take his child.

    I. So he would have to take responsibility?

    R. Of course, he wrong.

However, women who lean towards European ideals of 'respectability' might find the man's infidelity and outside children hard to bear. An older middle-class woman speaks of what it was like for her own mother:

    R. The relationship was bitter for her. It was not easy for her to know that, it wasn't one child, it was two, it was three, it was four, it was five, during the course of our growing up . . .

    I. When did your mother learn this?

    R. His first child was about two or three years younger than I. I was the last, out of three, you see, so this came after her childbearing or probably she chose not to have any more children after this, I don't know. But you sense as a child growing up the anguish that she had because of this relationship, because when a man comes in late, he would come in, say, one or two, you would hear. I mean there weren't many bitter rows. The sort or person she was, she wouldn't row with him, at least not openly for us to be involved, but you sense as a child that something was not right.

A 43-year-old professional woman, who seems to have come from a very close-knit family, explained her father's infidelity and what she perceives as the reason for it:

    R. When I had my first child he had his first outside child. I think it's my mother's fault, eh. All our life they were living sharing one bedroom. Well, after I got married there was separation. My mother said, this is what daddy told us, right, that I am a big woman now and she cannot be doing the same thing I am doing, so she never slept with daddy again till he died three years ago.

    I. So it was after that . . .

    R. That he went out and got the child.

However, women have differing perspectives of what might be regarded as promiscuity on the part of the male and of the female. Male promiscuity seems to be taken for granted — as long as the man supports his children. Some women also appear to be tolerant of what appears to be female promiscuity — many children for different fathers — and rationalize it on the grounds that children are a natural outcome of the search for support.

A young woman in her early twenties, who was raised by her aunt and who was poorly treated by her foster family, nevertheless was tolerant of her mother's behaviour:

    I. How do you view your mother with thirteen children and five different fathers. Have you thought about that?

    R. Yes. I wouldn't think she was a bad woman, right, because I know in those days probably she had it hard. Sometimes women might be fooled by men, you know.

    I. Is it painful for you to think about it, does it sadden you or shame you or hurt you?

    R. I'm not really ashamed because we have our children and although they're

for five men, you can look at them and say they're five different children and
they belong to me, especially with me.

I. Would you like to live your mother's life?

R. No, I don't think I could do that.

I. Why not?

R. Well probably she did not understand certain things in life and the first kid
she had . . . the worst thing her mother ever did was to throw her out and
she was young.

I. So her mother threw her out?

R. Yes.

I. Where did she go?

R. I don't really know, I never asked questions about anything. I heard somebody saying that the first child she had, her mother threw her out.

The same woman was asked:

I. What about your father, he had five children for five mothers?

R. Well you know they use to say that he was sharp but I don't think so. He
don't have any feeling for women, that's what I say. Because any man that
have feelings for a woman wouldn't want to go around having children like
that and know the women don't like those kind of things, right. Next thing
he settled down with a woman that does not have any kid for him, she has
a lot of big kids, right, big children old enough to be my father . . .

A close reading of the interviews suggests that there exists a female mythology
that, while the practice of men going around having many children with different
women might be condemned, similar conduct on the part of the woman can be
rationalized. Blame is laid on the woman's own ignorance, man's exploitation of
this and the lack of social supports. In other words, childbearing is seen as both
resulting in and as a result of female dependency. However, there does not seem
to be general condemnation of men who have children with many women as long
as they take a responsible attitude towards the women and children.

A 49-year-old explained about her mother, who had her children for a married
man:

I think they just bumped into each other and she start having one child and she
continued until she had four, four she had until my father died and left her pregnant with my last sister. And I suppose if he was still alive she will be still having
children because the way she always talking about it, he treating her well and
you know when women are getting good treatment from men how it is.

She was asked what kinds of things he did for her mother: 'I suppose he supported
his children well and he spend time with her, he doesn't sleep out, I know that well.
You know he just stay late like midnight with her and when he was sick before his
death you know he bought her a cow and it's because of the cow she got a house.'

Sharing relationships

A significant number of women in the Caribbean are in 'sharing relationships', that
is, they knowingly or unknowingly share a man with whom they have a steady relationship with another woman (or other women). Children by the various women
are frequently the outcome. Such sharing relationships exist at all levels; it is not
uncommon in middle- and upper-class families for there to be a set of 'inside'

children of the 'real' or legal family and 'outside' children with another woman. Sometimes these parallel families exist unknown to each other, or at least unknown to the 'inside' family; others might be aware but turn a blind eye. Such situations quite often are tolerated by the wife because, it is felt, she has the ring, the prestige and the security and she is unable/unwilling to break up the marriage. Shared relationships are nevertheless frequently the cause of bitterness and unhappiness to the women involved, as the WICP interviews demonstrate:

R. He would sleep here one night, there one night with other women. That wasn't good enough at all.

I. Did he have children with any of these other women?

R. None, he didn't have none with me neither.

I. But what did you think of that, he was sleeping here, sleeping there . . .

R. Sleeping all about.

I. Did you ever meet up with any of the women he was sleeping with?

R. I know them, all around here.

I. They were your friends?

R. They use to come. He use to bring things from the garden and leave it here for them and they will come for it.

I. Did you and the women ever have any quarrels?

R. Never with one.

I. Why not?

R. I ain't quarrelling with nobody.

I. Did any of them ever quarrel with you?

R. They never quarrel with me but they would tell him I say this and I say that whether I say it or not and then he would come home and fret. 'Why did you meet so and so and say so and so and so?' But I don't worry with he, you know.

This woman was an agricultural worker in her sixties, whose independent attitude to men and life was perhaps shaped by the fact that she had started to work at the age of 15. Her husband left her after six years of marriage and she remained single.

Another woman was asked:

I. What kind of a relationship did your stepmother have with your sister's mother?

R. They're always at war, they're always at war, always cursing, they never have a fight as far as I know but they always cursing wherever they meet.

To explore more deeply a woman's feelings and experiences in a 'sharing' relationship, we will examine in detail one case, that of a 38-year-old former domestic, now a farmer, who is sharing her children's father:

R. From the third go down to the seventh, the same father, he look after them okay because he have a lot of children. He have six with me, and he have seven with a next woman.

I. How do you feel about that?

R. Well I feel funny but have to work it out.

I. Do you still love him?

R. Yes.

I. Is he in the same town?

R. Same village.

I. So you see him?

R. Yes, well we does live next door, you know.

I. What! So close?

R. Yes, but not now. He move now. Just one year ago he move from there.

I. So how did you and the other baby mother get along?

R. Well we get along terrible I must tell you. We went all to the Court . . . [this was as a result of a pushing incident between the two women].

I. Who had the first baby for the fellow?

R. I.

I. Alright, and then . . .

R. She came between.

I. How many babies you had for him before she came about?

R. I had two.

I. So when she comes into the picture, how do you feel about it?

R. Me feel badly, mortify, I feel me could a box she up.

She was in a visiting relationship with this man when he brought the new woman into the village to live with him. She was asked to explain her reasons for continuing the friendship:

R. Because me love he. After he came back he talk to me and say that he don't prefer her more than me, only because her mother died and she want help, how he sorry for she.

I. You believed him?

R. Yes. I don't like to run around, nah run around. I always say I would like to have my children with one person. I did have the intention to settle down with that one.

I. So you thought he would marry you?

R. Yes, but since he get in with that one, the woman kind a little bright [implying that she has resorted to black magic or obeah].

These two 'baby mothers' were having children almost at the same time. Our informant was actually pregnant with her second child for this man when the other woman came on the scene:

She have one the same year too with that second one, so when I have mine the early part, she have hers the later part. I have mine the January and she have hers the November. Sometimes both of us have children the same, like I have one this year she have one this year too, so he does have two children born a year . . . The fourth one she have one born the same year again too and both of us did have our children the same time, I have mine October the 6th, and she have hers September the 9th. Mine was a little girl and hers was a little boy.

The children of both mothers took the father's surname and most go to the same school and, says our informant, they all look alike. The children are in and out of each other's homes; she and the other children 'pull nice'. But as for their mother:

R. We all pull terrible, me and she can't get along at all. Me nah have no bad mind for her, right, but she like she's a devil. She interference. She will meet me and she will laugh and she first will interfere with me but I don't pay her any mind.

I. So you just see her on the street and she mess with you, interfere, and then you curse and go on about your business?

R. Yes.

I. How do you feel about this? Here's this one man and these two women and she's interfering with you?

R. Well me feel bad. Me feel me can bang she.

I. That you could bang her?

R. Yes, when she trouble me.

I. You want to bang her?

R. Yes, waan wrap she up.

I. But you hold back?

R. Yes, because me fraid of trouble. If me go box her you know what the Government ga do?

I. Yes.

R. Just cuff off.

I. How do you feel about him?

R. Well, me nah really lock up with he right now. When he nice I nice too but when he bad me bad too.

Changing attitudes of women vs. men

The Caribbean has not been untouched by the winds of change, including the growing freedom for women. Education, which gives an increasing number of women entry into professional status and economic independence, is also altering the status of women versus men. Even in small island societies, women are beginning to assert their sexual equality. A middle-class WICP informant recalled:

R. Women prided themselves or called themselves sort of middle-class by virtue of the education they had got out of the Church that they were affiliated to. They suffered in that home in silence. Many of the women nowadays in our society, they're not prepared to do that you know. They have outlets. They can go off to family in the United States and the Virgin Islands and so on. A lot of the women are not tolerating it any longer. Some of them are staying and having outside affairs and are making new liaisons. I mean not just having outside affairs within the marital circle, you know. They're just splitting up and moving out into a house with another man.

I. Middle-class women?

R. Middle-class women.

I. How can a society so small cope with that situation?

R. I know a case just recently, you met the girl too, this young woman now and then turns up to parties with her ex-husband. She might call him and ask him to take her but she has an affair at one end with another married man and he has his own woman, you know, there's an accommodation in some cases.

I. Now there's always been this notion that women can contend with knowing that husbands are having an outside affair, but it's difficult for men to contend with knowing wives are having outside affairs, does that kind of notion exist here, how prevalent is it?

R. Yes, that does exist but things are changing now and I think men are just accepting it.

Barrow's male informants showed concern about the progress being achieved by the 'young women of today' and the implications for men. 'Rather than waiting at home on their menfolk, they are perceived to be out fulfilling their own ambition and desires' (Barrow WICP 1986b, p. 60). Barrow notes that 'During the group discussion the men expressed their views in a fashion which indicated that they felt threatened by today's women who seem to present a challenge to their ability to control their female partners and thus to their concept of manhood' (Barrow WICP 1986b, p. 61).

Analysing the contradictions

In trying to explain why Caribbean women 'put up with a lot' from their men, the need for warmth, love and tenderness cannot be ignored as significant elements in their behaviour, as our informants have revealed. Hermione McKenzie observed that 'the need for warm and satisfying emotional and sexual relationships exists on both sides. In a social structure which so often defeats fidelity and tenderness, the shift from partner to partner by both men and women may still be seen as a persistent quest for exactly these qualities in a relationship' (McKenzie 1977, p. x). Women's emotional vulnerability lies precisely in this desire for satisfactory 'relationships' and a susceptibility to male charms, despite everything:

R. He loved women obviously; there must have been at least four women that he had relationships with before my mother, and this is where I blame my mother . . . perhaps she wasn't educated enough to realize that she had no right to get involved with a man with a roaming eye.

I. That would rule out all Caribbean men then.

R. So this man had about four or five children before and I'm sure there are more but I really don't know.

Yet, even as she described the pain her father's infidelities brought on her mother and on the family, this same woman confessed:

R. I admired my father in a sort of secret way.

I. You didn't let your mother see it?

R. No. The thing about it is, I think she admired him too and she loved him. No man could have done what he did and still be treated as he was treated all through his life, this is the whole paradox of the thing.

I. How did she treat him?

R. Well I mean she loved him, nuh. This is all I can say. She probably must have loved him. She treated him good because when his sort of gay days were over, she had to be saddled with him then.

Another woman explained of her husband who 'ran around': 'He was lovable, he wasn't ugly like me. He had a nice countenance, he always smiling and you know people love people that smiling. He always friendly. He always have a lot of friends, men also.'

One informant who knowingly shares her common-law husband with another woman living near by, explained:

R. There are more women than men.

I. Okay so there are more women than men, and you said these women have feelings, alright? So that's one reason why women share. Why are you sharing?

R. Well sometimes, just love.

I. So you love him?

R. Of course.

I. And he loves you, and you've been together for about fourteen years or so.
What does he do for you?

R. He just act as a husband of mine.

I. In acting as a husband what kinds of things does he do?

R. Give me what I ask for, makes me happy.

I. What do you ask for?

R. Anything I want I ask.

I. Like what?

R. Anything for my home or my children.

The vast majority of women in the WICP study in fact indicated that they were seeking emotional support in their relationships with men (Anderson WICP 1986).

The attitudes and behaviour of Caribbean men and women towards each other is of course culture-specific. Part of the context is the history. The 'concentration of moral authority in the person of the woman' is seen as a powerful force in influencing relations between men and women of African descent in the Caribbean (Hodge 1977, p. 115). The socio-psychological dimension is also frequently cited, as in this quotation from a Caribbean psychiatrist: 'The traumatic socialization practices, the absent father . . . and the dual image of the mother (as satisfier and as depriver) constitute a situation which could call forth from males in such a confrontation only responses like hostility, withdrawal, status envy, rejection and schizophrenic fear of the female' (Elder 1968, p. 40, quoting M. Beaubrun). Implicit too is the strong role played by economic factors. The vacillation between dependence and independence displayed by many women has a strong economic base. A high level of female unemployment leads to dependency relationships with men and increased vulnerability of the female. Women who are economically dependent are far more likely to 'put up with a lot' from men. For example, one result of a pilot project in Jamaica to train women as construction workers and place them in reasonably well-paying jobs has been that, once the women get jobs and start earning, they leave unsatisfactory males. 'As soon as they start earning an income,' someone who works with the group states, 'they then have a choice as to who to live with.' Some chose to return to live with their mothers. These were women from ghetto areas, who might have entered into sexual relationships out of economic necessity, and, with their new skills and jobs, for the first time in their lives were able to exercise options (*Women Speak!* 1985, pp. 8–11).

But the behaviour of men too is conditioned by economic factors. A man's sole control over family resources might turn him into a dictator over his woman and children. On the other hand, a man's self-image and consequent treatment of his woman might also be a direct result of his economic powerlessness: 'where the society contains many demoralizing and alienating economic and social conditions, these deeply affect the quality of the relationships between men and women. At the same time . . . insecure male/female relationships themselves exacerbate difficult social and economic conditions' (McKenzie 1977, pp. ix–x).

Finally, the vacillation in women's behaviour might be seen as expressing the dichotomy of their cultural inheritance, where the stereotypes are European (protected/dominated female) but the role models and role performance are West African (woman as independent actor). Thus part of the vacillation arises from contradictions within the society itself.

The processes resulting from these contradictions might be summarized as follows:

1 While black women especially achieved *de facto* sexual equality on the plantations

and after through their economic contributions and their resistance to enslavement and other forms of oppression, the pervasive ideology at all levels has been male dominance.

2 The ideology of male dominance has been subverted by the reality of male marginality. This has led to increasing female self-reliance.

3 The strong impulse to female self-reliance is continuously subverted by contradictory female socialization and its results. While 'the resourceful woman is the cultural ideal' (Justus 1981, p. 446), fulfilment of this ideal is subverted or modified by strong cultural expectations towards childbearing and child-rearing (and, as Patricia Anderson (WICP 1986) reminds us, women's strong consciousness of nurturing extends to their menfolk). Early fulfilment of such expectations often leads to a lack of preparation for earning a livelihood. Coupled with this are the structural inequalities of these societies, where women's access to resources are limited by occupational statuses and earnings.

Caribbean economies do not provide the infrastructure to support female independence and hardship is often the lot of poor women especially, who end up with families to support. This leads to a further vicious cycle of (i) dependency relationships with men; (ii) a distortion of male–female relationships since there is for the woman a strong economic motive for seeking and maintaining such relationships. Such behaviour on the part of the woman breeds male distrust and reinforces the image of woman as 'trickster', 'schemer', 'manipulator'. Women, on the other hand, will argue that if they are scheming and manipulative they are forced to be so in order to extract from irresponsible males the economic assistance they need for their children.

The nature of male–female relationships is further modified by the fact that women are able to derive power and authority from non-sexual relationships and this helps to reduce emotional dependence on men. This also makes male–female relationships more complex than at first might appear.

It can be argued that the real power and status of women *vis-à-vis* men inhere in the following factors:

1 Male lack of responsibility and commitment to family life and women's commitment to family invest moral authority in the woman; this is heightened by the fact that, in these societies, the mother role is traditionally regarded as more central than the wife/partner role.

2 Women's network of kin and others (described more fully in chapter 7) and their ability to manipulate these enable them to counter male neglect and the relative instability of conjugal unions. There is a historical dimension to this, as Brodber shows in her study of post-emancipation Jamaican society: 'there was a persistent inner network of grandmothers, mothers, daughters and sisters bound together in economic activities. Men impinged upon this economic unit and its activities, as providers of the economic base, or as occasional and often contracted helpers' (Brodber WICP 1986, p. 34).

3 The striving by women for economic independence. There is a tradition of Afro-Caribbean women, like West African women, being managers of their own economic resources, which they do not necessarily merge with those of their partners (Mintz 1981; Sutton and Makiesky-Barrow 1981; Durant-Gonzalez 1982). Some observers have noted that marriage relationships are often characterized by secrecy and distance between husbands and wives regarding their economic affairs (Sutton and Makiesky-Barrow 1981). Women, as we have seen in chapter 6, constantly

emphasize the need to be independent; this is part of the female self-concept, even though independence is not always achievable.

4 Although women's public roles are limited, women do have access to prestige- and status-bearing roles independent of their mates through community affairs, religious societies, family ties, etc. These can help to reduce tensions — or exacerbate them when they are seen by males as conflicting with women's duties in the home.

5 Finally, there is the nature of the female strategies adopted. Although this has not been much studied, there is the suggestion that the Caribbean woman relies less on feminist confrontation in dealing with her mate and more on subtle 'subterranean' strategies (see, for example, Carolyn Cooper 1985). According to Louise Bennett:

> Jamaica oman cunny, sah!
> Is how dem jinnal so?
> Look how long dem liberated
> An de man dem never know?

(Bennett 1982)

Patricia Anderson also argues that the seemingly dependent behaviour on the part of the Caribbean woman might be a part of her strategy: 'Such behaviour does not necessarily reflect a psychological inability to act autonomously, but may itself be a situational strategy, utilising ideological conceptions of appropriate female behaviour . . . The immediate goals of securing material and emotional transfers are the means to achieving the major objectives of social reproduction and emotional satisfaction' (Anderson WICP 1986, p. 313)

Many Caribbean women do not seem preoccupied with gaining sexual equality *per se*, perhaps because they do not have a consciousness of sexual inequality. Many women in the WICP study asserted their consciousness of equality with men or at least an acceptance of their gender (see chapter 8). This of course can be interpreted as displaying a lack of feminine consciousness of the possibility of choice and free will, i.e. an acceptance of the status quo. There is in fact a widespread acceptance of patriarchic structures among women members of newer religions such as Rastafarianism (see Rowe 1980; see also Pentecostal woman's comments above).[1]

As is the case in other Third World countries, the perception, conscious or unconscious, that the sexual oppression of women is part of the larger forms of oppression based on economics, race and class might also serve to defuse focus on sexual oppression at the individual level. Filomina Steady in examining the experience of the black woman cross-culturally reminds us that: 'The experiences of the majority of black women represent multiple forms of oppression rather than simple sexual oppression. Race and class are important variables in her experience and are significantly more important barriers to the acquisition of the basic needs for survival than is sexism' (Steady 1981b, p. 3). The same conclusions were drawn by Roberta Clarke in studying the public roles of women in the eastern Caribbean (Clarke WICP 1986).

Ultimately, male–female relationships are power relationships. If men feel inadequate in one sphere, they might be forced to express their desire for power and control over women in other ways, through either (i) elevation of the male or (ii) devaluation of the female, or both. Derision and devaluation of the female takes

---

1 Though women in Rastafarianism seem not to be unaffected by growing feminist consciousness; some are now seeking to assert their identity, as are Hindu women in Trinidad (see Reddock 1989).

place at social levels throughout the region by various means: through the mass media (male-owned and controlled); in the world of entertainment through songs of derision and derogatory portrayals of women on the stage and screen; through the exploitation of female bodies to sell products in the world of advertising, to sell newspapers, posters or other products, or television time. Female lack of protest at such exploitation reveals one dimension of women's powerlessness.

At the individual level, men express their desire for control over women in many negative ways: in domestic violence and in rape and other acts of physical violence against women, which are widespread, and in various forms of mental cruelty, including extremely insulting private or public behaviour to their own and strange women: 'Young men at a loose end (usually unemployed — the devaluation of black manhood is perpetuated in economic frustration) will position themselves on a culvert, at a street corner, on a pavement, and vie with each other in the ingenuity of their comments to embarrass women going by. The embarrassment of women is part of the national ethos' (Hodge 1974, p. 117). These expressions are visible to anyone who lives in or travels through the Caribbean.

What we do not know at this stage is women's real consciousness about them-selves and about their relationships with men. We are still handicapped by ignor-ance of some critical aspects of feminine consciousness. For instance, as Anderson suggests, we know virtually nothing about how the class system or the growing upward mobility of women is affecting gender relations (Anderson WICP 1986). The fact that there was throughout the Caribbean, until recently, little public outcry of even the grossest abuse of the female body or psyche suggests that, in male–female and other relationships, women had not found the means of articulat-ing their oppressions.

The situation began to change rapidly in the 1970s and 1980s as the influence of the international women's movement began to be felt. Reddock argues that:

> many of the first women to be influenced were the stalwarts of the traditional women's organisations from the era of the 1950s, many of whom were heavily involved in the nationalist political parties which emerged at that time. It should be said that the new con-sciousness seeping into the region reminded these older women activists of the marginal position they still had within their political organisations and the governments which their parties formed.
>
> (Reddock 1989, p. 4)

A great deal of the women's activism of the 1970s took place within the frame-work of political parties in Jamaica and Guyana especially, where there were socialist governments, and through other small but active left-wing parties and organizations in these and other countries such as Trinidad. It was during the 1970s too that the national and regional structures mentioned earlier were all estab-lished and helped to provide a broader focus for women's activities. The university-based WAND in particular has been in the forefront of these activities, especially in the eastern Caribbean, collaborating with government and non-governmental organizations, with community development agencies and with other women's organizations.

In the period of the 1970s, several autonomous women's groups also came into being and all had active but short lives. Most comprised middle-class women (see Reddock 1989). The Sistren Women's Theatre Collective, which emerged in Jamaica in 1977, was the first of the feminist autonomous women's groups and the first to be predominantly working-class. Sistren's use of drama for consciousness-raising and entertainment has since then earned it international acclaim. By the

1980s, many small activist women's groups had emerged throughout the region. These groups have concentrated on consciousness-raising internally and to the wider society through a variety of media and techniques. They mounted several successful campaigns mentioned earlier (chapter 8). But as Reddock (1989) has pointed out:

> The issue of sexual violence has been a key factor in mobilising women throughout the region. This issue which includes domestic violence — sexual abuse of children, rape in marriage/unions, wife-battering, rape, incest, sexual harassment in the workplace and other forms of sexual assault has served to be the one issue capable of uniting women of all classes, races and ethnic groups. In the Caribbean region it has been the one factor which has brought to women some understanding of body politics and its relationship to the wider socio-political and economic system. (p. 10)

A few prominent examples include the rise of rape crisis centres (e.g. in Trinidad and Tobago), the hosting by women's bureaux of seminars on violence against women (e.g. Barbados, Dominica), public demonstrations against rape (e.g. Barbados), public requests by women's groups, umbrella organizations, women's bureaux for trial in camera for rape cases (most countries).

These examples illustrate that women are beginning to come together to raise their voices publicly, to articulate their grievances, to develop a notion of 'women's issues'. Additionally, changes have been observed in the activities of traditional women's organizations and in women's religious groups which are believed to be a response to the new feminine consciousness (Reddock 1989). At another level, there have been projects like the WICP, the introduction of a programme of Women and Development Studies at the University of the West Indies and the formation of the Caribbean Association for Feminist Research and Action (CAFRA) — a network of Caribbean feminists and feminist organizations which includes women in the Dutch, English, French and Spanish Caribbean as well as Caribbean women overseas; CAFRA is largely engaged in research and documentation, communication and information as well as action.

Despite these recent developments, there is not yet what can be called a women's movement within the Caribbean. Reddock observes that 'Daily, women activists are coming to terms with the fact that achievements so far have only scratched the surface and the lives of the majority of women are yet to be touched.' (p. 13)

10 *Conclusion*

Throughout this work we have sought to look at the reality of the lives of Caribbean women by viewing key issues in relation to the life cycle. We have used previously published and analysed data, as well as material from literature, folk culture and the life-histories of women. We have relied heavily on data generated by the multi-disciplinary Women in the Caribbean Project (WICP) and used a broader range of published material to attempt our own analysis. Our choice of material, our emphasis and our conclusions are no doubt coloured by the fact that we are ourselves a product of the culture we describe.

We are aware of some of the omissions and shortcomings of this work. Many important topics relating to women's lives, for instance health, ageing and sexuality, have not been covered at all. There were constraints of time and space but the most significant determinant has been the availability of information. Factual data are greatest in the topics on which the WICP and others have concentrated.

There were significant omissions in the available literature. We would have liked to include more about the effect — and the messages — of indigenous popular culture — especially reggae music and its widespread influence in the 1970s and 1980s. We would also have liked to include more about religion and its influence. Even a passing knowledge of Caribbean culture shows what a potent force religion is and always has been on the everyday lives of women, especially on their socialization and behaviour. Religion can significantly affect male–female relationships and modify community norms and expectations, for example, in relation to childbearing and marriage. We are referring here to both orthodox religions and the newer and faster-growing unorthodox churches and sects, both imported and indigenous. While the older churches and many of the newer religions such as Rastafarianism seek to enforce the patriarchy, Afro-Caribbean religions on the whole have been a powerful agency for securing women access to power and authority in their communities. Religions such as Shango or the Shouters of Trinidad and the Revivalist and Kumina cults of Jamaica, do offer women key leadership positions, important offices and a significant role in rituals and ceremonies. The impact of religion in its varied forms on the lives of women in the Caribbean is an area that would no doubt bear fruitful study.

Other areas in which we are conscious of the inadequacies and the tentative nature of what we have proffered and therefore of the need for further research were in the areas of childhood socialization and gender-role stereotyping in the home, the educational system and the wider society. Although we have referred to these as key issues and have speculated about them, we are aware that some of the information

185

we have used has been patched from very old cloth — primarily the family studies of the 1950s and 1960s. It is clear that a great deal more attention also needs to be focused on the role of the male within the family and his contribution to the socialization of children.

The greater reliance on data from Jamaica in some subject areas is due partly to the fact that Jamaica has probably been studied more than the other territories and partly to my living there, which enabled easy access to the data. We feel, however, that this has been compensated for by the fact that the WICP research concentrated on the eastern Caribbean and the voices of women heard have been mainly those from the smaller islands. In reading and re-reading these life-histories and the extended interviews with women in public life, I experienced no sense of strangeness about these women: it was as though I already knew them. They affirmed for me the commonalities of experience shared by Caribbean women.

Nevertheless, this should not obscure the fact that in the region there are vast differences obtaining not only within countries, i.e. between urban and rural areas, between races and classes and between age-groups, but also between countries, in terms of socio-economic development and infrastructure. The degree of the differences can perhaps be highlighted by one example from the three WICP project territories, in which Barbados would be regarded as the most 'developed' followed by Antigua, with St Vincent the least developed. While only 20.7 per cent of the sample in St Vincent had secondary schooling, there were almost twice that number in the other two countries — 41.7 per cent of women in Antigua and 38.9 per cent in Barbados.

Despite such variations, there is a level at which the peculiar history and culture of the individual territories is synthesized into what can be called a Caribbean culture, and there are enough shared elements to enable us to generalize about a Caribbean woman.

At the start of this work we set out to establish woman's 'true' situation, i.e. how her actual role performance and status differed from the stereotype. We also said that we would use, as a yardstick to judge women's rights and status, the declaration of equality embedded in the Guyanese constitution. Although the WICP study and this work were not concerned with women's status *per se*, women from the Caribbean do rank high in overall status compared with others in both developed and undeveloped nations. In a country ranking of women in 99 countries, the three largest Caribbean nations — Jamaica, Trinidad/Tobago and Barbados — ranked 15th, 23rd and 36th respectively in terms of social equality. Where specific indices were considered, Jamaica ranked second in the world in terms of education and Barbados fifth in terms of employment status (Population Crisis Committee 1988[1]).

In the Caribbean, there are few or no official barriers to female achievement, though there are still discriminatory laws which affect her domestic status and, as we have seen, many sexist barriers remain. But, compared with many parts of the

---

1 The Population Crisis Committee [1988] provides the following explanation of how their country rankings of the status of women were arrived at:

Measurements of women's well being and the gender gap between men's and women's status combined to provide a ranking — in a single figure — of the differences in women's condition between countries.

Each country's score was compiled by adding 20 measures of women's status related to the categories of 1) health, 2) marriage and children, 3) education, 4) employment, 5) social equality.

In each category, three measures are related to women's general well being and the fourth gauges the gender gap. Each of the twenty measures has a maximum of 5 points, 5 indicating the highest status. The maximum possible score was 100, 75 for women's status and 25 for gender gap.

world, there is for the most part equality of opportunity. Indeed, the progress of Caribbean women, especially young women, is quite remarkable, though it is far more so in the larger territories where women have greater access to education and job opportunities. In these countries, females are now prominent in government and administration and in some of the professions, and are proving themselves as entrepreneurs and businesswomen. There are in some of our larger cities and towns numbers of highly visible, well-dressed, apparently self-confident women, who in their life styles and manner appear to have gained equality with their male counterparts.

It is apparent, though, that the majority of these women are young, well educated and largely from the middle class or have adopted a middle-class life style. This admittedly subjective profile of women who are 'making it' in the system both points to the access route and also masks a wider reality, that, at the lowest end of the scale, the lives of women have not changed substantially. The vast majority of Caribbean women remain in subordinate positions within their societies. The very visible achievement of some women as successful actors obscures the reality of the many — those who are unemployed, dependent, unable to break out of the endless cycle of childbearing and relationships with men that are based entirely on the material support they can offer. These women are trapped in an endless cycle of poverty and despair.

Because the majority of women are 'miracle workers', labouring long hours both inside and outside the home, creating 'something from nothing', making incredible sacrifices for their children and tolerating the vagaries of their men, yet are capable of 'raising their voice up' when aroused, the general belief is that Caribbean women are 'strong', 'powerful', 'matriarchic', etc. The corollary is, at what price? High blood-pressure, for instance, is so common that it is taken for granted as something that goes with the territory.

Some aspects of women's condition of course derive from the economic status of these societies. Despite a 'modern' sector and a sophisticated life style for the top layer, the Caribbean still remains a poverty-stricken enclave with small, fragile economies characterized by dependency relationships with the metropolis. Rapid changes over the past thirty years or so mean that race is perhaps now a less significant indicator than socio-economic status, but the social and economic structure is still shaped like a pyramid, and while some women are moving upwards, and very rapidly too, most women remain at the bottom.

Women still have the highest rates of unemployment and are still mired in the lowest-paying jobs. In the widespread absence of male support for children, many assume the twin burdens of child-caring and household maintenance. The high visibility of women in the economic system is an outgrowth of the need to fulfil their family responsibilities since they are still both mothers and fathers. The economic crises since the 1970s and the 'structural adjustments' which governments locked into the capitalist world economy are forced to make at the behest of the International Monetary Fund and other banking and 'development' agencies, have had their heaviest impact on women since they are the ones forced to make the corresponding structural adjustments in the domestic economy. In a world of escalating living costs and eroding living standards, a world where a materialistic ideology prevails, woman's traditional weapon — her capacity to 'make do' — is simply not enough. Yet she is so busy 'making do' that she has little or no direct influence on the decisions taken at successive levels of government which will so radically affect her life: decisions such as how much money is to be borrowed and what it is to be spent on.

The WICP has argued that 'While recognising that Caribbean women can and do act independently of official policy to improve their situation . . . their ability to do so is considerably hampered by a gender ideology which consistently ascribes low status to their activities' (Massiah WICP 1986c p. 165). Indeed, the WICP has identified 'the low and possibly deteriorating value attached to women's multiple roles' (Massiah *ibid*). While the formal political ideology seeks to provide equal opportunities to all individuals, we have seen that in practice women are still systematically excluded from several areas of activity. Where they are included, their contribution either is not recognized or is afforded low priorities and rewards. The WICP has provided ample evidence of 'the inability of women to exploit the apparently favourable, but male-dominated infrastructural arrangements in order to improve their competence to function more effectively in their societies' (Massiah *ibid*).

Woman's very success at 'making do', at managing without a male partner, is probably the very factor that masks her true condition: the heavy toll it takes in terms of her own health and well-being and the stifling of her own opportunities for self-improvement, leisure and participation in public life, and of her ability to provide love and tenderness to her children and to her men. It is obvious that many women do not want to play the subordinate, submissive feminine role. They want to be independent, autonomous actors. What they need are the social and economic support systems that will enable them to discharge their obligations without the high degree of stress to which they are now subjected. Why should women be called upon to work miracles every day? Although the powerful role played by 'my mother who fathered me' is universally recognized, Caribbean societies are still backward in their provision of even the basic social amenities that would enhance women's ability to discharge that responsibility, provisions such as widespread child-care facilities, adequate and accessible health centres, facilities for continuing education and opportunities for the acquisition of better job and income-earning skills in a broad range of occupations.

The cultural expectation regarding motherhood is central to an understanding of the lives of Caribbean women because the choices they make in terms of childbearing will ultimately influence all their other interactions with society: it will affect their schooling, their job opportunities, their personal autonomy, their relations with men, and their participation in the wider society — in political and public life. In some ways, it is women's failure to appreciate these interactions and alter their behaviour accordingly that contributes to their continued subordination.

What is remarkable is that although early motherhood without male support will push large numbers of women into assuming heavy economic burdens, and although this fact is so visible, the Caribbean girl is largely unprepared for the economic role she will end up playing. This is mainly due to the serious role conflict that girls experience between childbearing and education. This is a conflict for women in all countries but is perhaps most acute in the Caribbean because of the strong cultural focus on childbearing as the symbol of adulthood and the strong push towards getting an education as the route to economic mobility. In large segments of the society motherhood usually comes before marriage and often means single-parenting; the girl, usually unprepared to earn a living since school drop-out is the inevitable consequence of pregnancy, often ends up dependent on her family or in a dead-end job. This sets up a cycle which makes her particularly vulnerable in her relationships with men since at this stage there is economic dependency: to enlist male support for her children, she might fall into the trap of having additional children for different men in the expectation that each new one will become the provider. This emphasis on the material breeds cynicism and distrust in relationships and often leaves her with several children and none of the support.

Although there is widespread official support for family planning programmes and these have led to falling birth-rates in the region, it is still difficult to counteract beliefs so deeply rooted in the culture and psyche as those pertaining to childbearing. For, in the absence of other or better societal rewards, or alternative role models, it is in bearing and rearing children that most women play what they perceive as their most important role in life; they derive not only emotional satisfaction but power and authority from parenting.

The style of mothering is sacrificial but it is expected that this self-sacrifice will pay off in the long run, and that children will support their mother in her old age and provide her with upward social mobility. This doesn't always happen but it happens often enough to be an inspiration to others and, when it does, it gives the mother the societal and community rewards she lacks otherwise: she can die happy, knowing she has been a 'good mumma'.

What is a 'good mumma'? One who first of all provides discipline, especially of the girl child, teaches her to have manners and show she has 'broughtupcy', to be able to do things in the home, to get an education and stay away from men, but to bear children and get a good man and to provide for her mother in her old age. The style is usually authoritarian and frequently accompanied by physical punishment. Reasoning is usually out since children who engage in 'back talk' or answer back are regarded as 'facety' and 'force-ripe'. When the girls 'fall' — often as a result of their own ignorance — the 'good mumma' will be disappointed but will nevertheless accept the inevitable, 'for she love grandchildren plenty'. She — or other female kin — will usually be there to help the daughter through pregnancy and birth. If a man does not come forward to say he is the 'baby-father', she will accept the responsibility of finding ways and means of feeding the new mouth in the household, which has now become three-generational. But by now she is a strategist in these matters for it is in this dimension, the dimension of providing, that her ingenuity and diplomatic and political skills come into play; she will persuade the entire world, if need be, to assist her. If she is lucky she will already have a network of family and kin she can call on for material and emotional assistance. Family is her most important resource. But she will turn to every and any opportunity that presents itself to enhance her ability to mind the child, even if this means giving the child away to someone who is better able to mind it for longer or shorter periods. Parenting as an activity for women is highly regarded: hence the high level of informal adoptions and child-shifting — among strangers and within families.

Even in marriage, a woman regards the children as her responsibility; children are the focus of her primary emotional investment as her primary faith continues to be in her kin; men will come and go but the family will always be there for her to fall back on. She herself as part of this network will also give assistance and help others as far as she can. 'Family' is not the narrow nuclear family but a complex network of far and near relations, sometimes spread across many continents.

Despite the ideal image of man as protector and provider which women say they hold, women do not really look to men as their guardians and protectors. Often the woman herself is the head and manager of her own household and economic affairs. Where there is an adult male present in the household, she — and society — will acknowledge him as head even if this is not objectively so. For, as Helen Safa points out, women feel that it 'looks better' if they fulfil societal norms. (Safa WICP 1986). For the same reason, women and their daughters will assume housekeeping chores — and will not ask their menfolk to help because it 'looks bad' for a man to do housework.

Even in households with a male partner as the main economic contributor, the woman's domestic status is close to egalitarian — many household decisions are made by women alone or women and men together; few family decisions are made by men alone. Yet women will pretend otherwise and refuse to acknowledge their own power and status. This adherence to gender-role stereotyping and social norms might in fact be part of woman's strategy. Her style is frequently based not on confrontation but on cunning, guile and subversion to get what she wants from men to further her own ends — which in most cases is tied up with her children. Such strategies, she argues, are necessary in order to extract child support from reluctant fathers.

Men are aware of this and male–female relationships are often marked by mutual distrust and antagonism. Part of this antagonism is because men know they really do not 'control' the women, although they might desire to do so; women will be financially dependent on men if they have to be, and will keep their mouths shut and defer to them and assume a subordinate position as long as it is necessary. But women play this role out of necessity; this is not what women really want. What women really want is their own financial autonomy. Thus even in partnerships there is secrecy between husbands and wives as to the true nature of their earnings and most women will try as hard as possible to put aside something of their own. Some women prefer visiting relationships with men to a residential union because they then have total control over their own resources. Part of men's perceived unreliability might be due to the fact that many men engage in multiple partnerships and many women put up with sharing their men with other women. The nuclear family status and single partnerships apply to a relatively small percentage of the total population.

In many societies women derive power and status from their menfolk. This would describe the situation of a small group of Caribbean women — those at the very top of the social and economic system and those from ethnic groups which stress traditional values. These are women who function within the nuclear family system and come closest to fulfilling the stereotyped female role. Women in such households do not work outside the home and their men wield economic control. There is also increasingly a number of professional single or married women who have power and status in their own right — deriving from their work status. Some women acquire power and status in their communities from their own economic activities, as is the case of traders such as the traditional market higglers or the more recent 'informal commercial importers' or 'traffickers'.

Most Caribbean women are not in that situation. Yet we have seen that they are not necessarily powerless. In their economic lives, they are able to harness resources from many areas to supplement their own activities. They end up deriving power and authority through successful child-rearing and are often moved to higher status by the social mobility of their children. In the domestic situation, they have power in the home, for it is their duty to 'make the money stretch', and they make their own decisions in some areas of domestic activity and are consulted by their mates in others; very rarely are they excluded from any form of household decision-making. Since one-third of Caribbean working women are heads of their own households, this automatically confers decision-making power on them.

Yet the kind of power women have has been thrust upon them by circumstances, is not apparent to the wider society and does not have a great impact, if any, at the level of national decision-making, even at the level where it affects their lives and well-being. It has been suggested that women's failure to run for and secure public office can be attributed to the social conditioning, which puts men first or in the 'highest rank', plus a political system which sets up such barriers that women feel that they have to be 'more men than men' to overcome them. There is evidence that women get little encouragement from the male-dominated political machinery and, although they do the donkey-work in politics, they face role conflicts and lack economic resources and support in their drive for a more prominent role. For these reasons and because the female electorate do not yet see issues in terms of gender, women are often divorced from the policy-making processes in these societies.

Part of the problem is that, for many women in poor Third World societies, bread-and-butter issues and racial and class oppression are still seen to be of more importance than gender oppression. As Helen Safa notes, 'Female identification with class issues may help to explain the absence of a strong women's movement in Caribbean society comparable to that developing in some Latin American societies' (Safa WICP 1986, p. 15). Women's preoccupation with child-rearing and with earning a living, with sheer survival, also do not give them the time needed to participate in community or group activities at a national level. Thus the women who participate tend to be older women, who are freed from such activities, or women in higher-income groups, who have more leisure because they employ other women to undertake their domestic duties. The fact that many women workers are domestic workers, i.e. are employed by other women in jobs that are perceived throughout the entire society as of low status, has widened the class cleavage and prevented women from uniting to defend their interests.

Women play a strong economic role but, as we saw in chapter six, this is not always officially quantified; thus women's contribution to the economy as a whole is undervalued and underrated. Since GNP and other measures are used in planning national economies which affect peoples lives, we perhaps need to develop more appropriate tools for measuring the labour of half the population.

The phenomenal increase in education, coupled with the diversification of these economies over the past thirty years or so, has created new opportunities for women, and the female labour-force participation rate compared with other Third World countries is high. While women with the highest levels of education are making breakthroughs in the system, the majority of working women are still found clustered in low-paid 'feminine' occupations — in teaching, nursing, clerical/secretarial work and services. The rapid entry of women at high levels in the workforce of some countries also masks their continued subordination and exploitation. Many women in high executive and administrative positions have got the opportunity to be there not just because they are highly qualified and capable but because they are willing to accept far less in salaries and perquisites and operate under conditions that men of much lesser qualifications and capabilities would consider insulting. Women's promotion to such levels is therefore not simply to be taken at face value, as an indication of the liberal new policies of male-dominated enterprises, but rather as evidence that, even at the highest levels, 'woman is a donkey'. In Jamaica, for instance, where women have made the greatest strides in reaching the highest levels of the workforce, male employers will attest that they prefer to hire women because women 'work harder', are 'more responsible', are 'steadier workers', etc. But the same employers will happily pay women less and extract far more out of them, simply because the women themselves acquiesce in this. Women at all levels still allow themselves to be exploited because of their social conditioning, which prevents them from acknowledging their true worth or that their labour is a commodity which has value in the market-place. Women at all levels also find it difficult to raise the issue of salaries and other matters affecting their working conditions with employers; they are far more willing to accept what they are given than men are. At the same time, the bargaining power of women as a whole is weakened by many factors related to gender, such as women's dual work role and her responsibility for social reproduction, and the adherence to a patriarchic value system which assigns her an inordinate share of domestic burdens. And, as we have seen, women are still being conditioned to value the social aspects of education and work over the instrumental. A great many women workers are not covered by any union organization and those who are will not necessarily find their interests put forward since the union hierarchies, like those of the political parties, are mostly controlled by men. Women's desire for economic independence is continually subverted by the fact that her subordinate position in the workplace combined with her domestic responsibilities means that it is often difficult for her to garner the resources she needs to save, invest, or own property — in other words, to acquire mobility through her own efforts. Where she is in a partnership, she is legally discriminated against in some respects in the sharing out of communal property.

Woman's economic role is partly forced on her by the cultural emphasis on childbearing; there is a strong link between female familial responsibility, her partner's contribution to the home or lack of it and the woman's economic activities. Where there is male support, the woman might have the option to stay at home or engage in more 'informal' income-earning activities as an alternative to seeking a job; for poor women who lack education and skills, work in the labour force is usually unattractive because it often signifies low-paid drudgery.

On the whole women still lack the technical and technological skills that will give them access to a broader range of more rewarding and lucrative jobs, which are opening up in, for instance, the minerals sector. Lack of any skills at all is creating increased marginalization of those at the bottom end of the scale, who are being forced out of agriculture and other low-skilled jobs but who are not equipped for other jobs. While new sectors are opening up to provide jobs for large numbers of women, as in export-processing industries, they are also bringing with them new stresses and strains.

There is a historical dimension to women and labour: women have always worked and hard manual labour has been the lot of poor black women since slavery and of Indian women since their indentureship. In the past, race and class determined women's place in the labour force; today it is determined largely by education. While socio-economic factors do continue to limit or enhance educational progress, there are also internal barriers to women's achievements and occupational choices. Part of this relates to gender-role stereotyping in the home, school and the society at large. While nowadays educational egalitarianism is the norm, women's education still suffers from the fact that girls' schools are not as well equipped as boys' schools for science and technical teaching and that, even in coeducational schools, there are still curriculum differences, as boys are still heavily concentrated in vocational and technical training, while girls learn domestic and other non-marketable woman-centred skills. Where choice is available, we do not know how it is arrived at — whether it is forced on girls by their parents, teachers and the way the school system is structured, or whether girls 'perceive' what is appropriate to their gender and act accordingly. There is considerable evidence that gender-role stereotyping does affect women's choices.

A fundamental question is: what is the ideal of womanhood that is being projected and absorbed in the Caribbean today? In chapter 2, we looked at how girl children were still being socialized into a Victórian ideal of the subservient woman whose place is in the home and whose role is that of the good wife and mother. Historically, this idealized image is what informed female education and has been the one projected over time by institutions such as the church and the media. This image is largely an imported one which bears little relation to the reality of the lives of the majority of women, either historically or in the present time.

Although we have some awareness of what images are being projected, we have no way of measuring precisely what role these images play in female self-concept and identity formation and how self-concept affects women's choices, behaviour and attitudes. One of the things we need to do, perhaps, is to look at women of high achievement in our societies and try to establish how they managed to attain their goals, what were the motivating factors and who or what facilitated their progress through the school system and in their careers. Such knowledge would perhaps help women in setting different goals and fighting the stereotypes.

Although we have placed contemporary women in perspective through historical analysis, we are nevertheless aware that we have been unable to factor in the dynamic effects of change as much as we would have liked. Caribbean societies in the last few decades have been caught up in world-wide changes and are probably more buffeted than most, given their smallness, openness and exposure to metropolitan culture, especially North American. Even in the most remote villages of the Caribbean there are overseas connections, there is frequent travelling back and forth, and there is widespread access to modern communications facilities — radio is almost universal, in the towns, television is becoming widespread and satellite dishes are becoming ubiquitous. Cinemas are flooded with foreign films and, in the absence of strong indigenous publishing, news-stands are flooded with foreign publications. Because of the long historical significance of external migration and the influence of the mass media and tourism, a 'foreign' life style and mode of behaviour is widely admired and imitated, especially by the young. At the same time, the rise over the last few decades of a strong and assertive indigenous popular culture, manifested, for example, in reggae and 'dub', in a new breed of socially conscious calypsonians and in the widespread practice of Rastafarianism, must be taken into account.

However, it could be that in some respects we are overestimating the level and nature of change. The world economic crisis beginning in the 1970s has had a heavy impact on these societies and their standard of living is falling, not rising. This has mostly affected the poorest of the poor. Undeveloped or deteriorating infrastructure has a heavy impact on women, as it increases the burden of domestic work and child care, in which older children may be forced to share, limiting their own access to opportunities. Lack of piped water means fetching it from a stand-pipe or river; lack of electricity means lack of labour-saving devices as basic as an electric iron. The WICP survey showed that in St Vincent, the poorest of the countries, 35.2 per cent of the homes were without their own water supply, 31.4 per cent were without electricity, and 63.9 per cent of households used either charcoal, wood or kerosene for cooking and lighting. Only 3.4 per cent of households had cars. It was found that 'The privately owned bus system provided an inadequate service. For some respondents, visits into Kingstown, the capital, was a whole day's trip.' (White 1986) This highlights the transportation difficulties that most poor people experience, even on a relatively small island, and the impact this must have on their use of time and their ability to work away from home.

Given conditions like these, it is possible that younger women are not in fact being freed from the household drudgery of their mothers and grandmothers as fast as we would suppose. The women in the WICP sample were in the age range 20–60, but many of the experiences derived from poverty which they described could also be the experiences of their own daughters and granddaughters, which would not leave them well placed to take advantage of those areas where rapid changes are definitely occurring, such as in educational opportunities.

Change might also be having an adverse impact on interpersonal relationships, as a more materialistic culture is eroding the social and friendship networks that were the basis of women's autonomy; a cash economy is replacing one built on exchanges and a more visible middle-class life style in all the territories is emphasizing the need to acquire cold cash as the facilitator of the outward trappings of mobility and status.

We should be better able to measure the qualitative effects of the visible changes in women's lives and thinking. As more and more women take on wage labour in manufacturing, hotels and offices, we can only speculate as to how this is affecting their desire for economic autonomy or their relationships with men. Is what Erna Brodber said becoming more common?

> men and women are . . . aware of the 'white' style of behaviour for women and for male–female relationships. Whether they accept this form depends on whether they have the economic wherewithal to operationalize it and the desire for social mobility. With the increase in the number of academically trained black men and their acceptance into the white collar jobs has come the cash base with which to acquire the 'necessary appendage'. Upwardly mobile women have become willing to design their lives to fit the stereotypes.
> (Brodber WICP 1982a, p. 21)

If young white-collar and professional women are jettisoning the model of the independent working-class mother who put them there and are redesigning their lives to fit the stereotype of the dependent female, what impact is this likely to have on the future development of a feminist consciousness in the region and changes in the patriarchic structure?

Is change having an impact on the socialization of children and gender-role training and, if so, how? What part do racial and class factors still play in the advancement of women? We also need to look at those women who are succeeding in the system. Who are the successful women and what criteria are being used to measure their success? In terms of the female value system, which seems to emphasize social and expressive traits and interpersonal relationships, do 'successful' women retain these values or do they find them impediments which need to be jettisoned in their path upwards? Finally, we need to know, do women really need to be 'more men than men' to crash the institutional barriers in Caribbean society?

Bibliography

WICP publications

Primary sources (WICP material collected 1979–1982, located at Institute of Social and Economic Research, UWI, Cave Hill, Barbados)

WICP, Interviews.
—— Life-histories of 38 women in the WICP territories
—— Interviews with women in public life (eastern Caribbean)
—— Questionnaire Survey

Published articles and unpublished conference papers

Anderson, Patricia (1984) 'Introduction' to *Women, Work and Development*, Cave Hill, Barbados: Institute of Social and Economic Research, UWI. WICP, Vol. 6.
—— (1986) 'Conclusion: WICP', *Social and Economic Studies* (Special Issue: Women in the Caribbean, Pt. 1) 35:2, June.
Barrow, Christine (1986a) 'Finding the support: strategies for survival', *Social and Economic Studies* (Special Issue: Women in the Caribbean, Pt. 1) 35:2, June.
—— (1986b) 'Male images of women in Barbados', *Social and Economic Studies* (Special Issue: Women in the Caribbean, Pt. 2) 35:3, September.
Brodber, Erna (1982a) *Perceptions of Caribbean Women: Towards a Documentation of Stereotypes*, Cave Hill, Barbados: Institute of Social and Economic Research, UWI. WICP, Vol. 4.
—— (1982b) 'Afro-Jamaican women and their men in the late nineteenth and early twentieth century.' Paper prepared for WICP Conference, Barbados, 12–16 September 1982.
—— (1986) 'Afro-Jamaican women at the turn of the century', *Social and Economic Studies* (Special Issue: Women in the Caribbean, Pt. 2) 35:3, September.
Clarke, Roberta (1986) 'Women's organizations; women's interests', *Social and Economic Studies* (Special Issue: Women in the Caribbean, Pt. 2) 35:3, September.
Cole, Joyce (1982a) 'Official ideology and the education of women in the English-speaking Caribbean, 1835–1945, with special reference to Barbados', in *Women and Education*, Cave Hill, Barbados: Institute of Social and Economic Research, UWI. WICP, Vol. 5.
—— (1982b) 'Female education in the contemporary Caribbean — major trends and issues'. Paper prepared for WICP Conference, Barbados, 12–16 September 1982.
Cummins, Diane (1982) 'Pilot survey: methodology and select findings'. Paper prepared for WICP Conference, Barbados, 12–16 September 1982.
Drayton, Kathleen (1982) 'Introduction' to *Women in Education*, Cave Hill, Barbados: Institute of Social and Economic Research, UWI. WICP, Vol. 5.
Duncan, Neville and O'Brien, Kenneth (1983) *Women and Politics in Barbados 1948–1981*, Cave Hill, Barbados: Institute of Social and Economic Research, UWI. WICP, Vol. 3.
Durant-Gonzalez, Victoria (1982) 'The realm of female familial responsibility', in *Women and the Family*, Cave Hill, Barbados: Institute of Social and Economic Research, UWI. WICP, Vol. 2.

Forde, Norma Monica (1981) *Women and the Law*, Cave Hill, Barbados: Institute of Social and Economic Research, UWI. WICP, Vol. 1.

Gill, Margaret (1984) 'Women, work and development: Barbados 1946–1970', in *Women and Work*, Cave Hill, Barbados: Institute of Social and Economic Research, UWI. WICP, Vol. 6.

Hodge, Merle (1982) 'Introduction' to *Perceptions of Caribbean Women*, Cave Hill, Barbados: Institute of Social and Economic Research, UWI. WICP, Vol. 4.

Jackson, Jean (1982) 'Stresses affecting women and their families', in *Women and the Family*, Cave Hill, Barbados: Institute of Social and Economic Research, UWI. WICP, Vol. 2.

LeFranc, Elsie (1983) 'Overview and conclusions', in *Report of the Conference on the Role of Women in the Caribbean, Barbados, 12–16 September 1982*, Cave Hill, Barbados: Institute of Social and Economic Research, UWI.

McKenzie, Hermione (1982) 'Introduction' to *Women and the Family*, Cave Hill, Barbados: Institute of Social and Economic Research, UWI. WICP, Vol. 2.

—— (1986) 'The educational experience of Caribbean women', *Social and Economic Studies* (Special Issue: Women in the Caribbean, Pt. 2) 35:3, September.

Massiah, Joycelin (1982) 'Women who head households', in *Women and the Family*, Cave Hill, Barbados: Institute of Social and Economic Research, UWI. WICP, Vol. 2.

—— (1984) 'Indicators of women in development: a preliminary framework for the Caribbean', in *Women, Work and Development*, Cave Hill, Barbados: Institute of Social and Economic Research, UWI. WICP, Vol. 6.

—— (1986a) 'Work in the lives of Caribbean women', *Social and Economic Studies* (Special Issue: Women in the Caribbean, Pt. 1) 35:2, June.

—— (1986b) 'Women in the Caribbean project: an overview', *Social and Economic Studies* (Special Issue: Women in the Caribbean, Pt. 1) 35:2, June.

—— (1986c) 'Postscript: the utility of WICP research in social policy formation', *Social and Economic Studies* (Special Issue: Women in the Caribbean Pt. 2) 35:3, September.

Mohammed, Patricia (1982) 'Women and Education in Trinidad and Tobago', Paper prepared for WICP Conference, Barbados, 12–16 September 1982.

—— (1984) 'Educational attainment of women in Trinidad–Tobago 1946–1980', in *Women and Education*, Cave Hill, Barbados: Institute of Social and Economic Research, UWI. WICP, Vol. 5.

Odie-Ali, Stella (1986) 'Women in agriculture: the case of Guyana', *Social and Economic Studies* (Special Issue: Women in the Caribbean, Pt. 1) 35:2, June.

Powell, Dorian (1982) 'Network analysis: a suggested model for the study of women and the family in the Caribbean', in *Women and the Family*, Cave Hill, Barbados: Institute of Social and Economic Research, UWI. WICP, Vol. 2.

—— (1986) 'Caribbean women and their response to familial experiences', *Social and Economic Studies* (Special Issue: Women in the Caribbean, Pt. 1) 35:2, June.

Powell, Dorian; Jackson, Jean and Bernal, Margaret (1982) 'Social networks: a resource base for urban women'. Paper prepared for WICP Conference, Barbados, 12–16 September 1982.

Safa, Helen (1986) 'Economic autonomy and sexual equality in Caribbean society', *Social and Economic Studies* (Special Issue: Women in the Caribbean, Pt. 2) 35:3, September.

White, Averille (1986) 'Profiles: women in the Caribbean project', *Social and Economic Studies* (Special Issue: Women in the Caribbean, Pt. 1) 35:2, June.

Other references

Anderson (Manley), Beverley (1985) 'Caribbean women and the political process', *Concerning Women and Development*, 2/85, WAND, Department of Extra-Mural Studies, UWI, St Michael, Barbados.

Antrobus, Peggy (1981) 'Caribbean women in the media', in Marlene Cuthbert (ed.) *Women and Media Decision-Making in the Caribbean*, Kingston, Jamaica: Caribbean Institute of Mass Communications/Unesco.

Astin, Helen S. (1982) 'The meaning of work in women's lives: a sociopsychological model of career choice and work behaviour', *Counselling Psychologist* 12:4.

Augier, F.R. and Gordon, S.C. (1962) *Sources of West Indian History*, London: Longman.

Bacon, E.M. and Aaron, E. (1890) *The New Jamaica*, New York: Walbridge and Co.

Barbados, Government of (1978) *National Commission on the Status of Women Report*, Bridgetown: Ministry of the Attorney General, 2 vols.

Bell, Jeannette (1985) 'Women and entrepreneurship', *Concerning Women and Development*, 4/85, WAND, Department of Extra-Mural Studies, UWI, St Michael, Barbados.

Bennett, Alvin (1973) *God the Stonebreaker*, London: Heinemann.

Bennett, Louise (1982) *Selected Poems* (ed. Mervyn Morris), Kingston: Sangster's.

Blake, Judith (1961) *Family Structure in Jamaica: the Social Context of Reproduction*, New York: The Free Press of Glencoe. (Also London: Greenwood Press, 1980)

Boland, Barbara (1974) 'Labour force', in George Roberts (ed.) *Recent Population Movements in Jamaica*, Paris: Committee for International Coordination of National Research in Demography (CICRED).

Braithwaite, Lloyd (1953) *Social Stratification in Trinidad*, Mona, Jamaica: Institute of Social and Economic Research, UWI (reprinted 1975).

Brathwaite, Edward Kamau (1971) *The Development of Creole Society in Jamaica 1770-1820*, Oxford University Press.

—— (1974) *Contradictory Omens*, Mona, Jamaica: Savacou.

—— (1977) *Wars of Respect: Nanny and Sam Sharpe*, Kingston, Jamaica: published by the API (Agency for Public Information) for National Heritage Week Committee.

Brodber, Erna (1968) 'Family structure and sex-role learning. A study of socialization in Jamaica', M.Sc. (Soc.) thesis, Mona, Jamaica: UWI.

—— (1974) *Abandonment of Children in Jamaica*, Mona, Jamaica: Institute of Social and Economic Research, UWI.

—— (1975) *A Study of Yards in the City of Kingston*, Mona, Jamaica: Institute of Social and Economic Research, UWI.

—— (1984) 'The second generation of freemen in Jamaica 1904-1944', Ph.D. dissertation, Mona, Jamaica: UWI.

—— (1986) 'The pioneering Miss Bailey', *Jamaica Journal* 19:2, May.

Campbell, George (1981) 'History makers', *First Poems*, New York and London: Garland Publishers.

Carmichael, Mrs (1833) *Domestic Manners and Social Conditions of the White, Coloured and Negro Population of the West Indies by Mrs. Carmichael, Five Years a Resident in St. Vincent and Trinidad*, London: Whittaker Treacher and Co., 2 vols.

Clarke, Edith (1957) *My Mother Who Fathered Me*, London: Allen and Unwin (paperback edition 1972).

Cohen, Yehudi A. (1955) 'Character formation and social structure in a Jamaican community', *Psychiatry: Journal for the Study of Interpersonal Processes* 18:3, August.

Cooper, Carolyn (1985) '"That cunny Jamma Oman": the female sensibility in the poetry of Louise Bennett', *Jamaica Journal* 18:4, November.

Cross, Malcolm and Schwartzbaum, Allan M. (1969) 'Social mobility and secondary school selection in Trinidad and Tobago', *Social and Economic Studies* 18:2, June.

Cumper, Gloria (1972) *A Survey of Social Legislation in Jamaica*, Mona, Jamaica: Institute of Social and Economic Research, UWI.

Cumper, Gloria and Daly, Stephanie (1979) *Family Law in the Commonwealth Caribbean*, Mona, Jamaica: Department of Extra-Mural Studies, UWI.

Cuthbert, Marlene (ed.) (1981) *Women and Media Decision-Making in the Caribbean*, Kingston, Jamaica: CARIMAC/Unesco, (mimeo.).

Drayton, Kathleen (1983) 'Caribbean women in politics', *Concerning Women and Development*, 10/83, WAND, Department of Extra-Mural Studies, UWI, St Michael, Barbados.

Durant-Gonzalez, Victoria (1976) 'Role and status of rural Jamaican women: higglering and mothering', Ph.D. dissertation, Berkeley: University of California.

—— (1983) 'The occupation of higglering', *Jamaica Journal* 16:3, August.

—— (1985) 'Women and industry', *Concerning Women and Development*, 3/85, WAND, Department of Extra-Mural Studies, UWI, St Michael, Barbados.

Elder, J.D. (1968) 'The male/female conflict in calypso', *Caribbean Quarterly* 14:3, September.

—— (1973) *Song Games from Trinidad and Tobago*, Port of Spain, Trinidad: National Cultural Council Publications (revised edition).

Emmanuel, Patrick (1979) *General Elections in the Eastern Caribbean: a Handbook*, Cave Hill, Barbados: Institute of Social and Economic Research, UWI.

Feldman, Harold (1969) 'Parent–child separation in Jamaica', Paper presented at Joint Meeting of Caribbean Psychiatric Association and American Psychiatric Association, Ocho Rios, Jamaica, May 1969.

Feldman, H. and Marriott, J.A.S. (1979) 'Diagnostic patterns and child/parent separation in children attending the Jamaican Child Guidance Clinic', *British Journal of Psychiatry* 4:4.

Gloudon, Barbara (1981) 'How media values affect Caribbean women', in Marlene Cuthbert (ed.) *Women and Media Decision-Making in the Caribbean*, Kingston, Jamaica: CARIMAC/Unesco.

Goodison, Lorna (1979) 'My mother', *Tamarind Season*, Kingston, Jamaica: Institute of Jamaica.

Gordon, Lorna (1981) 'The portrayal and participation of women in the Caribbean mass media', in Marlene Cuthbert (ed.) *Women and Media Decision-Making in the Caribbean*, Kingston, Jamaica: CARIMAC/Unesco.

Gordon, Shirley C. (1963) *A Century of West Indian Education: a Source Book*, London: Longmans.

—— (1968) *Reports and Repercussions in West Indian Education 1835–1933*, London: Ginn and Co.

Grant, D.R.B. (1974) *Living Conditions of Some Basic School Children: Pointers to Disadvantage*, Mona, Jamaica: The Bernard Van Leer Foundation Project for Early Childhood Education (mimeo.).

—— (1980) *Life Style Study: Children of the Lesser World in the English-Speaking Caribbean*, Mona, Jamaica: Bernard Van Leer Foundation Project for Early Childhood Education, 5 vols (mimeo.).

—— (1984) 'Poverty from generation to generation', *Sunday Gleaner* (Jamaica), 30 September.

Grantham-McGregor, Sally M. and Desai, Patricia (1975) 'A home-visiting intervention programme with Jamaican mothers and children', *Developmental Medicine and Child Neurology* 17:5.

Great Britain (1945) West India Royal Commission (Moyne Commission), Cmd. 6607, London: HMSO.

Gregory, Marie (ed.) (1985) *Caribbean Women for Democracy* 1:4, December, Kingston, Jamaica: Bustamante Institute of Public and International Affairs.

Hadley, C.V.D. (1973) 'Personality patterns, social class and aggression in the British West Indies', in David Lowenthal and Lambros Comitas (eds.) *West Indian Perspectives: Consequences of Class and Colour*, New York: Anchor Press/Doubleday.

Hamilton, Marlene A. (1976) 'A study of certain personality, educational and environmental variables associated with science orientation in a selected group of 5th form students in secondary schools in Jamaica', Ph.D. dissertation, Mona, Jamaica: UWI.

—— (1979) 'An investigation of the relationship between social class, success in the common entrance examination and performance in the G.C.E. "O" level examinations', *Social and Economic Studies* 28:3, September.

Handler, Jerome (1974) *The Unappropriated People: Freedmen in the Slave Society of Barbados*, Baltimore: Johns Hopkins University Press.

'Harassment at the workplace: unions to fight sexual abuse' (1985) lead story, *Daily Gleaner* (Jamaica), 2 April, p. 1.

Henriques, Fernando (1953) *Family and Colour in Jamaica*, Granada Publishing Company Kingston: Sangster's edition, 1976.

Henry, Frances and Wilson, Pamela (1975) 'The status of women in Caribbean societies: an overview of their social, economic and sexual roles', *Social and Economic Studies* 24:2, June.

Herskovits, Melville J. (1958) *The Myth of the Negro Past*, Boston: Beacon Press edition (first published 1941).

Higman, B.W. (1975) 'The slave family and household in the British West Indies, 1800–1834', *Journal of Interdisciplinary History* 6:2.

Hodge, Merle (1974) 'The shadow of the whip', in Orde Coombs (ed.) *Is Massa Day Dead? Black Moods in the Caribbean*, Garden City, NY: Anchor Books.

—— (1977) 'Young women and the development of a stable family life in the Caribbean', in L. Mathurin (ed.) *Savacou* (Caribbean Women) 13.

—— (1985) 'Whither the young Caribbean women?' in *Women Speak!* 17 April, WAND, Department of Extra-Mural Studies, UWI, St Michael, Barbados.

Jackson, J.V. (1979) 'An exploratory study of achievement need among girls attending secondary school in Jamaica', MA (ed.) thesis, Mona, Jamaica: UWI.

Johnson, Tina (1988) 'The impact of women's consciousness on the history of the present. The case of Clause Four', *Concerning Women and Development*, 1/88, WAND, Department of Extra-Mural Studies, UWI, St Michael, Barbados.

Justus, Joyce Bennett (1981) 'Women's role in West Indian society', in Filomina Steady (ed.) *The Black Woman Cross-Culturally*, Cambridge, Mass: Schenkman Publishing Co.

Katzin, Margaret Fisher (1959) 'The Jamaican country higgler', *Social and Economic Studies*, 8:4, December.

—— (1960) 'The business of higglering in Jamaica', *Social and Economic Studies*, 9:3, September.

Kerr, Madeline (1952) *Personality and Conflict in Jamaica*, London: Collins.

Lamming, George (1970) *In the Castle of My Skin*, Harlow: Longman (first published London: Joseph, 1953).

Landman, Jacqueline; Grantham-McGregor, Sally and Desai, Patricia (1983) 'Childrearing practices in Kingston, Jamaica', *Caribbean Quarterly*, 29:3/4, September/December.

Leo-Rhynie, Elsa (1978) 'An investigation into the relationship of certain cognitive, environmental, experimental and motivational variables to the academic achievement of selected Jamaican sixth form students', Ph.D. dissertation, Mona, Jamaica: UWI.

—— (1984) 'The status of women in education in Jamaica, midway in the United Nations decade for women 1975–1985'. Paper prepared for the symposium sponsored by the Women's Studies Working Group of the University of the West Indies, 13 December 1984.

Leo-Rhynie, Elsa and Hamilton, Marlene (1982) 'Life-style as a measure of socio-economic status: the development of an instrument for use in Jamaica', *Social and Economic Studies* 31:2, June.

—— (1983) 'Professional Jamaican women — equal or not?', *Caribbean Quarterly* 29:3/4, September–December.

Livingstone, W.P. (1899) *Black Jamaica*, London: Sampson Low, Marston.

Lowenthal, David (1957) 'The population of Barbados', *Social and Economic Studies* 6:4, December.

McKenzie, Hermione (1977) 'Introduction' in L. Mathurin (ed.) *Savacou* (Caribbean Women) 13.

Manley, Beverley (1985) 'Women and the process of social change', *Concerning Women and Development*, 9/85, WAND, Department of Extra-Mural Studies, UWI, St Michael, Barbados.

Manley, D.R. (1963) 'Mental ability in Jamaica', *Social and Economic Studies* 12:1.

Massiah, Joycelin (1982) 'Female-headed households and employment in the Caribbean', *Women's Studies International*, no. 2, July.

Mathurin (Mair) Lucille (1975) *The Rebel Woman in the British West Indies During Slavery*, Kingston: Institute of Jamaica.

—— (1977) 'Reluctant matriarchs', *Savacou* (Caribbean Women) 13.

Miller, Errol (1967) 'A study of body image, its relationship to self-concept, anxiety and certain social and physical variables in a selected group of Jamaican adolescents', MA thesis, Mona, Jamaica: UWI.

—— (1969) 'Body image, physical beauty and colour among Jamaican adolescents', *Social and Economic Studies* 18:1, March.

—— (1973) 'Self-evaluation among Jamaican high school girls', *Social and Economic Studies* 22:4, December.

Mintz, S.W. (1955) 'The Jamaican internal marketing pattern: some notes and hypotheses', *Social and Economic Studies* 4:1, March.

—— (1971) 'Men, women and trade', *Comparative Studies in Society and History* 13:3, July.

—— (1981) 'Economic role and cultural tradition', in Filomena Steady (ed.) *The Black Woman Cross-Culturally*, Cambridge, Mass: Schenkman Publishing Co.

Mintz, S.W. and Hall, Douglas (1960) 'The origins of the Jamaican internal marketing pattern', *Yale University Publications in Anthropology* 57.

Mohammed, Patricia (1983) 'Domestic workers in the Caribbean', *Concerning Women and Development*, 11/83, WAND, Department of Extra-Mural Studies, UWI, St Michael, Barbados.

—— (1985) 'The women's movement in Trinidad and Tobago since the 1960s', *Concerning Women and Development*, 11/85 and 12/85, WAND, Department of Extra-Mural Studies, UWI, St Michael, Barbados.

Moses, Yolanda T. (1981) 'Female status, the family and male dominance in a West Indian community', in Filomina Steady (ed.) *The Black Woman Cross-Culturally*, Cambridge, Mass: Schenkman Publishing Co.

Nettleford, Rex M. (1970) *Mirror, Mirror: Identity, Race and Protest in Jamaica*, Kingston: William Collins and Sangster Ltd.

Phillips, A.A. (1973) *Adolescence in Jamaica*, Kingston: Jamaica Publishing House.

Pollard, Velma (1974) 'My mother', *Jamaica Journal* 8:4, October.

Population Crisis Committee (1988) *Country Rankings of the Status of Women*, Population Briefing Paper no. 2, New York, June.

Population Reports: *Youth in the 1980s: Social and Health Concerns* 13:5, Population Information Program, Johns Hopkins University.

Powell, Dorian (1982) 'Parent–child relationships: the experiences of pregnant teenagers', unpublished ms.

—— (1984) 'The role of women in the Caribbean', *Social and Economic Studies* 33:2, June.

Reddock, Rhoda (1986) 'Indian women and indentureship in Trinidad and Tobago', *Caribbean Quarterly* 32:34, September–December.

—— (1988) 'Women and the slave plantation economy in the Caribbean: with special reference to Trinidad and Tobago', in S. Jay Kleinberg (ed.), *Retrieving Women's History: Changing Perceptions of the Role of Women in Politics and Society*, Berg/Unesco.

—— (1989) 'Women's organisations and movements in the Commonwealth Caribbean in the context of the world economic crisis of the 1980s'. Paper prepared for Research Group, 'Women's Movements and Visions of the Future', Development Alternatives with Women for a New Era (DAWN).

Richardson, Mary F. (1982) 'Socialisation and identity', *Social and Economic Studies* 31:2, June.

Roberts, George W. (1955) 'Emigration from the island of Barbados', *Social and Economic Studies* 4:3, September.

—— (1957) *The Population of Jamaica*, Cambridge University Press.

—— (1975) *Fertility and Mating in Four West Indian Populations*, Mona, Jamaica: Institute of Social and Economic Research, UWI.

Roberts, George W. and Sinclair, Sonja (1978) *Women in Jamaica: Patterns of Reproduction and Family*, Millwood, NY: KTO Press.

Rodman, Hyman (1971) *Lower-Class Families: the Culture of Poverty in Negro Trinidad*, Oxford University Press.

Rodney, Walter (1981) *A History of the Guyanese Working People 1881–1905*, Baltimore and London: Johns Hopkins University Press.

Rohlehr, Gordon (1970) 'Sparrow and the language of the calypso', *Savacou* 2, September.

Romer, Nancy (1981) *The Sex-Role Cycle: Socialization from Infancy to Old Age*, Old Westbury, NY: Feminist Press.

Rowe, Maureen (1980) 'The women in Rastafari', *Caribbean Quarterly* 26:4, December.

Royale, Gloria (1981) 'Images of women in Caribbean TV ads', in Marlene Cuthbert (ed.) *Women and Media Decision-Making in the Caribbean*, Kingston, Jamaica: CARIMAC/Unesco.

Rubenstein, H. (1984) 'Occupational complexity in an Afro-Caribbean village', *Journal of Caribbean Studies* 4:1, fall.

Rubin, Vera and Zavalloni, Marisa (1969) *We Wish to be Looked Upon: a Study of the Aspirations of Youth in a Developing Society*, New York: Teachers College Press, Columbia University.

Safa, Helen I. (1983) 'The CBI and women workers', *Concerning Women and Development*, 9/83, WAND, Department of Extra-Mural Studies, UWI, St Michael, Barbados.

Seacole, Mary (1984) *Wonderful Adventures of Mrs. Seacole in Many Lands*, new edn, London: Falling Wall Press (first published London: James Blackwood, 1857).

Semaj, Leahcim (1984) *Child Development in the Caribbean: an Annotated Bibliography*, Mona, Jamaica: Regional Pre-School Child Development Centre, UWI.

Senior, Olive (1986) *Summer Lightning*, Harlow: Longman.

Sistren (with Honor Ford-Smith ed.) (1986) *Lionheart Gal: Life Stories of Jamaican Women*, London: Women's Press.

Smilowitz, Erika (1983) 'Una Marson: woman before her time', *Jamaica Journal* 16:2, May.

Smith, M.G. (1960) 'Education and occupational choice in Jamaica', *Social and Economic Studies* 9:3, September.

Smith, R.T. (1975) 'Class differences in West Indian kinship: a geneological explanation', in F. Marks Arnaud and A. Römer Rene (eds.) *Family and Kinship in Middle America and the Caribbean*, Institute of Higher Studies in Curacao, Netherlands Antilles and the Department of Caribbean Studies of the Royal Institute of Linguistics and Anthropology at Leiden, Netherlands.

Steady, Filomina Chioma (ed.) (1981a) *The Black Woman Cross-Culturally*, Cambridge, Mass: Schenkman Publishing Co.

—— (1981b) 'The black woman cross-culturally: an overview', in Filomina Steady (ed.) *The Black Woman Cross-Culturally*, Cambridge, Mass: Schenkman Publishing Co.

Stone, Carl (1974) *Electoral Behaviour and Public Opinion in Jamaica*, Mona, Jamaica: Institute of Social and Economic Research, UWI.

—— 1985 'The free zone issue', *Daily Gleaner* (Jamaica), April.

Sutton, Constance and Makiesky-Barrow, Susan (1981) 'Social inequality and sexual status in Barbados', in Filomina Steady (ed.) *The Black Woman Cross-Culturally*, Cambridge, Mass: Schenkman Publishing Co.

Walcott, Clotil (1984) 'Domestic workers' rights', *Women Speak!* 13/84, WAND, Department of Extra-Mural Studies, UWI, St Michael, Barbados.

Warner, Keith Q. (1982) *The Trinidad Calypso*, London: Heinemann.

Williams, Eric (1973) 'Education in the British West Indies', in David Lowenthal, and Lambros Comitas (eds.) *Consequences of Class and Colour: West Indian Perspectives*, Garden City, NY: Anchor Press/Doubleday.

Wilmot, Swithin (1984) 'Not "full free": the ex-slaves and the apprenticeship system in Jamaica 1834–1838', *Jamaica Journal*, 17:3 August.

—— (1986) 'Emancipation in action: workers and wage conflict in Jamaica 1838–1840', *Jamaica Journal* 19:3, August.

Women Speak! (1985) Quarterly newsletter of WAND, Department of Extra-Mural Studies, UWI, St Michael, Barbados, no. 18, July–December.

Wray, S.R. and McLaren, E. (1976) 'Parent–child separation as a determinant of psycho-pathology in children: a Jamaican study', *West Indian Medical Journal* 25:4.

Index